EVERY-
WHERE
I GO

EVERY-WHERE I GO

ED YOUNG

Artwork by Jo Beth Young

WINNING WALK
family

EVERYWHERE I GO

Published by Winning Walk Family

Copyright © 1999 by H. Edwin Young

International Standard Book Number: 0-7417-0001-8
Publisher Standard Address Number: 631-7286

For information contact: Winning Walk Family
                             6400 Woodway
                             Houston, TX 77057

Printed in the United States of America

This book is dedicated to the staff
of the Second Baptist Church of Houston, Texas,
whose members have served faithfully
with me for so many years.

ACKNOWLEDGEMENTS

The devotionals in this book were gathered from twenty years of sermons preached at the Second Baptist Church of Houston. Not all of the illustrations used originated with me, nor can I recall where I first heard many of them. I openly acknowledge my debt to those whose writing and speaking has influenced my own; I am grateful for their insight and inspiration.

I am also grateful for the contribution my wife Jo Beth made to this book. Her paintings add color and beauty to these pages, just as her love has colored and enriched my life for nearly 40 years.

I would also like to thank Leigh McLeroy, who took masses of manuscripts and gleaned from them the illustrations and vignettes she felt would touch people's hearts in a meaningful way. Leigh is a gifted writer who took the stories I spoke "off the cuff," and gave rhyme and rhythm to their re-telling. Not only did she work tirelessly on this project—she did a great job!

FOREWORD

Daily time spent in God's Word is essential for Christian growth. *Everywhere I Go* is your guide book for spending time with God each day, reading His Word, memorizing key scriptures, applying the Word to everyday life and meditating on its meaning.

The four section titles (and the book's main title) come from a song I heard my mother sing hundreds of times: *"In the morning I see His face; in the evening His form I trace; in the darkness His voice I know; I see Jesus everywhere I go."* When we prayerfully read and apply God's Word, and hide it in our hearts, we *do* see Jesus everywhere.

You may begin this book at any point during the year, and work straight through the 365 devotions it contains. Each one is designed to focus your mind and heart on a single concept. Read the title, then read through the devotional section with an open heart. Go to your Bible again and read the suggested scripture passage, asking yourself, "Is there a command for me to obey, a sin to avoid, an example to follow or a promise to claim?" Each devotion ends up with an action step: either a practical application, a thought for further reflection, or a question to be answered. Jot down any comments you may have in response to this action step.

My mother has graduated from this earth and has realized the benediction I heard her pray every day of my boyhood: *"When Thou art through with us on earth, take us to our home which is in heaven."* She now sees Jesus face to face. My prayer for you as you begin this book is that you will learn how to see Jesus…everywhere you go.

His and yours,

Ed Young

IN THE MORNING...

This painting was a gift to a special friend, and its light is a reminder of how God brightens our lives through relationships. Just as sunshine warms this tabletop scene, we are warmed by the love of God as it is expressed through our closest friends and family members.

Jo Beth Young

What Is A Christian?

"...if you confess with your mouth Jesus as Lord, and believe in your heart that God raised Him from the dead, you shall be saved."

ROMANS 10:9

A Christian is a Christ-follower. He is someone who has said "I confess my sins to the Lord, turn from them, and ask Christ to come in and take over my life." I am amazed at how many believers have never told another person how to receive the eternal life that they enjoy. If someone asked you "What is a Christian?", could you rightly respond? Would you?

Several years ago a friend of mine was giving the commencement address at a Kentucky high school. A young man in his congregation was the class valedictorian, and following the ceremony he said to my friend, "Pastor, I want to talk to you. I want you to tell me what it means to be a Christian." This pastor was surprised at the question, since the young man had attended church all his life. But he agreed to meet with him the next morning so they could talk. You've probably guessed by now that that meeting never happened. The young man died that night in an automobile accident. His father recounted that his son regained consciousness before he died, and asked his Dad the same question he had asked my friend. His father could not answer. Could you?

There is no more important question than this: "What is a Christian?" Make sure you know the answer, and be ready to give it without hesitation.

Read: Acts 8:25-37

Memorize these verses: Romans 3:23, Romans 6:23 *and today's verse,* Romans 10:9.

None Righteous

"As it is written, there is none righteous, not even one."

ROMANS 3:10

It is relatively easy for us to recognize sin in one another. It is much more difficult to recognize it in ourselves. But "none of us is righteous," Paul tells us, *"not even one."* We tend to think of ourselves as the exception, but when it comes to sin, there are no exceptions. Until we understand the holiness of God, however, it is almost impossible for us to see clearly our own sin.

Years ago, the *London Times* ran an article encouraging its readers to respond to the question, "What is wrong with the world?" I am sure the editor must have read the following reply more than once before its profound truth sunk in:

Dear Sir:

In response to your question, "What is wrong with the world?", I am.

Yours Truly,

G. K. Chesterton

We are what is wrong with the world! God's standard is absolute righteousness, and when we begin to see His holiness, we understand our own impossible shortfall. No matter how skilled we may be at hiding our sins, we cannot make them disappear. Only God is able to save us, and His opinion of us—His assessment of our hearts—is the only one that matters.

Read: *Romans 3:10-20*

 Are you trying to cover up your sin, or even denying it? Remember, Jesus died to forgive it.

Prepare The Way

"For of His fullness we have all received, and grace upon grace."

JOHN 1:16

People who came to hear John the Baptist preach heard the straight truth. John didn't pull any punches, or dress up his message to please his audience. He was simply a herald, sent to prepare the way. He said, "Make ready for the way of the Lord, and make His path straight. Every ravine shall be filled up, every mountain and hill shall be brought low, and the crooked shall become straight, and the rough roads smooth...and all flesh shall see the salvation of God." In other words, someone awesome is coming!

Years ago I was visiting Williamsburg, Virginia, and was impressed with its careful preservation and restoration. Every detail was considered. But even at Williamsburg, I was surprised to see ground crews meticulously combing the gravel paths that cross the historic settlement, smoothing them and removing any rough stones. When I asked a worker what was going on, he said "Next week the emperor of Japan is visiting, and this is the route he will travel. We're just making sure all the pathways are smooth and straight for the emperor."

There is only one thing we must do to prepare the way for our King, the awesome Son of God: we must repent of our sin. It is repentance that prepares the way for us to receive His fullness, grace upon grace.

Read: *John 1:6-16*

Have you experienced genuine sorrow and repentance for your sin?

It's A Salvage Operation

MEMORIZE

"There is salvation in no one else; for there is no other name under heaven that has been given…by which we must be saved."

ACTS 4:12

Several years back I was on the interstate and my car just ceased operation. The red dashboard light that says "HOT" came on, I slowed down, coasted to an exit and lifted the hood to a cloud of smoke. Not a good sign. It was a short walk to a garage that towed my car in, and the problem turned out to be a belt that had come loose. They put the belt back on, did a few other tweaks, and before you know it, my car was salvaged: it was restored to the purpose for which it was intended, i.e., for driving.

That's what salvation is. It's a salvage operation. Through the blood of Jesus Christ, lives are restored to the purpose for which they were made. Some people think salvation is merely a supernatural insurance policy that reserves a place for them in heaven. But when we are saved, we begin to ful-fill the purpose for which we were made, right here and now. My car was made to transport me…to get me somewhere. When it ceased to function, it had to be salvaged…saved. It's easy to become bogged down in theolog-ical terms like "salvation," and "sanctification" and "propitiation." But Jesus is in the salvaging business, plain and simple. New lives for old. It doesn't get any clearer—or better—than that, does it?

ACTION

Read: *Matthew 9:1-8*

Thank Jesus again today for salvaging your life and making something wonderful of it.

Getting Priorities Right

MEMORIZE

*"But seek first His kingdom and His righteousness;
and all these things shall be added unto you."*

MATTHEW 6:33

I f someone asked you to list your top ten priorities in life, given enough time, you could certainly name them. On the other hand, if your life was examined on the basis of those priorities, the order of some might change, and others would disappear entirely. The truth is, we may give noble lip-service to the things that really count, but be weak in their actual life application.

At the Fido Dog Food Company's annual convention, all of its salesmen, marketing managers and officers were gathered. At the appropriate time, Fido's President and CEO took the podium. "I want to ask you something," he said. "What is the greatest dog food company in the world?" The employees bellowed "FIDO!"

"What dog food company offers the best salaries and fringe benefits in the dog food industry?" Again the crowd roared their answer: "FIDO!" He went on. "What dog food company has the most effective, well trained sales staff in the world?" They responded "FIDO!" with gusto.

"Well then," he said, "Why is it that out of 18 dog food companies, we rank 18th in sales?" From the back of the room, a single voice was heard: "The dogs don't like it!" First things first. For the Christian, nothing precedes the pursuit of God Himself.

REFLECTION

Read: *Matthew 6:25-34*

Determine today what things you may be placing before the pursuit of God.

Covering The Bases

MEMORIZE

"There is therefore now no condemnation for those who are in Christ Jesus."

ROMANS 8:1

Every one of us knows what it means to "cover the bases." Covering the bases is an attempt to satisfy every eventuality...and to keep from being caught short. I saw a wonderful example of this in a Jerusalem bus station, of all places. Ironically, it was located at the foot of Golgotha, or "skull hill," believed to be the place of Christ's crucifixion.

A bus parked in this station was decorated with an eye on the windshield, directly above the driver's seat. The eye had a mirror behind it, and when I asked, I was told that the mirrored eye protected you from the evil eye of another. In other words, if someone gave you the evil eye, you "mirrored" it right back at them! Also on this bus were four horseshoe stickers, two on the right, and two on the left. Between them was a prayer written in Arabic: "May Allah protect us." Now there's a driver who's covering his bases. His bus is parked on the spot where Jesus died, he's got the eye to ward off evil, he's hoping for luck, and praying to Allah!

I talk to people like this all the time. They say something like, "Oh, my grandfather was a Presbyterian preacher, and my mother took us to church every Sunday. I was baptized way back when, and I try to do good." They think they have the bases covered, or hope they do. But in reality, there is only one base. Paul says that the man or woman who is in Christ has covered it. There is no condemnation for the one who repents of sin and puts his faith in Jesus Christ.

QUESTION

Read: *Romans 8:1-5*

Are you trusting in anything but Christ for your salvation?

Time With God

"As the deer pants for the water brooks, so my soul pants for Thee, O God."

PSALM 42:1

David hungered for time alone with God. He looked forward to it the way we look forward to being with a beloved. When my oldest son was dating his wife-to-be, he would come in late and say, "Dad, I didn't know how late it was. The time just flew." That's the way it is with lovers. They want to be together and are never ready to part. Can you imagine a boy saying to his girl, "I would've come to pick you up sooner, but the evening news was on."? Neither can I. Lovers make time to be together.

Not only do those who are in love want to be together, they also find ways to communicate when they are apart. They'll write letters, or call, or send electronic mail...anything to stay in touch. Now let me ask you a question or two. Do you love God? Really love Him? Then do you make time to be alone with Him? Does that time drag, or does it seem to fly? Do you love to talk to Him, and listen carefully for His voice? When you pick up the Bible, which is God's love letter to you, do you hang on every word because you adore its Author?

If we say we love God but do not yearn to be with Him, maybe our love is not as strong as we think. Because you see, it's impossible to love God and not delight in time spent with Him, time spent reading His word, or listening for His voice. Make time for Him today.

Read: *Psalm 42:1-11*

 Don't let over-ambition sabotage your time with God. If you do not have a regular time of devotion, start small. Begin with five minutes, not thirty. But begin.

Marks of the Master

"...for I bear on my body the brand-marks of Jesus."

GALATIANS 6:17

I f you and I are Christians, we will be marked by what rules our lives. Paul's "marks" were dramatic: "Five times I have received from the Jews thirty-nine lashes. Three times I was beaten with rods, once I was stoned, three times I was shipwrecked...I have been in labor and in hardship, through many sleepless nights, in hunger and thirst, often without food, in cold and exposure." None of us can match Paul's physical marks, but is there anything else about us that "gives us away" as followers of Christ?

Tolstoy tells an old story of a czar who opened his palace to any peasant with calloused hands. Any poor man or woman could present himself at this rich man's gate and be given admittance if they bore the marks of a worker. In Tolstoy's tale, if your hands were smooth the way mine are, you would be given bread and water and sent away. But if your hands had done hard labor, you would be invited to eat at the great table, and enjoy the delicacies of kings.

What are the marks of a Christian? Mercy. Truthfulness. Love. Faith. Patience. Longsuffering. Forgiveness. Can others tell by the marks on your life that you follow Christ? Is your character being conformed to His? Are His priorities your priorities? Is there enough of Jesus in your life to give yourself away as His?

Read: II Corinthians 11:23-33

 Ask someone who knows you well what "marks" he sees on you.

God Answers Prayer

"Ask, and it shall be given to you; seek, and you shall find;
knock, and it shall be opened to you."

MATTHEW 7:7

There is no reason to be shy about asking God for what we need. James says we must ask in faith for what we need, and Jesus Himself encouraged His followers to ask. I've talked to a lot of folks who say God never answered their prayer, but God answers every son's or daughter's prayer. Sometimes He gives that which we ask. Sometimes He refuses. Sometimes He tells us the timing is wrong...that we must wait. But He always answers.

The father of a young family lost his job. He and his wife began to pray that God would provide for their needs, and encouraged their children to pray as well. Their son Bobby took them at their word. "God," he prayed, "I need a shirt, size seven." He wanted a special kind of shirt, in a particular size. Night after night he prayed. "God, I need a shirt. Size seven, don't forget." Finally, a phone call came in the middle of the day. It was a man they knew from church, who owned a downtown store. "I know you're having a rough time," he said. "Why don't you come down here and go through some boys clothes you may be able to use? They're mostly one size—seven—but maybe you can make do." The mother could have told her son ahead of time what they were going to do, but she had heard his prayer for weeks, and she wanted him to see it answered for himself. When they arrived at the store, the owner brought out one size seven shirt, then another, then another, until there were twelve shirts—all sevens!—on the counter. We learn to believe in the power of prayer by praying. Our job is to ask. God's desire is to answer. Ask!

Read: James 1: 5-8

Lay your requests before God today, and don't stop until they are answered, yes or no or wait.

You Can't Argue With Experience

"Whether He is a sinner I do not know; one thing I do know, that, whereas I was blind, now I see."

JOHN 9:25

The ambassador from Holland to Siam was once talking to the King of Siam. "You know, King, it gets so cold in my country that water freezes into ice...and the ice is so hard that herds of elephants could run across it." The King of Siam couldn't imagine such a thing. "Nonsense!" he said. "Until you told me this, I believed you to be honest. Now I know you are a man who is not to be trusted!" You see, what the ambassador told the king was beyond his experience. But the ambassador *had* seen it, and he knew it to be true.

You can't argue with experience. The man in our scripture had a first-hand experience with Jesus Christ. He was born blind, and when Jesus touched his eyes, he could see! The pharisees got right in his face and began to question him. "You claim to have been blind since birth?" Well, yes. He did. "And you say that this man gave you sight?" Yes. That's right. "Do you know that this man is a sinner?" Hmmm. I don't know about that. "Who is he, then?" Don't rightly know. "Well, what do you have to say?" Just this: I was blind. And now I see.

If you have had an encounter with the living Christ, you have first hand experience of His power to change a life. No one, no matter how powerful, intelligent or antagonistic, can argue with what He has done for you.

Read: John 9:13-30

Praise God today for the changes He has made in your life. Then tell someone about them.

What In The World Is Real?

MEMORIZE

"...for the things which are seen are temporal, but the things which are not seen are eternal."

II CORINTHIANS 4:18

When my oldest son Ed was about seven and his brother Ben was about five, Jo Beth and I listened to their prayers each night...an experience I highly recommend to parents of small children. One night Ben prayed first. He prayed for everyone, from aunts, uncles, and our dog Barney to Batman, Robin, the Joker and Mr. Freeze. When Ed's turn came, he began to pray for various people and situations, but Ben couldn't be still. Finally, he opened one eye and punched his big brother: "Ed, don't forget to pray for Batman—he needs it!" Ed stopped his prayer, and with all the worldly sophistication of a seven-year-old, said, "Ben, don't you get it? Batman is *not real.*"

We live in a day where it has become increasingly more difficult to discern between what is real and what is not. Wouldn't it be great if we grownups could have the clarity and certainty that little Ed had back then? Then we could easily distinguish what is real and what is artificial; what is valid and what is useless; what is eternal and what is temporal. There are endless demands on our time, requests for our resources, suggestions for our priorities and competition for our devotion. How in the world do we decide what is real?

Let me offer two guidelines. First, we must hold everything up to the plumb line of scripture. What does God's Word have to say about my priorities? My resources? My time? Second, what does the Holy Spirit, who lives in me, direct me to do? Never ignore the Word of God or His still, small voice. He knows what is real, and He can see the unseen, eternal things better than you or I.

ACTION

Read: *II Corinthians 4:16-5:4*

Ask God to search your heart and show you whether you are focusing more on the temporal, or the eternal.

Giving Your Best

"Give and it will be given to you; good measure, pressed down, shaken together..."

LUKE 6:38

I t is true that we reap what we sow, but this verse from Luke also hints at another spiritual truth: sometimes we reap more than we sow. The wise man or woman knows that giving is not the occasion for stinginess, because the goodness that we sow in giving often comes up in areas we never dreamed.

My son Ben illustrated this for me at a very young age. When he was a boy, Ben's best friend was a little guy named Greg. One day Ben came home from playing with Greg, and Jo Beth realized he'd left something behind. "Ben," she asked him, "where's your favorite car—the little blue one you like so much?"

He kind of shrugged and said, "I gave the blue one to Greg." When she asked him why, his explanation made perfect sense. "Mom, I thought you were supposed to give what you like the most." You see, Ben loved his friend Greg, but Greg was not a Christian. But years later, Ben won Greg to Jesus Christ. Then Greg went home and won his mother and dad to the Lord. And his mother and father won his grandparents to Christ. Greg's sister subsequently became a Christian, and now Greg is the pastor of a church in South Carolina. We reap more than we sow. When we give our best—even if it's only a little—God multiplies our gift in ways we could never imagine...for our good and for His glory. So give!

Read: *Luke 6:30-38*

In what areas of life are you giving less than your best? Are you willing to change?

Be Slow To Anger

MEMORIZE

"But let everyone be quick to hear, slow to speak, and slow to anger..."

JAMES 1:19

Years ago no one on the PGA tour wanted to play with a golfer by the name of Bobby Cole. It seemed Cole was angry all the time. He made cutting remarks. He was bitter. And he made the golfers around him mad, too. Sam Snead was Cole's partner at the Master's in Augusta, Georgia, one year, and Snead's reputation for graciousness was as well-known as Cole's reputation for obnoxious behavior. But after ten or twelve holes, even Snead was disgusted with Cole.

As they approached the next hole, Snead took out a three iron and laid up right down the middle. As Cole took out his iron, Snead said, "Son, when I was your age, I would take my driver and fade my shot right over those pine trees. It would save me about 100 yards, but that might be a little tough for you." Cole's anger flashed as he took the bait. "I can do anything you've ever done," he said. "Get out of my way, old man." Then he took out his driver and hit a fabulous shot with a slight fade. The ball hit the top of the pine trees and fell in a deep rough. As both golfers were walking toward their shots, Snead looked back at Bobby Cole and said, "Nice try, son. But I forgot to tell you that when I was your age, those pine trees were only shoulder high."

Solomon wrote in Proverbs that a hot tempered person stirs up strife, but one who is slow to anger can head off contention. The wise person is never in a hurry to give in to anger.

ACTION

Read: *Ephesians 4:17-27*

Ask someone close to you if you are "slow to anger." Listen to his or her response.

Whose Values?

MEMORIZE

*"Do we then nullify the law through faith? May it never be!
On the contrary, we establish the law."*

ROMANS 3:31

No one likes to talk about the law much anymore. And values, well—they've become a cultural antique! Today's education system doesn't instruct children on what is right and wrong. Instead, they learn "values clarification." And the "values" that are "clarified" may not be yours or mine, and almost certainly will not be God's.

A college religion instructor uses a peculiar little test to illustrate to his students that each of us operates under an innate system of values. He offers them a list of fifteen items and asks them to rank them using whatever scale they choose. They review the list—"mouse, boy, sun, angel, ant, crab, Norwegian pine, corn, amoeba, hamburger, potato, Rolls Royce, Moby Dick, Taj Mahal, the idea of good"—and plunge in. The results, he says, are always fascinating. But the fact that the students do rank the items somehow illustrates that a value system—even an unconscious one—is at work.

How does the Christian make value judgments? He relies on God's word, which is His law. The fact that Christ died for our sins does not give us license to sin more, or to ignore His commands. In fact, Paul argues, it is grace that establishes God's law in our hearts and makes His values our own.

REFLECTION

Read: *Exodus 20: 1-17*

 Read the Ten Commandments in Exodus 20. Are these ancient laws written on your heart?

DAY
15

Do You Really Love God?

MEMORIZE

*"You shall love the Lord your God with all your heart,
and with all your soul, and with all your mind."*

MATTHEW 22:37

St. Augustine asked his followers if they really loved God. "Do you love Him with all your heart, soul, mind and strength?" he asked. Then he told a story as a way to discover the answer. Suppose God came to a man and said, "The world and all that is in it is yours. I will give you perfect health. Whatever your heart desires is yours. I will even do away with sin and death and enable you to live forever." Sounds good, doesn't it? The whole world at your disposal—no sin, eternal life? Too good, perhaps. "There is only one thing you will not have," God would say in this imaginary exchange. "You will never see My face. The choice is yours. I will respect your wish."

Augustine said if there were a quiver in a person's heart at the words "you will never see My face," it is quite possible that he might really love God. If a man decided to turn away from all that the world could offer for the joy of seeing God's face, his love might be true. Sounds like a pretty good test to me!

The only satisfaction to be found in this life is found in the love of God. We can choose Him through His Son Jesus Christ and know Him as we are known. Only then does satisfaction come—but then, it comes from everywhere. Because when the soul is satisfied, all the other things in life may be enjoyed for what they are: gifts from a God who is unchanging and good, and whose love endures forever.

QUESTION

Read: *Matthew 22:34-40*

What would you choose in Augustine's story? Do you believe that God alone is enough?

The Sacrifice of Fools

"God is spirit, and those who worship Him must worship in spirit and truth."
JOHN 4:24

Once I spent a fabulous morning of private worship in my study at home. God came down in a wonderful way and gave me fresh new insight in my study time, and a renewed energy for the day. I showered, dressed, kissed Jo Beth at the door and said "Have a great day!" She stopped me and asked, "Would you mind taking out the trash?" Is there anyone on this planet who actually enjoys taking out the trash? I was irritated, and she could tell. For one thing, the trash was overflowing. And I couldn't find the little "twistie thing" to tie the bag.

Here I am, the spiritual leader of this home, the head of this household, elbow-deep in garbage. I was mad about it. Then it hit me: How can it be that the man who was so prayed up and carefree five minutes ago is now fit to be tied? How could this be the same guy? All that praying, all that listening, all that studying and crying and cleansing and confessing…how can it be? Nothing that I got in the quiet of the study had transferred to the chaos of my kitchen. Not one thing.

A fool gives God the sacrifice of singing and praying and giving and sharing, then goes out and lives as he pleases. The fool's worship never changes him. When we go through the motions of church and Christianity, and our hearts remain the same, we have offered the sacrifice of fools.

Read: *John 4:19-26*

How long does your quiet time last? Only as long as you are "quiet"?

Our God Is Awesome

*"You who fear the Lord, praise Him...and stand in awe of Him,
all you descendants of Israel."*

PSALM 22:23

Real worship begins with awe of God—not a frightened fear, but a reverent fear. Anyone who has lost this awe for who God is and what He has done, has lost the ability to worship.

My granddaughter LeeBeth taught me a great deal about this in Disneyworld, of all places. Her "Mimi" and I had taken her to the theme park, and after a long day, settled into our room. I noticed a card by the phone that said at 10:00 p.m. there would be a parade on the lake outside our window, complete with lighted boats and fireworks. I casually asked LeeBeth if she might like a parade before we turned in. She thought I was teasing, but I insisted this was serious, and pretended to phone room service to request our parade. (It was almost 10:00.) Then I pulled the drapes open and started counting, and before I could say "three", there were lights and rockets and the sounds of a parade. Her face filled with wonder and awe. I felt like a king. (Thank you, Disney.)

LeeBeth at sixteen would not have been awed that her "Goosie" (that's me) had ordered a light parade. But at six, she was. If God does not "wow" us, if wonder at Him does not move us to gratitude, something is deeply wrong with our hearts. I agree wholeheartedly with the man who said he pitied the atheist because he had no one to thank for the good things he received. Have you thanked Him today?

Read: Psalm 22: 22-26

 What has God done that has "wowed" you today? Worship Him in wonder and awe.

He's A Big God

"O God, Thou art awesome from Thy sanctuary. The God of Israel Himself gives strength and power to the people. Blessed be God!"

PSALM 68:35

Babylonian literature tells the story of a man who wanted to believe in God, but did not. He went to a Jewish teacher, saying, "If you'll show me God, I'll believe. Just show Him to me." The teacher said, "I will show you God—but first, go outside and gaze at the sun for five minutes." The man went outside, but he could not look at the sun for more than a few seconds. He told the rabbi that he had failed...that the sun was too bright to gaze upon.

The teacher nodded in agreement. "You could not look on a minor creation of God for even a minute—and yet you want to see Him who put the brilliance in the stars. You cannot. He is too big."

What a great word about the nature of God. He *is* a big God—too big for us to easily grasp or readily comprehend. And too majestic for us to take in more than a glimpse of His awesome character. Because He is so big, the distance between us is great. For me to understand all about God would be about as reasonable as expecting our Schnauzer Sonny to understand all about calculus...and Sonny's a smart dog! How grateful I am that God sent His Son Jesus Christ to live in the flesh and show us what He is like, up close. Jesus said, "He who has seen me has seen the Father." Through Him, we can gaze on God to our heart's content.

Read: Psalm 68:32-35

Have you seen God in His Son Jesus Christ? If you have, you can never be the same.

What Are You Listening For?

MEMORIZE

*"The heavens are telling the glory of God;
and their expanse is declaring the work of His hands."*

PSALM 19:1

Two men were walking down the sidewalks of Manhattan, one a Native American and the other a born-and-bred New Yorker. The noise was incredible: cars, buses, horns, sirens, people talking loudly in the midst of the chaos. Suddenly, the Native American said, "Listen! I hear a cricket! Do you hear it?" The New Yorker was incredulous. "No way! You couldn't possibly hear a cricket on a Manhattan sidewalk during rush hour." His friend disagreed, and to prove his statement, he bent down and retrieved a chirping cricket from a crack in the sidewalk. "How could you hear it?" the New Yorker asked. "Easy," said his friend. "I've lived outdoors all my life. I can hear a cricket over any other kind of noise. That's not amazing. If you want to see amazing, watch this!" And with those words, he reached into his pocket, pulled out a quarter, and dropped it on the pavement. As soon as he did, heads began to turn. It seemed as if every Manhattan-ite for blocks heard the coin as it hit the sidewalk. He had proved his point: you hear what you are listening for. Our ears pick up the sounds to which they are tuned.

Let me ask you a question. What are you listening for? Do you hear God's voice amidst the cacophony of every day living? Do you see His hand at work all around you? Is your heart tuned to sing His praise? We can either listen to the din of the world, or strive to hear the voice of God. The choice is ours.

QUESTION

Read: Psalm 19:1-6

Have you heard God's voice today? Through what sound did it make its way to your ears?

The Thread That Holds Us

MEMORIZE

"And He is before all things, and in Him all things hold together."
COLOSSIANS 1:17

A Danish philosopher tells the story of a spider that dropped a single strand down from the top rafter of an old barn and began to weave his web. Days, weeks, months went by, and the web grew. It regularly provided the spider food as flies, mosquitoes and other small insects were caught in its elaborate maze. The spider built his web larger and larger until it was the envy of all the other barn spiders. One day, as this productive spider was traveling across his beautifully woven web, he noticed a single strand going up into the darkness of the rafters. *I wonder why this is here*, he thought. *It doesn't serve to catch me any dinner.* And with that, the spider climbed as high as he could and severed the single strand that was his sustenance. When he did, the entire web slowly began to tumble to the floor of the barn, taking the spider down with it.

The apostle Paul wrote that Jesus Christ is before all things...and that in Him all things hold together. He was present at creation. He is the head of the church. He is the first born from the dead, and it is in Him that all the fullness of God dwells. When we try to sever our lives from the sustaining thread of Christ, everything falls apart.

Every man or woman who has clipped the strand that unites us with God and sought to find meaning and satisfaction and sense in life has been disappointed. There is simply no coherence in a life lived out on our own terms with no reference to the divine.

ACTION

Read: *Colossians* 1:15-20

 Thank God for sending us Christ, through whom all things hold together.

Remember Who You Are

MEMORIZE

"For we are His workmanship, created in Christ Jesus for good works, which God prepared beforehand, that we should walk in them."

EPHESIANS 2:10

When I left Laurel, Mississippi, to go to the University of Alabama, my dad said to me, "Son, remember who you are." I am ashamed to say today that I snickered at those words. I thought, "Remember who I am? I'm the son of a country store merchant. What does *that* mean?" But during the next few years, in moments of tremendous tension and pressure and temptation, I would hear his voice saying, "Remember who you are." Through those words, I recalled times of family altar, where my mother read the Bible, and compelled me to read along with her. And although I was far from home, I never forgot my upbringing.

When we remember who we are, we always know what to do and how to live. When we forget who we are, we become uncertain of what is right and are easily swayed by the world. Who are you? Well, if you are a Christian, you are a child of the King. You are adopted into God's family as a son or daughter, and you have a place at God's table. You are an "alien" in this world, but you have a home in heaven. Also, you are God's workmanship. He designed you, created you as a one-of-a-kind testimony to His excellence, and you have been made for "good works," and not for evil.

When the world tries to squeeze you into its mold, remember who you are!

ACTION

Read: *Ephesians 2:1-10*

 Determine to let who you are affect all of your choices and actions today.

Give Us This Day Our Daily Bread

MEMORIZE

*"And my God shall supply all your needs
according to His riches in glory in Christ Jesus."*

PHILIPPIANS 4:19

When the Israelites fled Egypt and were making their way to the Promised Land, they subsisted on a very unusual diet. It was called "manna," and it fell from heaven every day. The Israelites were instructed to gather only enough for that day...and the next morning, manna would fall again. Those who disobeyed and gathered more found that the "extra" spoiled, and became unusable. Thus, they depended on God day-to-day for their survival. And so do we.

I'm a rather particular eater. When I travel, I'm faced with the challenge of finding food that I like (and recognize!) that will be good for me. I remember being in a restaurant in Amman, Jordan, and pointing to different dishes saying "What is it? What is it? What is it?" The word "manna" literally translated means "What is it?" Can you imagine eating "what is it" every day for forty years?

God has promised to supply all of our needs, according to His riches in glory in Christ Jesus. He does this daily...but sometimes we don't recognize His provision. It looks like nothing we've seen before, and we say, "What is it?" Regardless of what He provides, we can be certain of two things: first, that it comes from a loving, wise Father, and second, that it will be good for us. What more could we ask?

QUESTION

Read: *Exodus* 16:1-7

What has God provided for you today? Did you receive it thankfully?

A Well-Fitting Yoke

MEMORIZE

"Come to Me all who are weary and heavy-laden, and I will give you rest."
MATTHEW 11:28

The words "come to me...and I will give you rest" strike a note in my heart, and in the hearts of many. We need a place to go where we will be received and cared for, and we need rest. Jesus offers all that—but with a strange twist. We would expect Him to say, "Come to me, Edwin or Bill or Susie, and I will give you rest—and let me take that heavy yoke that you've been laboring under." Instead, He says, *"take My yoke upon You and learn of Me."* Wait a minute, Lord! I want rest, and You are asking me to put on a yoke? That's exactly right.

The yoke is a symbol of toil, and Jesus says, "I know you're burdened. That is why you've come to me. So here: take My yoke with its burdens and pressures and responsibilities, and put it on." Strange, isn't it? But do you know why it works? It works because the yoke of Christ is the perfect combination of peace and disturbance, because it fits us so perfectly, and because Jesus Christ Himself pulls next to us all the way!

We're all different in personality, abilities, likes and dislikes. Some of us crave change. Some need the comfort of steady repetition and sameness. Some are energized by people. Others are drained by crowds but fed by solitude. But Jesus knows us, and when we allow Him to, He puts a yoke on us that fits perfectly and fills us with a sense of purpose, power and direction. When we put on the well-fitting yoke of Christ, our weakness is swallowed up in His strength, and we discover that His yoke is easy, and His burden is light.

QUESTION

Read: Matthew 11:25-30

How is His yoke fitting you these days?

Navigating Change

MEMORIZE

"For I, the Lord, do not change; therefore you, O sons of Jacob, are not consumed."

MALACHI 3:6

The key to surviving and thriving in an atmosphere of change is *perspective*. We can view change in one of several ways, but the view we choose will determine whether change becomes an obstacle or an opportunity for us.

One response to change is to fight it. Sears, one of the leading retailers in America, resisted marketing pressure to change their way of doing business for many years. In 1970, Sears stock was $62 a share, but at one point in the 1980's, it traded for as low as $14. As retail sales dropped, Sears executives began examining possible causes for the decline. This operational "gut check" revealed layer upon layer of unnecessary bureaucracy and a growing insensitivity to the marketplace. You see, we can resist change around us, but that resistance often draws a costly penalty. We fall behind those who are more willing to be flexible, and instead of leading, we find ourselves in the position of playing catch up.

No one should be more secure in the face of change than the Christian. Why? Because our God is the one who remains unchangeable. He is our constant, our North Star, our anchor...and His character, His love and His precepts will never vary one iota. Isn't that a comfort? With Him in control of our lives, change is not an obstacle...it's an opportunity.

QUESTION

Read: Malachi 3:1-7

Does change frighten you? Ask yourself why, and remember that God is changeless, even when nothing around us remains the same.

Investing In The Eternal

"The righteous will never be shaken, but the wicked will not dwell in the land."

PROVERBS 10:30

When the ground around San Francisco shook, rumbled and broke open in September, 1989, Americans held their breath as they watched televised reports of destruction and death. Days after the quake, when all hope for survivors had died, workers wept with joy and weary relief at the sight of one man, miraculously preserved, pulled from the heap of twisted metal and pulverized brick that had been his home. When life falls to pieces around us, God preserves.

Scientist and inventor Thomas Edison was 67 years old and at the pinnacle of his career when his laboratory was destroyed by fire. As the fire raged out of control, Edison's son remembers seeing his father running toward him shouting, "Son, go get your mother and bring her here. She'll never see another fire like this as long as she lives." The next day Edison called his employees together and began making plans to rebuild. As he sifted through the ashes of his office, he found a picture of himself, charred around the edges, but with the image still intact. Picking up the picture he turned to his son and said, "See, the fire never touched me. It never touched me."

We may lose all we have materially in this life, but if we have invested in spiritual things, no tragedy that can happen in this fallen world will ever touch us. The beloved hymn "Amazing Grace" says it best: "Through many dangers, toils and snares I have already come; 'Tis grace hath brought me safe thus far, and grace will lead me home."

Read: *Proverbs* 10:27-32

 Your world can be shaken, but you cannot. God holds you securely in His hand.

The Red Lizard of Lust

"But put on the Lord Jesus Christ, and make no provision for the flesh in regard to its lusts."

ROMANS 13:14

A uthor C. S. Lewis spins a remarkable story about a little red lizard that a certain ghost carried on his shoulder. The lizard twitched its tail and whispered continually to the ghost, who urged him all the while to be quiet. When a bright and shining presence appeared and offered to rid the ghost of his troublesome "baggage," the ghost refused. He understood that to quiet the lizard, it would be necessary to kill it, and that seemed too harsh. Maybe the lizard need not die, but could be trained, he reasoned. The presence responded that training would not work; it must be all or nothing. Finally, with the ghost's permission, the presence twisted the lizard away from him, breaking its back as he flung it to the ground. Then an amazing thing happened. The ghost became a perfect man, and the lizard became a beautiful silver and gold stallion, full of power and grace. The man leaped astride the great horse, and they rode into the morning as one. Lewis ends the story with these words: "What is a lizard compared with a stallion? Lust is a poor, weak, whimpering, whispering thing compared with that richness and energy of desire which will arise when lust has been killed."

Pastor John Piper, in his excellent book *Future Grace*, says that to successfully conquer lust, we must fight fire with fire: "If we try to fight the fire of lust with prohibitions and threats alone—even the terrible warnings of Jesus—we will fail. We must fight it with a massive promise of superior happiness. We must swallow up the little flicker of lust's pleasure in the conflagration of holy satisfaction. Our aim is not merely to avoid something erotic, but to gain something excellent."

Read: *Psalm 119:9-16*

Lust cannot be eliminated in our lives without being replaced by something stronger and more desirable: the love of Jesus Christ Himself, and the purity of sex rightly enjoyed.

Unclaimed Guilt

MEMORIZE

*"Having canceled out the certificate of debt...against us...
He has taken it out of the way, having nailed it to the cross."*

COLOSSIANS 2:14

Someone once wryly described guilt as "the gift that keeps on giving." We can attempt to alleviate our guilt with rationalization, activity, and the passage of time, but nothing changes the fact that sin not dealt with by God lives forever. We can rename it, bury it, ignore it, or try to explain it away, but the bottom line is that sin—and the guilt that accompanies it—never dies until God gets hold of it. Until He does, we can expect to see our same tired sin all over again in a different time and place, like the recurring sequel to a movie we never liked to begin with!

I have seen more damage done to individuals and relationships by the ghost of guilt than from any other source. Frequently, the guilt of some past sin is carried from generation to generation, affecting the lives of those who may be totally unaware of its origin. In the world's major airports, unclaimed baggage or parcels are seized by authorities, because terrorists have been known to hide explosives in luggage, then abandon it. Psychologists tell us that the baggage of guilt and shame do not go unclaimed either. If a parent refuses to deal with his or her own guilt, a child will often subconsciously pick it up and carry it. There is a solution for unclaimed guilt. Let Jesus have it. Guilt that is nailed to the cross is canceled. "He breaks the power of canceled sin, He sets the prisoner free."

REFLECTION

Read: *Genesis 45:1-15*

 Are you carrying around a load of guilt? Would you like to set it down and let Jesus claim it? Confess your sin to Him, and receive His forgiveness.

War And Peace

*"He who is slow to anger is better than the mighty, and he who rules his spirit,
than he who captures a city."*

PROVERBS 16:32

I know a spot in North Carolina where two rivers come together. From a high bluff you can see them moving calmly toward their meeting point, but where they converge, the waters are raging. These two strong, independent rivers ultimately combine to form a wider, even more impressive one.

A good marriage is like this natural phenomenon. One independent person meets another independent person, and they decide to merge their lives into one. The trouble begins when they try to decide which one! Actually, the answer is...neither. Like these rivers, two marriage partners become a new and separate creation—stronger, wider, more impressive—that bears the marks of both. And strong people do not join easily or without conflict, any more than rivers do.

Conflict is inevitable in any close, extended human relationship...and that includes marriage. Even good ones go through rough spots. The good news is, conflict does not have to hurt a good marriage. The difference between a good one and a troubled one is not the presence of problems, but how those problems are handled. Conflict can either become the source of greater isolation...or greater intimacy.

Read: *Ephesians 4:25-32*

 How do you handle anger in your closest relationships? Can you view it as an opportunity for deeper understanding?

What Love Overlooks

MEMORIZE

"Love bears all things, believes all things, hopes all things, endures all things. Love never fails."

I CORINTHIANS 13:7

A woman celebrated her 50th wedding anniversary with her husband. She was a wonderful wife, mother and grandmother, and on this special occasion, one of her grandchildren asked her the secret to her happy and enduring marriage. She smiled and said, "Well, sweetheart, when your granddaddy and I married, I made a list of ten things I would overlook in his personality. Just ten things I didn't like, but was willing to forgive. I decided on that day that anytime one of those ten things would come up, I would overlook it for the sake of harmony in our marriage." One of the grandchildren said, "Granny, tell us the list. We want to know what was on the list." She paused and said, "You know, to be honest with you, I never really wrote them down. But every time your grandfather would do something that made me mad, I would think to myself, 'Lucky for him that's one of the things on my list.' "

Relationships are hard work, and difficulties and conflicts will come. But they are not the end of the world. Real love is willing to overlook slights, annoyances, and petty disagreements, choosing instead to take a long term view. "We love," the apostle John wrote, "because He first loved us." Our only hope as human lovers is to allow the love of Christ to flow through us. We can hope, believe, and endure because we have been perfectly loved.

QUESTION

Read: *I Corinthians 13:1-7*

Are you holding grudges over petty things? Take the long view of love today.

Fruit-Bearing

MEMORIZE

"The fruit of the righteous is a tree of life, and he who is wise wins souls."

PROVERBS 11:30

You and I were made to bear fruit. For the Christian, our "fruit" is changed lives...our own, and others. Yet some believers' lives are "barren" for long stretches of time, bearing no fruit at all.

Author James Michener was raised on a farm. He recalls from his childhood that a neighboring farmer raised apples. One day, young Michener was passing by his orchards and witnessed a strange thing: the neighbor was driving nails in some of the trees that were not bearing fruit. He watched in curiosity as this farmer approached a barren tree and drove four large, rusty nails into the base of the tree, north, south, east and west. Then he moved higher on the trunk of the same tree and repeated the process. When Michener questioned the neighbor, he told the boy, "Just wait until next spring. You'll understand it then." When spring rolled around, Michener said that apple tree produced the biggest, reddest apples he had ever seen. The farmer said, "You see, those rusty nails remind the tree that it was made to produce apples. Sometimes it forgets."

Some of us need a jolt to remember that we were made to produce good fruit for the kingdom of God. And sometimes pain or hardship is the "nail" that reminds us. You'd be surprised at how many of us bloom and bear fruit in places where we once felt the sting of a nail.

REFLECTION

Read: John 15:1-8

 Does the fruit of your life testify that Jesus Christ lives in you?

Overwhelming Evidence

MEMORIZE

*"For since the creation of the world His invisible attributes,
His eternal power and divine nature, have been clearly seen..."*

ROMANS 1:20

One of the favorite questions posed by skeptics and unbelievers is this one: "What about those who've never heard the Good News? God wouldn't condemn them in their ignorance, would He?" They usually go on and give you a few examples, just to drive home their argument. "What about the guy who's never been to a church, or that person in India, or Alaska, or Central or South America or Africa?" The next time someone asks you that, open your Bible to Romans, chapter one, and say, "That's an interesting question. Let's see what God has to say about it."

What Paul says in Romans is this: "For the wrath of God is revealed from heaven against all ungodliness and unrighteousness of men who suppress the truth in unrighteousness." In other words, anyone on this planet who rejects God is suppressing the truth. They may not have come in contact with the Bible, or had someone share their faith with them, but they have had plenty of contact with God's *general revelation.* "Because that which is known about God" said Paul, "is evident within them, for God made it evident to them." We are born with an inclination toward God! It's built in! And furthermore, "Since the creation of the world, His invisible attributes, His divine nature *have been clearly seen.*" In creation and in our hearts alone, there is overwhelming evidence for God!

QUESTION

Read: Romans 1:16-20

How long has it been since you have considered the overwhelming evidence of God's existence?

Enough Power?

*"For the word of the cross is to those who are perishing foolishness, but to us who are
being saved it is the power of God."*

I CORINTHIANS 1:18

D o you and I have enough power to live the Christian life? Consider
this: we have the power of the Holy Spirit within us...the third
person of the Trinity who raised Jesus from the dead. Don't you
think that's enough power to keep our minds set on the Spirit, and to have
life and peace? I think it's more than enough power...if we use it.

An old cartoon dating back to the World War II depicts a soldier with an
M-1 rifle aimed at an oncoming enemy tank. The tank is poised to roll right
over the comparatively tiny soldier with his rifle. In the next frame there is
a picture of a soldier with a rocket launcher. The soldier in the cartoon is
now giant-sized, and the tank relatively small. The idea is that a soldier with
a rocket launcher is more than adequate to defeat a tank.

That's our situation. We live defeated lives when we say, "Boy, all I've
got against Satan and the world is this little old M-1 rifle and my own determination. I've got to really bear down if I'm going to survive." And all the
time we possess the resurrected power that brought Christ out of the
grave...we have the Holy Spirit inside us, with the power of a rocket launcher! All we need to do is appropriate it.

Read: Acts 1:1-8

*Have you forgotten the power of the Spirit and tried to live for Christ on
your own steam?*

Watch Your Mindset

MEMORIZE

*"For the mind set on the flesh is death;
but the mind set on the Spirit is life and peace..."*

ROMANS 8:6

Let me ask you something about your mindset: Are you a feeler or a springer? When you get up in the morning, are you a feeler or a springer? I'm a feeler. I don't just jump out of bed and go from zero to sixty in nothing flat. I need to lie still for a little bit and wake up gradually. But Jo Beth is a springer. She wakes up and does not linger. She's up and out before I can get one eye open. Generally, springers go to sleep quickly...like between "good" and "night." That's it. They're down and out in a matter of seconds! But we feelers ease into sleep the same way we ease into waking. Regardless of whether we are feelers or springers, the time to set our minds is when we first wake. At that moment we must turn our thoughts toward God.

If we ignore this opportunity to set our minds on the things of God, we give the devil a foothold, and soon—without our even knowing it—we have set our minds on the flesh. And the mind set on the flesh, Paul tells us, is death. But if we turn our minds and hearts God-ward, and set our thoughts on Him, what a difference it will make in the way we live. Which sounds better to you? A mind set on death, or a mind set on life and peace?

ACTION

Read: Romans 8:5-13

Choose tomorrow morning to set your mind on the Spirit of God, and allow Him to order your thoughts all day.

Accused!

*"...nothing good dwells in me, that is, in my flesh; for the wishing is present in me,
but the doing of the good is not."*

ROMANS 7:18

My wife and I were engaged in a normal, garden-variety disagreement. In the midst of it, I made one of those "terminal statements" counselors warn against...something like "That's the dumbest thing I've ever heard in my life." And she took offense. "Are you saying I'm dumb?" she asked. I should have stopped there. But I didn't. "Well, at that moment," I said, "you were not only dumb, you were stupid." She was hurt (and rightly so). I was mad. And since it was a Sunday morning, I got in the car and headed for church to preach. It wasn't long before a little voice inside me said, "So you're the spiritual dynamo who's going to speak to a few thousand people today, are you?" It persisted. "Who do you think you are? You're a hypocrite. A phony. You've blown it." I was accused. Have you been accused lately? It's not a good feeling, is it?

The Bible tells us that Satan is the accuser. When we sin, when we're down and feeling hopeless, he talks even louder than usual. Before long, we're depressed and despairing, thinking that we've failed Christianity 101 and can't possibly make up the work we've missed. We're hopeless failures. Accused. Paul understood. He wrote, "For the good that I wish I do not do; but I practice the very evil that I do not wish...". What hope do we have if Paul could not escape Satan's accusations? Good news! We have Paul's hope, and it is this: "Thanks be to God through Jesus Christ our Lord! There is therefore no condemnation for those who are in Christ Jesus."

Read: *Romans 7:18-25*

When Satan shouts "accused" at you, consider what Christ has done for you and say instead "acquitted...through the blood of Jesus Christ Himself."

Led By The Spirit

"The Spirit Himself bears witness with our spirit that we are children of God."

ROMANS 8:16

How does a person know that he or she is a Christian? How do we really know? I'll tell you. We know because the Holy Spirit "bears witness" with our spirit, confirming in our hearts that we are indeed children of God.

Beginning with my sophomore year in high school, I was an hour-a-week Christian. I went to church, I was in attendance, I was present and accounted for. I had received Christ as an 11-year-old boy, but during my high school years I became exceedingly cynical and apathetic. I showed up. That was about it. I even laughed at people who were considered "religious" by others in my little town, and went along with a lot of chicanery in which I had no business participating.

But there were some things I did not do. There were temptations as a teenager that looked incredibly good to me, but I did not give in to them. Looking back, I know why. Even with my cynical attitude, I still felt the witness of God in my life...that inner voice of the Holy Spirit saying, "You are mine. This is not for you." When I came back to Christ a few years later and gave myself anew to Him, He was with me as He had always been before. That is the inner witness of the Spirit. We may wander away or run from God, but there is a quiet place in which He deals with us and confirms that we are His own.

Read: *John* 14:16-21

If you have wandered from God, get still and listen for His voice. He is never far from you.

Which Dog Wins?

"Even so, consider yourselves to be dead to sin, but alive to God in Christ Jesus."

ROMANS 6:11

There is a never-ending battle in the life of every believer between the flesh and the Spirit. Have you noticed? Even when we surrender our lives to God, Satan continues to tempt us. We are never given a reprieve from temptation. So how do we wage this life-long battle? And who wins? I believe the answer is revealed in this story.

An Alaskan trapper owned several dogs, two of which he trained to fight. Every month he would bring the dogs—one white and one black—to town to fight. The townspeople would bet on the winner, sometimes betting on the black dog, sometimes on the white one. The owner of the dogs would bet, too...and he always won. One month he'd bet on the black dog, and the black dog would win. Another month he would gamble on the white dog, and the white dog would win. Some folks finally caught on, and asked the man his secret. "How do you know which dog is going to win?" they asked. "You're never wrong." The dog owner shrugged his shoulders, and said, "It's easy, really. The one who wins is the one I feed."

Who's going to win in the battle between the Spirit and the flesh? That's easy, too. The stronger one is the one we feed. So we must set our minds on the things of God, seeking to please Him and be obedient to Him in all we do. In that way, we feed the Spirit, and insure victory over sin.

QUESTION

Read: *Romans 6:6-14*

Which "dog" is being fed most in your life today? The Spirit, or the flesh?

The Amazing Appeal of Jesus Christ

MEMORIZE

"Now all the tax gatherers and the sinners were coming near Him to listen to Him."

LUKE 15:1

Does it seem strange to you that irreligious, ungodly people were drawn to Jesus? Does that strike you as unusual? What did Jesus have that drew the sinners and tax gatherers—the "dregs" of society—to Him? I believe it is the same appeal Jesus would have if He were alive in the flesh today, an appeal that would draw people who are fishing, hunting, playing golf, cutting their yards, or living under bridges or in jails or flophouses. What would it be?

First, supernatural power. Imagine that in the nightly news broadcast they told of a man in a nearby town who walked through a hospital and healed everyone of their sickness. That would be a draw, would it not? Jesus had supernatural power, and people saw it, and wanted to experience its benefits. Second, Jesus had hope about Him. He talked about life after life. He said this world is not all there is...there is more to life than this. All kinds of people want to live forever. All kinds of people are interested in life after life.

Also, Jesus spoke truth. His words had a ring of reality about them, and He was honest and candid and open. The naked truth is a powerful thing, and even the ungodly are drawn to someone who speaks the unvarnished truth. Finally, Jesus' life was permeated by love. They saw in Him a kind of supernatural love that was pure and sacrificial and revolutionary. And these are appeals that are still operative today.

QUESTION

Read: *Luke 5:30-35*

Are you the kind of person to whom the ungodly would be drawn? To the degree that you are like Jesus, you will have His appeal.

Acceptable Loss?

*"Or what woman, if she has ten silver coins and loses one coin,
does not...search carefully until she finds it?"*

LUKE 15:8

"Acceptable loss" is a military term many are familiar with. The idea is that there are some losses in any military endeavor, but that every mission has a level of loss that is acceptable, based on the risk undertaken and the goal to be achieved. Luke chapter 15 contains a trio of stories about people who have lost things. If you are a mathematician, you might hear these stories and consider the percentages. A man has a hundred sheep, he loses one. That's a one percent loss! That seems quite acceptable. A woman has ten coins and loses one—still only a ten percent loss, and really quite acceptable. A man has two sons, and loses one. A fifty percent loss, granted, but one that might be overcome in time.

But Jesus was not a mathematician or an accountant. He never considered percentages of "lost-ness." He considered people. And in these stories about searching for lost things, Jesus was saying that sinners are very, very valuable to Him. Sinners count with Jesus. There is no acceptable percentage of loss when it comes to the Son of God and sinners. He is not willing that even one "lost sheep" should perish. I wonder how different our world would be if you and I adopted Jesus' view of "acceptable loss?"

Read: *Luke* 15:1-10

Pray today for your friends and family members who are lost. Considering their value, why not organize a "search party" for them?

Road Signs

MEMORIZE

"And after He had said these things, He was going on ahead, ascending to Jerusalem."

LUKE 19:28

The scene described here is sometimes called the triumphal entry. It is Jesus' final return to the city of Jerusalem where he would be captured, charged, and crucified for His claims. Luke tells us that Jesus was going ahead, up to Jerusalem. I would be willing to say that no one reading these words today has Luke 19:28 underlined or highlighted in their Bible. It seems incidental, parenthetical, insignificant. But nothing could be farther from the truth. This powerful verse is a key road sign in God's eternal plan of redemption.

All of heaven and earth had been waiting for the moment when Jesus would go up to Jerusalem for the last time. When Adam and Eve disobeyed God in the Garden of Eden, the Bible says, "...the Lord God made garments of skin for Adam and his wife, and clothed them." With that act, a scarlet thread appeared that runs through all of history: without the shedding of blood, there is no remission of sin. Again at Passover, blood covered the door posts of Jewish homes...and the prophet Isaiah predicted one "who will lay down his life as a ransom for many—the suffering servant." Jesus' entry into Jerusalem meant that the time had come for God to reveal His plan for salvation...and Jesus knew well what that plan required. This was the time for His divine visitation. Many missed Him. But some believed. It is no different today.

REFLECTION

Read: *Luke 20:9-18*

 Have you recognized Jesus in His time of visitation? When He touches your life, are you thrilled by His presence?

Plan "A"

"There is none righteous, not even one; there is none who understands,
there is none who seeks for God..."

ROMANS 3:10-11

Theoretically at least, there are two ways to get to heaven. You might call them Plan "A" and Plan "B." The first way to get to heaven, Plan "A", is to live a life without error. A sin-free life. Never a wrong action, a wrong thought, a wrong desire. No errors. Not only does Plan "A" require you to live a life without error, it requires perfect righteousness. Every thought righteous. Every action righteous. Every word spoken pleasing to God. Every motive pure. In other words, Plan "A" requires that you bat a thousand...for life. If you live a life like that, when you die, God will say "You've done it! I'm admitting you to the Super Universal Eternal Colossal Heavenly Hall of Fame! You have made it in through Plan 'A'." Theoretically you could get into heaven like that. But only theoretically.

Theologically, Plan "A" is impossible because we're all born in sin. Billy Graham is a sinner. Mother Teresa was a sinner. Even the apostle Paul was a sinner. None of them are Plan "A" candidates. Maybe someone would want to hedge: "Now wait a minute pastor. I may not be a saint, but I'm no Ted Bundy or Unibomber. Are you saying God will not "grandfather" me in under Plan "A" because I've done my very best?" That's exactly what I'm saying! If you don't believe me, believe Paul: "There is none righteous, *not even one.*" Plan "A" is simply unworkable. No one has ever gotten right with God and made it to heaven on Plan "A." Are you ready now for Plan "B?"

Read: *Romans 3:21-28*

If you have not done so, abandon any hope you have placed in Plan "A"
for salvation.

Plan "B"

MEMORIZE

"Therefore having been justified by faith, we have peace with God through our Lord Jesus Christ."

ROMANS 5:1

Thank goodness for Plan "B." There is a way to get right with God. There is a way to be declared righteous and be received into heaven. Plan "A" is useless because the law tells us we are all sinners. No flesh will be justified; no man can be "good enough." That's why Plan "B" is strictly a gift. It is God's gracious answer to man's failure. And it is free.

In Plan "B", God Himself declares our worth, on no basis of our own. How does this work? Paul explains it this way: *"But now, apart from the law, the righteousness of God has been manifested being witnessed by the law and the prophets."* In other words, the righteousness of God has been manifested by the coming of Jesus Christ into the world. If you want to see righteousness, look at Jesus. He is righteousness that has put on flesh and blood. Through Him, God has said to each one of us, "_____, you are worthy." Through the death and resurrection of Jesus Christ, His righteousness can become our righteousness. When we place our faith in His sacrifice, a divine exchange takes place. How do we get right with God? By Plan "B"— by placing our faith in Jesus Christ, forever abandoning any misguided attempts at Plan "A."

QUESTION

Read: Romans 5:1-8

 Have you embraced Plan "B," trusting Christ alone for your salvation?

"He Stood In My Stead"

MEMORIZE

"For while we were still helpless, at the right time Christ died for the ungodly."

ROMANS 5:6

As a seminary student, I worked at a church in Winston-Salem, North Carolina. It was there I had the privilege of "debriefing" Mrs. Jane McCray, a missionary to the Gaza Strip. I don't remember much of that interview, except the story she told when I asked her to describe the toughest position she found herself in during her time in Gaza.

"A state-side church sent us some clothing for children," she said, "and as I unpacked the clothes, I saw they had placed a New Testament in the pocket of every piece of clothing." Because it was illegal to distribute Bibles there, she was forced to go through every item and remove them. "There were hundreds of them," she said, "and I put them in a sack, thinking to hide them somewhere safe. But as I was walking through town, some boys saw the sack and must have thought there was food in it. They grabbed it and ran." When the boys got around the corner and opened the bag, they found nothing but books, and were angry. So they ripped them up, tearing out the pages. "Then," she said, "pages of the New Testament began to fly all over the village. Just everywhere." It wasn't long before the books were traced to Mrs. McCray, and she was charged with distributing illegal literature. She was instructed to appear before a government official the next day, but that night, she had some unexpected visitors. "A little girl knocked on my door," she told me, "and with her was an army officer. He told me his daughter heard about my plight, and asked him to hear my side of the story. As I told him he paced the floor. When I was done he said this: "Mrs. McCray. This is very serious. But you cannot go to court. I will go and stand in your stead." And this army officer did just that, forfeiting his name, his career, everything he had to protect her. Then she looked at me with tears in her eyes, and said, "Eddie, he stood in my stead." And as she said it, I knew that was just what Jesus Christ had done for me.

QUESTION

Read: *Romans 5:9-15*

 What does it mean to you that Jesus Christ stood in your stead?

How To Receive Treasure

"Do not lay up for yourselves treasures upon earth, where moth and rust destroy, and where thieves break in and steal."

MATTHEW 6:19

I t is God, James tells us, who is the giver of every good and perfect gift. Treasure, real treasure, comes from God alone. How is it, then, that we fail to receive that which He would give us? Often the problem is not that God is *withholding*, but that we are *holding on*.

There's an old, bucolic story about a little boy who got his hand stuck in a delicate vase. It seems he reached into the vase to retrieve something, and then could not pull himself free without breaking it. Finally, he called out to his dad for help. They worked and struggled to ease his hand out, but to no avail. Seeing no alternative, the father made the inevitable decision: the vase must be broken.

Just before he struck the fatal blow to this heirloom piece, the father asked his son to try to slip his hand out one more time. Crying now, the little boy 'fessed up: "Dad, I'll do it if you make me, but if I do, I'll have to drop my dime." It's an antique story about an antique vase, but it illustrates a very basic spiritual principle: The hand that is closed cannot receive the treasure that God wants to give. It's just that simple.

Read: *Matthew 6:19-24*

What are you holding on to that keeps you from receiving? Are you willing to let go of it today?

The First Mile

MEMORIZE

"And whoever shall force you to go one mile, go with him two."

MATTHEW 5:41

I n our culture of over-achievers, we tend to focus on going farther...on going the second mile. And Jesus clearly said we are to be willing to do that. But to begin the second mile, we must complete the first. We must be ordinary before we can hope to be excellent.

A south Alabama track meet was a showcase for a fine, young athlete expected to shatter the state record in the mile. He was the race...no one else could come close to him in ability. No one in the packed stands gave a glance toward the pale, scrawny kid lined up on the outside. He was nobody special... nothing to notice.

The gun sounded. As expected, the star runner looped the track like a sprinter, pulling away from the pack with yards to spare. As he broke the tape, the crowd roared. Another runner finished second...then third...then fourth. The loudspeaker announced the winner's time, a new state record. But the race wasn't over. One runner was struggling for the finish line all alone. When he crossed it, he collapsed, gasping for breath. When coaches rushed over to lift him up, one of them chided him for running: "Son, what were you thinking? You're no miler, and this is a championship race. You couldn't hope to win."

"Sir," he said, "we had us a boy who could run the mile, but he took sick. Coach asked me to run in his place. He didn't send me down here to win...he sent me down here to run a mile, and Mister, I ran a mile."

QUESTION

Read: *Matthew 5:40-48*

Are you trying to run the second mile without completing the first? Run the first mile.

Lifestyle Evangelism

MEMORIZE

*"Sanctify Christ as Lord in your hearts, always being ready to make a defense to any-
one who asks you to give an account for the hope that is in you..."*

I PETER 3:15

Evangelism is not a program or the application of a method; it is a lifestyle. Some are naturally gifted at sharing their faith and others are not, but every Christian is called to testify to the good news that Jesus Christ came to seek and to save the lost.

A Canadian brigadier general was appointed Governor of the African Gold Coast following World War I. He was known as a wise, stalwart ruler and an inspiration to his subjects. A friend of the Governor once noticed a saying on his mirror that puzzled him. It said, "For God, For King, For Country." His friend said, "Sir, you see this every morning when you stand before your mirror. What does it mean to you?"

The Governor answered, "For God doesn't mean that much to me, but For King means a bit more. And For Country—well, that means everything to me." His friend answered, "I can see that king and country are important in your life, but Governor, you've never sought to know God." Touched by his friend's forthrightness, the Governor said, "How does one get to know God?" The man replied, "You get to know God by learning about His Son, Jesus Christ." Then he told him how to invite the Lord into his life.

There is no reason for us to be intimidated by worldly power. We are empowered by the Holy Spirit when we speak of Christ, and we must seize the moment when opportunities arise.

ACTION

Read Acts 8:25-38

 Watch today for opportunities to talk about your faith in Christ. Then seize the day!

Moving An Iceberg

"For if you love those who love you, what reward have you?
Do not even the tax gatherers do the same?"

MATTHEW 5:46

Ice-cold folks are among the toughest we encounter. Nothing moves them. Nothing seems to break through their frosty exterior. And if we're honest, their coolness repels us. They're hard to love. But are we excused? You know the answer. We are not. Not only are we called to love those who love us, we are called to love those who do not.

The Titanic was an engineering marvel: the largest, fastest cruise ship ever built. Her designers boasted that she was unsinkable. But history records that the great ship encountered an iceberg on her maiden voyage and sunk to the bottom of the sea, claiming over 2,000 lives. The iceberg was sighted before the collision, but the ship met it "full speed ahead" with disastrous results.

Sometimes we meet the "iceberg" folks in our lives in much the same way: we go full speed ahead, hoping to overpower them. We meet their barb with one of our own. We try to disarm them before they can disarm us. We match their chilly ways with our own brand of cool. But there is another way to deal with an iceberg. In time, the ice that wrecked Titanic broke away from its moorings and floated out to sea. Surrounded by the warmer waters of the ocean, it eventually melted away. When we love the unlovable with the warm and steady love of Christ, amazing things can happen.

Read: I John 4:7-12

Who in your life challenges you to love them? How will you do so this week?

The Sin of Partiality

MEMORIZE

*"My brethren, do not hold your faith in our glorious Lord Jesus
with an attitude of personal favoritism."*

JAMES 2:1

Isn't it good that you and I don't decide who is "worth saving?" We're too easily deceived by appearances. We may think the rich, profane executive who has the world by the tail would make a dynamite Christian if he were "cleaned up," but judge the down-and-out derelict as a more likely candidate for prison. Years ago a play called "Tobacco Road" caused a stir at its Atlanta, Georgia, premier because those in the audience were offended by its main character, Jeter Lester. Lester was the epitome of every bad southern stereotype: uncouth, swaggering, dishonest, mean. The city's elite were repulsed by the idea that the south might be full of Jeter Lester's, and re-dedicated themselves to social reform to remedy that possibility.

Oddly enough, the same crowd did not object to the equally wretched main character of another play, "Who's Afraid of Virginia Wolfe?". Virginia, too, was a mean, foul-mouthed bully, but she was wealthy. And well-connected. And educated. These two characters, whose demographics were miles apart, were actually more alike than different. How do we treat the Jeter Lester's and the Virginia Wolfe's? Usually, we ignore the Jeter's (hoping they'll go away) and show preference to the Virginia's. After all, they have *potential*. But to Christ, they're one and the same. He loves them, and died for them both. How can we then, choose one over the other?

QUESTION

Read: James 2:1-9

   How have you allowed appearances to affect your treatment of others?

Hindsight

MEMORIZE

*"Then I will take My hand away and you shall see My back,
but My face shall not be seen."*

EXODUS 33:23

Sometimes we just don't see God coming. We don't realize that He desires to meet with us, that He wants to be a part of every aspect of our lives. We've put Him in a box instead, and imagined Him to be much smaller than He is. And when He comes close, we're largely unaware.

Moses experienced the presence of God in some pretty spectacular ways. Once he asked God to show him His glory, but God warned Moses that what he asked was dangerous: "No one can see my face and live," He said. Instead, He offered an indirect alternative. He would hide Moses in the cleft of a rock, and shield him with His hand. Then, when God had passed by, He would allow Moses to see His back. Moses saw God, but only in hindsight.

Aren't we like that? We may say we want to see God, but we couldn't survive His direct approach. But when He has passed by, when we've had a brush with glory, we see Him in hindsight. We say, "Oh yes, that was the hand of God. He was with me there. He touched my life, and I didn't even realize it at the time." The apostle Paul said "For now we see in a mirror dimly, but then face to face; now I know in part, but then I shall know fully just as I have also been fully known." One day, our sight will improve...but until then, our view is constrained. Seek to daily stretch your awareness of God's glorious presence.

QUESTION

Read: *Exodus 33:18-23*

How can you be more alert to God's hand in your life?

The Secret of Greatness

MEMORIZE

"...but whoever wishes to become great among you shall be your servant."

MATTHEW 20:26

Some years ago I ate dinner with a well-known author. If I gave his name, many would know it. You've likely read and enjoyed his books, as have I. I anticipated an evening of stirring conversation and great dialogue, but I was disappointed. In fact, I have seldom been so bored. All this very intelligent, successful man did for two hours was talk about himself. On and on and on, story after story. Finally, he took a breath, and I thought we might be getting a break. Then he said, "Enough about me. What do you think of my latest book?"

Whether we admit it or not, we're all guilty to some degree of self-promotion and ego-inflating. But Jesus' teaching showed that these practices are worthless. "If you want to be great," he said, "learn to be a servant to others." Then He modeled that lesson Himself by serving those closest to Him in the simplest, most ordinary ways. The proud will be humbled in due time. But the reverse is also true. The humble, the quiet workers, the loving servants, will one day be exalted.

How about you? Are you grabbing the spotlight all the time, or are you content to work quietly in the wings while others shine? Servanthood is the secret of true greatness.

QUESTION

Read: John 13:3-15

 How much of what you do would you continue to do if no one looked or applauded?

Family Matters

"Grandchildren are the crown of old men, and the glory of sons is their fathers."
PROVERBS 17:6

The older I get, the more I love my family. My wife, my sons and daughters-in-law and my six grandchildren are more precious to me than anything else in this life. But if I were starting my family over again, I'd strive to do better. I would listen more. Love my wife more. Spend more quality time with my children. Praise them more often for doing right. If I had it to do over again, I'd let them know how grateful to God I am for each of them, every day. Because family matters.

Puritan reformer and preacher Jonathan Edwards married Sarah Pierpoint, and they had 11 children. Every day Jonathan and Sarah Edwards would sit down with each one of those children alone, and say "Let's talk a little about you." Also, every day, this husband and wife rode on horseback together for an hour or more. And 150 years after Edwards' death, his family was still growing strong. By 1900, the Edwards clan included 13 college presidents, 66 professors, a law school dean, 100 attorneys, 32 judges, 56 physicians, a medical school president, over 80 public office holders, over 100 missionaries, and a whole platoon of clergymen. Edwards' legacy was not his writings or the sermons he preached. It was the family he loved and led.

What about you? Is your family your number one priority? Do they know it? Tell them today, and let your actions prove that it is true.

Read: *Proverbs 23:13-25*

What things do you need to let go of so your family can be strong?

Forgiveness

MEMORIZE

*"In Him we have redemption through His blood,
the forgiveness of our trespasses according to the riches of His grace."*

EPHESIANS 1:7

None of us deserve the forgiveness that is ours when we place our faith in Jesus Christ. That's why it's called grace. We're not receiving the due penalty for our sins; Jesus Himself has already paid that penalty (death) on our behalf. How is it, then, that we who have been forgiven much have trouble forgiving others?

A distant relative of mine left home as a young girl to go to nursing school. Just before her graduation she became pregnant, but the man she loved and had hoped to marry refused to take responsibility for her or the child. She had a baby girl, and gave her up for adoption shortly after her birth. The daughter was adopted by a dear Christian couple, and she grew into a fine young woman who went to college, graduated, and married a fine Christian man. After the death of her adoptive parents, this woman (by now in her thirties) began to search for her birth mother. With her husband's help, the mother was found, and she agreed to meet the daughter she'd given up years before. A few days later, a reunion was arranged in a local hotel room, and the two began to establish a loving, caring relationship. Several years went by before the mother could bring herself to ask the question she'd longed to voice: "Can you find it in your heart to forgive me for what I've done?" The daughter did not hesitate a moment. She simply said, "Mother, I forgave you a long time ago."

Do you know what forgiveness is? It is the restoration of a relationship that was broken through sin and separation. Is there someone who needs your forgiveness?

ACTION

Read: *Psalm 51:1-19*

Ask God to point out any unforgiveness that is in your heart. Be willing to act on what He reveals.

God's Army

"Let us therefore lay aside the deeds of darkness and put on the armor of light."

ROMANS 13:12

I'm not much of a fisherman, but I've heard of a fisherman who always came back with a great catch. Every time he went out, he would return with chests full of bass, trout, catfish, etc. Nobody could believe his skill, especially not the game warden who lived down the block. Wondering how this guy did it, the warden invited himself along on the next fishing trip. The two made an appointment, headed for the water, and began to unload. The warden couldn't believe his eyes. His neighbor had no rods or reels, no bait, no trot lines…nothing. But he kept his mouth shut. He had come to learn.

They got in the boat, and went out in the middle of a large lake. When the boat was still, the great fisherman pulled out some dynamite, lit it, and threw it into the water. All kinds of fish began floating to the surface. "Do you know what you're doing?" shouted the warden. "You must be nuts! You've just broken every ordinance in the book. I'm sworn by the laws of this state, friendship or no friendship, to see that you are punished. I've never seen anything like this, I…" His buddy just kept scooping up fish as fast as he could, then lit another stick of dynamite, handed it to him, and said "Are you going to talk, or are you going to fish?"

We are called to be fishers of men. Too many Christians spend their time talking, but never wet a hook. (I'm not recommending the use of explosives.) God has a remnant of people He wants to use to claim lives and territory for Jesus Christ. So as God's army, let me ask you: Are you going to talk, or are you going to fish?

Read: *Matthew 28:16-20*

 Who do you know that needs to hear about Jesus Christ? Pray that God will prepare a time for you to share the gospel with that person.

The Healing Power of Fellowship

MEMORIZE

"For the body is not one member, but many."

I CORINTHIANS 12:14

The church of Jesus Christ should be a house of healing. Our fellowship should be nurturing and life-giving—not fearful and vengeful. Some have said that the church is the only institution that shoots its wounded...and sadly, many times she does. But that should not be the case.

We could take a lesson from nature in observing the mighty Sequoia tree. Sequoias are among the oldest trees in the forest...and they are strong. They grow straight because their root system is self-correcting, and their bark contains an acid that repels insect attacks. They withstand wind and violent rain because they grow in clumps, allowing their root systems to intertwine. To blow over one tree would mean blowing over an entire hillside of them!

Oh, if the church were as strong from within! In the fellowship of believers, there should be a spirit of openness to those who are hurting, confused, embarrassed, disenfranchised, lost. The down-and-out should be "in" in God's family, and the suffering should find comfort. Why? Because the Holy Spirit who lives in us empowers our hearts to love as Jesus loved. We have the resources to be strong, and to nurture the weak until they are strengthened, too.

QUESTION

Read: I *Corinthians* 12:12-27

How do you respond to those in your fellowship who are in need?

God Loves The Unlovely

*"But God demonstrates His own love toward us, in that while we were yet sinners,
Christ died for us."*

ROMANS 5:8

Down in South Georgia, a little family of sharecroppers struggled to make ends meet. They never seemed to have enough to go around, but one year they planted at just the right time, the rains were plentiful, and the market conditions were right. After they gave the landowner his share, they paid their bills and had a little bit left over. They decided to buy one thing the entire family could enjoy, and after shopping through the dry goods catalog, they selected something they'd never owned before: a mirror.

When it arrived, the husband, wife and children gathered round, and unwrapped it together. The wife looked in it first, and then the husband. Each child took a turn, down to the youngest named Willie...a small, deformed child whose mouth was misshapen and scarred. He stood before the mirror a long time before he turned to his mother. "Did you always know I looked like this...different from the others?" She said, "Yes, Willie." He said, "Momma, you mean I always looked like this, and you loved me anyway?" She said, "Yes, Willie. I love you because you are mine. You belong to me."

Isn't it a relief to know God has always known us, with our shortcomings, our flaws and sinful ways, and He loves us anyway? We were sinners when Christ died for us...not "cleaned up saints." He loves us because He gave His Son to die for us.

ACTION

Read: I John 3:1-3

List all your best assets. Now tear up the list. God could not love you any more because of them, or any less without them..

Wanted: Firsthand Experience

MEMORIZE

"and you shall know the truth, and the truth shall make you free."

JOHN 8:32

D r. E. Stanley Jones has said that mankind is on the verge of a spiritual renewal ushered in by the scientific method. What is the scientific method? In pedestrian terms, it is the belief that truth is revealed by experiment. In other words, it is proven deductively. Prior to the age of science, truth was determined philosophically—by debate. But the scientific method has brought the search for truth out of the lecture hall and into the laboratory. I happen to agree with Dr. Jones that this turn of events is conducive to revival. Why? Because we have a God whose presence and precepts stand up to investigation and experiment.

Our God became flesh. And the Lord Jesus invited (and still invites!) men and women to take Him into the laboratory of life and prove Him. When we do, we will discover that Christianity is real. It is true. Chesterton said, "If there is a story....then there is a storyteller." The Gospel is the truest story ever told. And God Himself is the Storyteller.

Are you a skeptic? Trust Christ. Try Him. Prove Him. He can withstand the fiercest intellectual investigation you can muster. But be warned: Some of the most powerful apologists this world has ever known discovered truth by experience, and began the journey as doubters.

REFLECTION

Read: John 1:35-49

Look for empirical evidence of the presence of God today. Record your findings and share them with someone else.

Any Old Bush!

MEMORIZE

*"Because the foolishness of God is wiser than men,
and the weakness of God is stronger than men."*

I CORINTHIANS 1:25

I can relate to Moses. When God appeared to him in the burning bush and commissioned him to lead God's people out of Egypt, he wasn't sure he was the guy. "Please, Lord," he said, "I have never been eloquent, neither recently nor in time past, nor since Thou hast spoken to Thy servant; for I am slow of speech and slow of tongue." History records that God was not deterred in His choice. As a young man, I had a strong fear of public speaking. If you had told me then I would preach, I would have given a defense very similar to Moses'. I was an unlikely candidate for the pulpit, to say the least.

Major Ian Thomas said in reviewing Moses' call that when God is in a thing, the ordinary is more-than-adequate. Moses may have thought the burning bush was a supernatural vision. But it wasn't. It was just an ordinary bush. And when God wants to speak, *any old bush will do*. The important thing is not the fitness of the instrument, but that it is God Himself who speaks, quite often, through foolish, weak instruments.

Sometimes we see someone alive for God, someone with extraordinary giftedness, and we say, "I wish I were like that! I wish I had his ability, his poise, his discipline." But the truth is, God can use any life. Our foolishness only highlights His wisdom, and our weakness testifies to His strength. You are someone God can use. "You don't know me," you might say. And maybe I do not. But I know God.

ACTION

Read: *Exodus 3:1-14*

Surrender your list of excuses today, and ask God to use you as He sees fit.

God With Us

MEMORIZE

"Behold, a virgin shall be with child, and bear a son, and they shall call His name Immanuel, which is translated 'God with us.'"

MATTHEW 1:23

What a name! Immanuel. "God with us." It is a promise, as well as a name, and it has been given to men and women of God throughout history, and given to us. Immanuel will be with us, and His presence is life-changing!

Desmond and his family lived at the Star of Hope mission in Houston, a temporary shelter for the homeless of our city. One summer our high school young people served as workers and counselors at a camp that allowed the children of families residing at the mission to spend a week in the country. Desmond was an inquisitive little guy of seven, who listened intently to the words of his counselors as they talked about Jesus and what it means to know Him. Each night before lights out, Desmond would ask his counselor Ray to sit by his bed until he fell asleep, because he was afraid of being alone in the dark. On the last night of camp, Desmond wanted to ask Jesus into his heart. He told Ray, who talked with him and led him in a prayer to receive Christ. That night, Ray sat down by Desmond's bed after lights out. After a few minutes, Desmond opened his eyes in the dark, looked at his friend and said, "It's okay, Ray. You don't have to stay. I know I'm not alone because God is with me now."

How can we know that God is with us? We receive His presence by responding to the invitation of His Son Jesus, who says "Behold, I stand at the door and knock. If anyone hears my voice and opens the door, I will come in to him and dine with him and he with Me." (Revelation 3:20)

QUESTION

Read: Micah 5:2-5

 Do you know "Immanuel?" Have you opened the door and let Him in?

Is That All There Is?

"Vanity of vanities, says the preacher. Vanity of vanities, all is vanity."

ECCLESIASTES 1:2

Serious fans of basketball will remember October 6, 1993, as a significant date in sports history. On that day, Chicago Bulls superstar Michael Jordan faced the assembled crowd of media with their microphones and notepads, and told them the game offered no more challenges to motivate him. He was ready to retire. Although Jordan would come back two years later, he was clearly disenchanted with the game that had been his life, although he was at the top, and the money he was making was phenomenal. Why would a man with everything under the sun walk away? Jordan, whose father was murdered earlier in the year, hinted at the answer as he told reporters, "One thing about my father's death was that it reinforced how [life] can be taken from you at any time." Basketball—and the fame, money and excitement it brought—was no longer compelling enough to get the superstar up in the morning. As he looked at the prospect of another long season, in his heart he must have said, "Been there. Done that. Now what?"

The key words that described Michael Jordan at his early retirement were these: "everything under the sun." You see, if our existence is only played out "under the sun," if there is no spiritual realm to life, then even fame and fortune will get old. That's right. King Solomon proved the same thing when he tried it all, and returned time and again to this phrase: "Vanity of vanities. All is vanity." In other words, "It's vapor. It's air. It's not enough." Can you relate to Jordan and King Solomon? Have you had your fill of "flatland living?" Then consider the adventure of pursuing the Creator Himself…that's an endeavor that never gets old.

Read: *Ecclesiastes* 1:1-11

Are you setting yourself up to say "Been there, done that, now what?" by the things you are pursuing?

The Brotherhood of Man?

*"That they may be one; even as Thou, Father, art in Me,
and I Thee, that they also may be in Us..."*

JOHN 17:21

There is a church in northern California that has portraits of famous people hanging in its vestibule. There is a portrait of Socrates and another of Eleanor Roosevelt. There are portraits of Abraham Lincoln, Ghandi and Jesus. These words are written in gold over the assembled portraits: "And we are all children of God..." I am sure people pass by those portraits every day and marvel at the universal brotherhood of man. There is only one problem: the universal brotherhood of man (and the universal "fatherhood" of God) is a lie. The quote in gold letters is even a quote from the Bible—but it is incomplete. "We are all children of God," the scripture says, "through our faith in the Lord Jesus Christ."

There is no universal brotherhood apart from Christ. But through Him, we are adopted into the family of God, and we become joint heirs with Christ to the very kingdom of God. We are like sheep, Jesus said, who have wandered away and followed our own schemes and desires. But we were created for something different...something more. The greatest lie perpetrated today is that God's way does not work. The second greatest lie is that man's way does. The truth is, there are no values working in this world today *but* God's. And there is no other way into His family but through His Son and our Savior Jesus Christ.

Don't let a sense of political correctness deter you from calling Jesus what He is: the way, the truth, and the life...and the only way in to the family of God.

Read: John 17: 18-26

Thank Jesus for adopting you into God's family...and tell someone who's not yet adopted how the process takes place.

Perspective Is Key

MEMORIZE

*"If any of you lacks wisdom, let him ask of God,
who gives to all men generously and without reproach..."*

JAMES 1:5

Sometimes things are not as they seem. A woman entered an airport gift shop with an hour or so to spare before her flight. She bought a newspaper and a small package of cookies, then settled into a chair near the gate to wait. As she opened the paper and began to read, a gentleman sat down opposite her, resting his briefcase and a cup of coffee on the small table between them. He opened his paper, too. As she read, she reached for a cookie from the bag in the center of the table, and popped one into her mouth. A few minutes went by and she reached for another cookie, but they had been moved. The package, near empty, was sitting on top of the man's briefcase. "How rude," she thought, taking another cookie and moving the package back to her side. Then she heard the rustle of cellophane and watched as her seat-mate ate the last cookie! She glared at him angrily above her paper, then gathered her things, gave him one last withering stare, and moved to the other side of the waiting area. Her fury did not subside until half an hour into the flight when she reached into her bag for a pen and found...her unopened package of cookies!

Perspective is critical, is it not? We do not always have the understanding we need to correctly evaluate the world around us. Even those of us who are Christians are guilty of having a "flatland perspective" that does not take into account the wisdom of God. He sees things we cannot, and His understanding is infinite.

ACTION

Read: I Kings 3: 3-15

 If you are in a confusing situation, ask God for wisdom to help you see it rightly.

Leadership And Judgment

"The fear of the Lord is the beginning of knowledge; fools despise wisdom and instruction."

PROVERBS 1:7

Deputy Sheriff Barney Fife of the television hamlet of Mayberry, North Carolina, was running for office in an old episode of "The Andy Griffith Show." Eager to learn some necessary skills from his trusted superior, Sheriff Andy Taylor, Barney asked Andy how he had acquired his unusually good judgment. "Well, Barn," Andy said, "I guess you could say good judgment comes from experience." Barney considered that for a moment. "Then where does experience come from?" he asked. "Experience," Andy replied, "comes from bad judgment."

Some leadership skills can be learned from experience, but the gift of leadership is given by God. King Solomon exhibited good judgment in the beginning of his reign, exercising the gifts of wisdom and discernment that were given to him by God. But the leadership principles he spoke of at the end of his life were those shaped from the crucible of experience—experience forged in the fires of bad judgment. He had lived in excess, tried it all, and made more than his share of bad choices.

The best leaders possess both natural gifts and skills honed by experience. How can you spot a leader? When a leader steps out, others follow—consistently and enthusiastically over time. Leadership is assuming responsibility for building relationships with grace.

Read: I Kings 3: 16-28

Pray for those you know who are in positions of leadership. If you are a leader yourself, ask a trusted friend to pray for you.

Following The Leader

"And He said to them, 'follow Me, and I will make you fishers of men.'"

MATTHEW 4:19

It takes two things to get something accomplished in this life: leadership... and incentive. My wife and I saw this precept in action on a stay at the Peabody Hotel in Orlando, Florida. One afternoon around 4:00, we observed a red carpet rolled out from the front fountain to the elevator. People were waiting on either side of the carpet—we supposed for a dignitary to arrive. But what arrived at 4:00 p.m. was not a dignitary, but a flock of ducks. And these ducks, accompanied by strains of "The Stars and Stripes Forever," marched right through the lobby, into the elevator, and all the way up to the roof. The crowd applauded wildly. We were amazed.

I asked the first employee I saw how these ducks were able to do such a thing. He said, "Well, the environmentalists make sure we don't keep a duck too long, but we put the ones who have already learned the drill at the front, and they're the leaders. The other ducks follow them because they know they're leading them to food. Food's the incentive, you know." There it was: leadership and incentive.

No Christian should ever live an ineffective life. We have all we need to make an impact on our world. We have a perfect leader—the Lord Jesus Christ—and a glorious incentive. He has promised to make us by grace what we are not by nature. We can become what He called us to be: fishers of men.

Read: Matthew 4: 18-25

 Have you obeyed Christ's call to become a "fisher of men?"

The Myth of The Self-Made Man

"Every good thing bestowed and every perfect gift is from above..."

JAMES 1:17

Never make the mistake of thinking you are responsible for all that you have. The triumphs of life are gifts, not merit badges. Sometimes people get what they deserve for their hard work and effort, but just as often they do not. James says that every good thing in life is from the Father above who is the source of life itself. The following story illustrates how we become confused about how we got what we have.

A newspaper reporter went to interview a successful entrepreneur. "How did you do it?" he asked. "How did you make all this money?" The entrepreneur was glad to tell his story. "You see, when my wife and I married, we started out with a roof over our heads, some food in our pantry, and five cents between us. I took that nickel, went down to the grocery store, bought an apple, then shined it up and sold it for ten cents. Then I bought more apples, shined them up and sold them for twenty cents apiece." The reporter was beginning to catch on, and thought this would be a great human interest story. "Then what happened?" he asked excitedly. "Then my father-in-law died and left us $20 million," the rich man said. He had fooled himself into thinking he had done something, forgetting that he had *received* something.

Don't forget all you have been given, and remember to thank the Giver for each and every good thing He bestows.

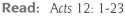

Read: Acts 12: 1-23

What have you taken credit for that came from God Himself?

A Dangerous Love Affair

"He who loves money will not be satisfied with money,
nor he who loves abundance with its income."

ECCLESIASTES 5:10

The place was Chicago, Illinois, the year was 1923. Nine of the world's wealthiest and most successful men gathered for a meeting at the city's Edgewater Beach Hotel. Almost anyone in that day would have exchanged places with any of these well-known executives. They were powerful and rich. The world was their oyster. But only 25 years later, all but two were dead. None had lived the easy life their tremendous resources seemed to promise.

Charles Schwab, the president of the nation's largest independent steel company, lived on borrowed money the last five years of his life and died bankrupt. Samuel Insul, the president of a giant utility company, died a penniless fugitive from justice in a foreign country. Gas company executive Howard Hopson suffered from insanity. Wheat speculator Arthur Cotton died destitute. Richard Whitney, president of the New York Stock Exchange, was released from Sing Sing prison. Albert Fall, a member of the president's cabinet, was pardoned from prison so he could die at home. Wall Street's greatest bear, Jesse Livermore, committed suicide, as did Ivan Krueger, the head of a great monopoly. Bank president Leon Fraser also took his own life.

The most dangerous love affair any man or woman will experience in life is a love affair with money. It is a deceitful object of desire, because it can never deliver what it promises. If you make money your primary aim, you are setting yourself up for a life of heartache.

Read: *Proverbs* 30: 7-9

Have you attributed more importance to money than it really deserves?

Boarding The Wrong Bus

MEMORIZE

"Sir, give me this water, so I will not be thirsty, nor come all the way here to draw."

JOHN 4:15

A man boarded a bus in New York City with every intention of traveling to Detroit. Unknowingly, he ended up in Kansas City, Missouri. When he got off the bus, he asked for directions: "Where is Woodward Avenue?" Nobody in Kansas City had heard of Woodward Avenue, of course, because it was in *Detroit*. The fellow thought people were not being very helpful or gracious, and he began to argue saying, "I know you're putting me on. Woodward Avenue is one of the main thoroughfares here in Detroit. Tell me how to get there." Bystanders and bus station employees insisted they had never heard of such a street. "Wait a minute," one man said. "Did you say *Detroit*?" The man turned to face him: "That's right. Detroit." A murmur began in the crowd. "Sir," he said. "That's your problem. You're not in Detroit. You're in Kansas City."

It's easy to catch the wrong bus in life...to have a destination in mind and think you are on the vehicle that will get you there. But if you are on the wrong bus, it is impossible to reach your destination. Jesus met such a woman at a well in Samaria. She had come at mid-day to draw water, but her whole life had been spent thirsting for love and belonging. She had pursued numerous relationships with men to quench her thirst...but she was on the wrong bus. When Jesus told her He could offer her water that would satisfy her for life, she responded with enthusiasm: "Sir, give me this water, so I will not be thirsty, nor come all the way here to draw." She still didn't quite understand. She thought the water was in the well—but it wasn't. It was in Jesus Himself. If you are thirsting for love and meaning in life, look to Jesus. He Himself is the way.

QUESTION

Read: John 4: 7-26

Are you looking to others for the kind of love that only Jesus can give?

A Time To Speak

MEMORIZE

"Like apples of gold in settings of silver is a word spoken in right circumstances."

PROVERBS 25:11

A wise person knows when to speak, and when to keep silent. I have wished many times that someone had whispered in my ear to be silent. There have been times, too, when I have been silent and should have spoken out, when I have wished someone had said, "Okay, Edwin, this is your cue. Speak up!" Those in attendance at the 1994 National Prayer Breakfast, held in conjunction with the National Religious Broadcasters' Convention, witnessed a time for speaking when Mother Teresa took the podium and pleaded for the lives of unborn children.

Barely tall enough to be seen over the lectern, this tiny nun began her address by reading a portion of scripture, then stunned the assembled dignitaries, including the President and Vice President of the United States, by saying, "The greatest destroyer of peace today is abortion...[for] if we accept that a mother can kill even her own child, how can we tell people not to kill each other?"

"Mother Teresa," wrote Charles Colson after the event, "was invariably polite and respectful. She did not flinch in speaking the truth. She demonstrated civility wedded to bold conviction, confronting world leaders with a message of biblical righteousness." Clearly, she viewed the breakfast as a time to speak.

REFLECTION

Read: *Ecclesiastes* 3: 1-8

Have you backed away in moments when you should have spoken? Resolve this week to speak boldly in the right circumstances.

On God's Time

MEMORIZE

"And in Thy book they were all written, the days that were ordained for me
when there was not yet one of them."

PSALM 139:16

The Creator, and not the creature, determines the length of life. The psalmist understood this when he wrote the words of Psalm 139. King Solomon echoed them when he wrote, "There is a time to be born, and a time to die."

Even retailers understand the impact of this idea. A recent Sharper Image catalog advertised a "Personal Life Clock"—a marble obelisk with digital numbers that flashed the number of hours, minutes and seconds remaining in one's statistical lifetime. "All lives are finite," the catalog glibly noted. "In fact, the average life lasts only 683,280 hours or 2.4 billion seconds. This new Timisis Personal Life Clock reminds you to live life to the fullest by displaying the…most profound number you will ever see." But it could be wrong by a mile.

You see, our days are God-appointed and God-ordained. God's Son, too, had an appointment with death. His cry, "It is finished" from the cross was the triumphant call of the God-man whose numbered days on earth had been fulfilled. There is a time to be born…and a time to die. And God selects them both.

QUESTION

Read: II Peter 3: 8-9

Do you live with a sense of urgency and gratitude, knowing that your days
are numbered?

Going Nowhere Fast

MEMORIZE

"What advantage does man have in all his work which he does under the sun?"

ECCLESIASTES 1:3

Have you been to the gym lately? Every time I work out, I am astounded by the array of exercise equipment—stationary bikes, recumbent bikes, treadmills, stair climbers—all designed to enhance fitness. You get on them, and you go...nowhere. In fact, going nowhere is part of their design. The point is not to get somewhere—the point is to expend as much energy as possible for as long as possible while you are going nowhere. Every time you step off the treadmill or the bike, you are in the same place that you began.

It seems we are a culture dedicated to getting nowhere fast. We want to know how to do things: to get fit, lose weight, achieve financial success, find love—and naturally we want to do them in the quickest possible way. "How" questions are the most frequently asked questions in this life under the sun. But the real question in life isn't "how?", but rather "why?". Why be successful? Why strive to gain power? Why spend your life searching for prestige or love?

King Solomon dared to ask the bigger questions. Is life really worth living? And if it is, why? He argued that a life moving in circles but going nowhere was pointless, and I agree. Life only makes sense when we include God in our thinking. Without Him it's just a lot of motion, going nowhere with no purpose.

REFLECTION

Read: *Ecclesiastes* 1: 3-9

What about you? Are you on a track or a treadmill? Climbing a staircase, or laboring on the stair climber? Where is God in your reckoning of life?

The Disease of Sin

MEMORIZE

"For the wages of sin is death, but the free gift of God is eternal life in Christ Jesus our Lord."

ROMANS 6:23

British journalist Malcolm Muggeridge had been faithful to his wife for the length of their marriage, but he carried in his mind the thought that if the right opportunity ever presented itself, he would be intimate with another woman, just for the experience. That opportunity seemed to present itself when Muggeridge was in India, away from his wife and family. Each morning when he rose, Muggeridge swam in the Ganges river. On one such morning, he saw a woman bathing herself, quite a distance away. "This is my moment," he told himself. "No one will know." He began to swim upstream to her, struggling not just against the water, but against the current of his own conscience. He went underwater, then surfaced when he was just a few yards away from the unsuspecting woman. When he saw her, it was Muggeridge, not she, who experienced the shock of a lifetime. The woman was a leper. Her nose was eaten away. There were sores and white blotches all over her skin, and the ends of her fingers were gone. She looked more like an animal than a human.

"What a wretched woman this is," he thought to himself—but at the same moment, he was overwhelmed with a devastating truth: "What a wretched man I am!" Though Muggeridge never expressed it in his autobiography, he must have come to understand a basic principle: Physical leprosy is crippling and terminal, but spiritual leprosy is deadly and eternal. Muggeridge's real-life, graphic experience illustrates an unalterable truth: When we walk away from the commands of God, we walk right into disease...the disease of sin.

REFLECTION

Read: I Corinthians 10: 7-13

Are you entertaining the possibility of committing a particular sin? Reconsider, and resolve today to obey God when the temptation comes.

Providence

"For I know the plans I have for you, declares the Lord, plans for welfare and not for calamity to give you a future and a hope."

JEREMIAH 29:11

The man or woman who trusts that God is in control has no need to "get even" or to hold a grudge. Joseph proved this when he was reunited with his brothers after they had sold him into slavery. His confidence in God allowed him to say, "But now, do not therefore be grieved or angry with yourselves because you sold me here; for God sent me before you to preserve life." (Genesis 45:5) Perhaps he had a right to blame his brothers for all the bad things that had happened to him, but he was wise enough to see beyond the immediate and discern God's purpose. This is the mark of a mature man.

While living in North Carolina, I had several occasions to visit Charlotte, "the queen city." The Myers Park section of Charlotte is an incredible maze of curving roads and cul-de-sacs, all confusing to a driver unfamiliar with the area. I soon discovered (with help from the natives) that the key to traffic flow in Myers Park is a throughfare known as Providence Road. This street is the hub that runs through the section, tying together all the tangled roads.

Providence expresses the idea that the hand of God is shaping our lives, and shaping history. We are not at the mercy of a cyclical, happenstance repetition of events or ideologies, moving aimlessly through time and space. Our destiny is not controlled by powerful nations, great men or circumstances. It rests securely and comfortably in the hands of God.

Read: *Jeremiah* 29: 10-14

Have you lost sight of the providence of God? Remember our lives (and these times) are in His hands.

"I Do."

*"For this cause a man shall leave his father and his mother,
and shall cleave to his wife; and they shall become one flesh."*

GENESIS 2:24

I think back on the girls I dated and thought at times I might marry, and I remember praying, "Oh, help her to like me," or "Let her want to marry me." I thank God that He, in His wisdom, did not affirmatively answer those prayers! So many single adults see marriage as *the* great goal of life. Then they meet someone they choose to marry and imagine they have somehow "arrived," only to find that marriage in and of itself is an unworthy goal. If marriage is the goal, what do you do for the rest of your life once you've attained it?

A young medical student was given a tour of the hospital where he would train. A resident led him into a semi-private room where two men were situated. The student spoke to both of them, but neither responded. One of them didn't even look up. As the student left the room he queried the resident: "What's wrong with them?" The resident replied, "Well, the guy in bed one is in good physical health, but he's severely depressed. He was head over heels in love with a girl who left him at the altar for another guy." The med student was taking notes. "And the other one? Did he lose his girl, too?" The resident shook his head. "Him? Oh, no. He's the guy that got her."

The moral of this story is simple: You can get into big trouble married; you can get into big trouble not married. Marriage can be a great journey, but it's a terrible goal.

Read: *Genesis 2: 18-25*

 If you're single, is marriage your primary goal? Reconsider. If you're married, what goals do you have for your marriage?

Staying On Track

"Wives, be subject to your own husbands, as to the Lord. Husands, love your wives, just as Christ also loved the church..."

EPHESIANS 5:22,25

Herman Miller Inc. manufactures office furniture and is consistently recognized as one of the best managed companies in the U. S. What makes Herman Miller Inc. a success? One thing: clearly stated values are supported and understood at every level. Virtually everyone in the firm, from assemblers to executives, can articulate their company's philosophy and goals—and an infrastructure has been allowed to develop that encourages open, honest communication, regardless of organizational rank or functional responsibility. What's it like to work at a place where goals are high, communication is prized, and people really care about one another? HMI's absentee rate is between 1 and 2 percent—well below the 6 percent industry standard. And the company's turnover rate of 7 percent is less than half of the 15 to 20 percent average of other U.S. firms.

What do you think might happen in a marriage partnership where "key executives" set high goals for their union, cultivated communication, and agreed upon their mission? I think it might be as big an attention-getter in our culture as Herman Miller Inc. is in the marketplace! Just like HMI executives give ownership away for the good of the enterprise, husbands and wives must realize that they do not "own" their marriage. In fact, they do not even have the rights to themselves, do they? They have been bought and paid for with a price, and are called to glorify God with all they are and all they will ever be. Husbands, loving your wives glorifies God. Wives, being submissive to your husbands glorifies God. Your marriage is His enterprise, and it can be a glorious one!

Read: 1 Peter 3: 1-6

If you are married, are you and your mate in agreement on your marriage mission?

How To Love Your Wife

MEMORIZE

"So husbands ought also to love their own wives as their own bodies."

EPHESIANS 5:28

Aman who loves his wife sacrificially loves her in a satisfying way. If husband and wife are "one flesh" in marriage, then to hurt her is to hurt himself, and to do good to her is to do good to himself. Husbands are to know what is satisfying to their wives, and to seek to give those things. So husbands, do you know those things?

To determine whether or not I knew the things that were satisfying to my wife, I gave myself a little test. Let me encourage you to try it, too. I wrote down on a piece of paper three things I believed my wife enjoyed. Then I gave her the paper, and asked her to "grade" it. I was one for three. It's funny—no woman, or very few, could live with a man for long and not score 100% on such a test. But we men are not so observant. Paul understood this gender difference and encouraged men to love their wives as they loved their own bodies. Men know their bodies. They know how much they weigh, and what they like to eat, and how many cups of coffee will keep them awake at night. They know how many miles they can jog before their knees begin to ache, and whether a nagging pain can be ignored or needs a doctor's attention. They listen to their bodies.

Imagine how many marriages would improve if a man attempted to know his wife as well as he knew his own body, and to treat her with as much care as his own flesh! Husbands…that's how to love your wife!

ACTION

Read: *Ephesians 5: 22-33*

If you are a married man, become a student of your wife. Seek to know her completely…and become an expert on her preferences, gifts and needs.

It's Not Fifty-Fifty

*"And be kind to one another, tender-hearted, forgiving each other,
just as God in Christ also has forgiven you."*

EPHESIANS 4:32

At nearly every wedding ceremony I perform, the bride and groom hear this verse from Ephesians as a part of my charge to them. Marriage is not a fifty-fifty proposition. It is two people each giving 100 percent, regardless of the performance of their mate. In other words, it is a husband's responsibility to be as kind, tender-hearted and forgiving to his wife as Christ has been to him. Likewise, it is the wife's responsibility to extend that same Christ-like kindness, tender-heartedness and forgiveness to her husband.

I wonder sometimes if this is truly understood as a bride and groom stand at the altar. I imagine if their thoughts could be broadcast, they would be more like this: *"Boy, I've got a gal here who will meet all my needs. I've had a poor self-image all my life, but now I have someone who really loves me, and I'm thrilled to be with her."* And the bride: *"I'm so glad I've found this guy who will meet all of my needs for life. When we're married, all of my troubles with family, friends, relationships, and work will just melt away!"* This is what I call a "two ticks/no dog" proposition. A tick is a parasite in the insect world. It sees a host, attaches itself to that host, and has itself a nourishing meal. But when a husband and wife both look to the other person as their "meal ticket" to lifelong satisfaction, what you have is two ticks and no dog, or to put it another way, two takers and no givers. It is not hard to see trouble ahead for a relationship of this sort.

Read: *Ephesians* 4: 25-32

If you are married, talk to your mate about this verse. If you are single, understand that this is the promise that marriage requires of the Christian.

Fill 'Er Up?

MEMORIZE

"Little children, let us not love with word or with tongue, but in deed and truth."

I JOHN 3:18

Everyone has basic needs, and God designed the home to be the primary place where those needs are met. Some have said the home is like a restaurant where people are "fed" with love. Others liken the home to a hotel—mostly a place for spending the night, but not where real living takes place, and sadly, that is sometimes true. But the best analogy I've heard compares the home to a full-service filling station. That's something I know a little about.

When I was growing up my dad had a country store, and next to it was a small building with gas tanks out front. The gas station was never operational until the summer dad said, "Edwin, I want you to go out and run the filling station." So that summer, I became a small businessman. I was fired up. Every morning for three months, I got up, put on my jeans, t-shirt and sneakers, and went to work. My dad taught me when a customer pulled up to say "Fill 'er up?", then to check under the hood, wash all the windows, check the tires and the oil. In that way, I sought to take care of all the customers who came to my full-service filling station.

I think the home should be just like that, because the world is a tough place. Whether you work outside the home, or you're a homemaker, it's tough out there. Toward the end of each day, the family begins to converge on the home. And everyone's tank is empty. Who is going to put on the attendant's uniform, rush out and say "Fill 'er up?" Mom? Dad? The answer is, everybody! You see, each one is to be customer AND attendant in his home. By imitating Jesus Christ, we learn to love one another in deed and fill each other up.

REFLECTION

Read: I John 3: 18-24

Have you been neglecting the "attendant's" duties in your home? How can you "fill up" those that you love today?

No Excuse

"If I had not come and spoken to them, they would not have sin,
but now they have no excuse for their sin."

JOHN 15:22

Writer Ernest Hemingway was the son of devout Christian parents. His writing was forceful, action-oriented and often brutal, but it exhibited none of the beliefs his parents tried to instill in him. Early in his life, he rejected the faith of his family as irrelevant. A letter from his mother written in 1920 illustrates how completely he had divorced himself from their beliefs: "Unless you, my son, Ernest, come to yourself, cease your lazy loafing and pleasure-seeking...stop trading on your handsome face...and neglecting your duties to God and your Savior Jesus Christ...there is nothing for you but bankruptcy; you have overdrawn."

Hemingway told a writer for *Playboy* magazine in 1956 that "what is immoral is what you feel bad after," and since not much made him feel bad, he was a self-proclaimed man of unimpeachable standards. "People with different ideas about morality would call him a sinner," the article read, "and the wages of sin, they say, is death. Hemingway has cheated death time and time again to become a scarred and bearded American legend...Sin has paid off for Hemingway." But the final years of Hemingway's life were marked with repeated suicide attempts, paranoia, multiple affairs, and finally, a successful suicide. Hemingway knew the truth. But he refused to surrender to it. The faith of our families does not automatically become our own. But we are responsible for the truth we have heard, and if we disregard it, God says we are without excuse.

Read: Romans 1:18-25

What have you done with the truth you have been shown? Remember, to do nothing is to reject it.

A Look, A Word, A Touch

MEMORIZE

"Better is open rebuke than a love that is concealed."

PROVERBS 27:5

There are three simple things that express care to our loved ones. They are not particularly complex or artistic like a chocolate souffle—they are more like bread: filling, simple, satisfying. What are these three things? A look. A word. A touch.

Several years ago I was in Dallas, Texas, at a basketball game for high school all-stars. My son Cliff and another young man from his school were competing with athletes from private schools across the state. Since all three of my sons played basketball, I have been to hundreds of games—and I have loved every one of them. In fact, it is a good thing there were never any games scheduled on Sunday morning, or our pulpit would have been empty!

This particular game would be Cliff's final game of his high school career. In the final moments of the game, he looked up at me in the stands—just a long, long look at his dad. And that look of love just filled me up! That was all it took. Just that moment, that look, and I was full. You can love someone, believe in them, think they are great, but unless you express that with a word, a look or a touch, they may never know it. It takes so little time, and costs us nothing, but these three things are an investment that pay dividends for life.

QUESTION

Read: I John 4:7-19

 Do those whom you love know it, or is your love concealed?

Let's Talk!

MEMORIZE

"A fool does not delight in understanding, but only in revealing his own mind."

PROVERBS 18:2

It should not come as a surprise to anyone that men and women are different! Therefore, husbands and wives need to remind themselves frequently that they have married a foreigner! One of the first things any husband needs to learn is how important talk is to the woman he has married. Women are natural communicators, and their love of sharing thoughts and ideas begins early. A few years ago I was spending an afternoon with my granddaughter, LeeBeth. We played games for a while, ran for a while...just did things together. But it wasn't long before she had another idea: "Goosey," she said, "let's go back in my room. I want to tell you something." So we went to her little room, and closed the door, and she said, "I have some secrets to tell you." She began to tell me some little things, and I listened...then she said, "Now you tell me some secrets." Now, I had three boys, and not one of them ever told me a secret or asked me to tell them one. But girls deepen relationships with talk and sharing of special secrets.

Applying this truth to marriage means that a part of showing a wife affection is communicating with her—not only talking, but really listening. How many men have suddenly heard their wives say, "Did you hear what I said?" or, "Are you listening?" I am often guilty here. Sometimes men, we just do not listen as we should. But by his attentiveness to his wife and his desire to communicate with her in a meaningful way, a man demonstrates affection. And affection is the number one need of a wife in marriage.

ACTION

Read: *Colossians* 3:12-19

The average married couple spends only 37 minutes a week in conversation with one another. Can you "up the average" in your home this week?

Is There A Father In The House?

MEMORIZE

*"Let our sons in their youth be as grown-up plants,
and our daughters as corner pillars fashioned for a palace..."*

PSALM 144:12

Fatherhood is a relationship...so a man who is uninvolved in the lives of his children and unaware of their struggles, dreams, and desires, is not really a father. Unfortunately, our society tends to applaud the successful man more than the family man—but the truth is, if you are genuinely a family man, you are a successful man.

Frederick Flick was a West German industrialist worth more than $1.5 billion. Prior to his death he controlled some 300 companies and interests. A profile of this powerful businessman in a national magazine said that he had made all the right moves when it came to accumulating wealth. But every one of his children was a failure. Peter Drucker might have called Flick a success, but according to biblical standards, he was a dismal failure. Why? Because he neglected to give his children what they needed from a father: love and leadership. When Flick's wife died, he buried her at 3:00 p.m., went back to the office at 5:00, and never broke stride.

As a pastor, I talk with so many parents who want the church to instill values in their children, and to educate them concerning life. The church can certainly help in these areas, but no church, school, or summer camp can be expected to rear children and successfully guide them through the maze of childhood and adolescence. There is absolutely no substitute for a parent's time and touch in the life of a child.

REFLECTION

Read: II Corinthians 8:1-7

Dads....how are you doing? Have you talked to your children today? Have you listened?

Give Yourself First

"And this, not as we had expected, but they first gave themselves to the Lord and to us."

II CORINTHIANS 8:5

Paul held up the Christians at Macedonia as an example to his Corinthian friends. The Macedonians (who had little) had given liberally to the Jerusalem church...and the Corinthians (who had much more) had promised aid, but done nothing. But Paul's most convicting description of these generous believers was not about money, but about heart. "They first gave themselves," he said.

God is not honored when we "tip" Him with our money but withhold from Him our selves. The gift without the giver is bare. Those Macedonian givers climbed into the offering plate with their gift. They didn't just nod at God with a few coins...they put their very lives at His disposal. What a radical act of faith! Jesus illustrated this best when He instructed His disciples to "render unto Caesar the things that are Caesar's...and to God the things that are God's." Well, what is God's? We are!

Jesus picked up a coin to drive home His point, saying, "Whose picture is on this coin?" They answered the obvious: "Caesar's." What has God's picture on it? You and I do. We are made in the image of God, and His picture is etched on your life and mine in an indelible way. When we give ourselves along with our gifts, our offering is sacrificial, spontaneous and spiritual. And we can be sure that God is honored by it.

Read: II *Corinthians* 8:1-7

 What kind of giver are you? Is God getting you, along with your gift?

French Fries

MEMORIZE

*"...all this abundance that we have provided to build Thee a house for Thy Holy Name,
it is from Thy hand, and all is Thine."*

I CHRONICLES 29:16

The Bible says more about money that it does about heaven or hell combined, and contains amazingly relevant principles regarding money management, stewardship, and budgeting. But the bottom line is this: every bit of what the Christian has belongs to God. He owns everything.

This principle was vividly illustrated to me in McDonald's of all places. I had gone to the home of the golden arches for lunch with my granddaughter, LeeBeth. We stood at the counter and placed our orders. She, with the confidence of youth and healthy arteries, ordered a "Happy Meal," including a hamburger, french fries and a drink. I, of the older and more "heart smart" generation, ordered a "McLean," with no fries. I paid for both of us, and we took our lunches to a nearby table and sat down. About halfway through our meal, I began to think how good one of LeeBeth's french fries would taste. As I reached across the table, she put her hand in front of mine and said with a stern warning, "No, Goosey, those are mine."

Now I bought every one of those french fries, and if I had wanted to, I could have marched back up to the counter and bought every french fry in the house. As I thought about her response, I began to understand how our child-like possessiveness of the things He provides must appear to God. He owns everything...and it is all at His disposal. He gives it to us to "do business with" for an undetermined time. May we be found faithful with what is His.

REFLECTION

Read: II Corinthians 9:6-11

 Have you become confused about who owns what? What are you holding onto that is God's?

Who's The Captain of Your Soul?

"That at the name of Jesus every knee should bow..."

PHILIPPIANS 2:10

A lot of people are foolish enough to think that they are captain of their own soul. They desire control in certain areas of life, and are unwilling to surrender to the sovereignty of Almighty God. Usually, pride or immorality feed this insistence to live life on our own terms, but it is always a dangerous business.

A golden eagle was seen regularly over a certain Hawaiian island for many years. This eagle had almost a seven-foot wingspread. It was a magnificent bird! Now the eagle is a very territorial creature, and it will challenge anything that invades its space. For years, small planes and helicopters would not violate this eagle's "air space" because they knew it would attack. Many times the bird would see a helicopter approaching and begin its screeching ascent. When this happened, the helicopter would flee—not out of fear, but out of concern for the eagle's safety. But one day a pilot unfamiliar with the area flew into the mighty bird's territory, and the eagle came at it with talons extended, ready to attack. When the helicopter landed, all that was found of the eagle was a single feather.

Mark it down. When we mock the truth of God, and suppress it for so long that we eventually exchange it for a lie; when we shake our fist at our Maker and deny the rule that is His by right, the ultimate confrontation will not be insignificant. In fact, there will be less left of us than the feather of a golden eagle. "Every knee shall bow," the Bible says. And it does not lie.

Read: Psalm 86: 11-13

In your attitudes or actions, are you denying the Lordship of Jesus Christ?

What Will We Be?

"Beloved, now we are children of God, and it has not appeared as yet what we shall be."

I JOHN 3:2

Not one of us knows what we will become. We can study for a certain career, plan for a certain vocation…but we do not know what we shall be. When we come to Christ, we become members of His family, and He takes us on as His divine project. He alone knows what we will become. He knows the precise blending of blessing and brokenness necessary to conform us to the image of Christ and allow us to be used by Him.

Suppose there is a certain aristocratic family in London, England, and the heir to this family's fortune is Lord Something-or-Other. He is wealthy and cultured. He and his wife and all of their children are graduates of Oxford and Cambridge. Lord Something-or-Other decides rather late in life to adopt a child—a young boy—from the Belgian Congo. He brings the boy to London and sets about indoctrinating him into the family. What a challenge! This foreigner will need language tutors, etiquette lessons, and instruction on how to dress and act in aristocratic circles. It will be no small challenge to make him into "one of the family."

In one sense, that's what God has done with us. We have been adopted into His family…born again. Right now we do not know where the journey is going to take us. We can only be certain that through blessings and buffetings, He will shape us into the man or woman He desires us to become…and He will not stop until the job is complete.

Read: I John 3:1-4

Ask God to do whatever it takes to make you the man or woman in Christ that He wants you to be.

First Fruits

MEMORIZE

*"And not only this, but also we ourselves, having the first fruits of the Spirit...
groan within ourselves... waiting eagerly for our adoption."*

ROMANS 8:23

What does it mean that we have the first fruits of the Spirit? That we groan, looking forward to our adoption? First fruits are the preview of an entire crop. Say you've planted several acres of corn. When the first ears of corn are harvested, they are considered the first fruits. You taste them and say, "This corn is delicious. It's wonderful." You taste the first fruits of all that was planted, and, because you have tasted it, you can say, "Let me tell you—this whole crop is outstanding."

The presence of the Holy Spirit in our lives is the first fruits, the fore-taste, of all that we will someday become. A similar passage in II Corinthians 5 deals with this same concept, calling these first fruits "the earnest of the Spirit," or a down-payment that insures the fulfilled contract of our Christ-likeness.

Paul says that even with these first fruits of glory in our lives, we groan within ourselves. Our present existence is similar to the pains of labor before birth. Have you ever seen anyone after the birth of their child say, "Let me show you a picture of my wife in labor."? No! We don't do that (and wouldn't live long if we did!) Instead we say, "Let me show you a picture of our beautiful new baby!" As we groan now, having these first fruits of the Spirit, we're looking forward to seeing the picture of our resurrected life with Christ in glory. "Blessed assurance," wrote hymnist Fanny Crosby, "Jesus is mine. Oh, what a foretaste of glory divine!"

ACTION

Read: *Romans 8:18-25*

Thank God today for the first fruits of His Spirit that are evident in your life.

Prayer 101

MEMORIZE

"Lord, teach us to pray…"
LUKE 11:1

I know very few Christian men and women who have not said, "I would really like to know how to pray…I'd like to have a disciplined, powerful prayer life." Most of us suspect that we don't pray as we could or should…but we don't quite know what to do about it. You see, prayer is both ordinary and mysterious. It is as ordinary as picking up a telephone and as terrifying and mysterious as discovering that God Himself is on the other end of the call!

Jesus' disciples knew He was a man of prayer. And they understood somehow that His prayer life was sustaining and life-giving to Him. They knew He derived power from His time alone with the Father, and that it was a priority in His life. So they asked for a lesson in prayer. And Jesus gave them a model to remember and practice.

I believe the six basic ingredients in the Lord's Prayer give us the secret of real communication with God. To help us remember them, I've used an acrostic: C-H-R-I-S-T. "C" is for concentrate. We are to focus on God as "our Father," and think about His character, His nature, His attributes. "H" is for hallowed. His name is hallowed, or holy, and we are to hold it above every other name. "R" is for rule. God is the ruler of everything that is, and every-thing that is to come. "I" stands for "I need." We are to tell God our needs, since He is our provider. "S" is for sin. As I forgive sin against me by oth-ers, God forgives my sin. "T" is for temptation. I am to ask God to keep me from temptation, and to not let me get trapped in situations I'll be unable to handle. That's the outline. This is not a rote, mechanical prayer, but a form, a model, for personal, heart-felt communion with God.

ACTION

Read: *Luke* 11:1-10

Ask God today to teach you to be a prayer warrior, so that you can "hear the phone ring," and answer with a sense of excitement and expectation.

Unbendable Laws

*"For the law of the Spirit of life in Christ Jesus has set you free
from the law of sin and death."*

ROMANS 8:2

Whether we acknowledge them or not, we live by laws. There is a law of the Spirit, and there is a law of sin and death, and Paul says that one has freed us from the other. In this world, we have the law of gravity. If I drop a book, it falls to the floor. That's gravity. But we also have the law of aerodynamics. When an airplane takes off, the law of aerodynamics frees its passengers from the law of gravity. Temporarily. But if you're in an airplane and decide it's rather stuffy inside, and you open the emergency exit and step outside for air, you'll discover that the law of gravity is once again in effect! When you exit the plane, the law of aerodynamics no longer rules.

It is the same with you and me in our spiritual lives. As long as we are in Christ and Christ lives in us, the law of the Spirit sets us free from the law of sin and death. But when we step outside of the leadership of the Holy Spirit and begin to walk in the flesh, we are subject again to the law of sin. It's just that simple. You may think you no longer operate in the realm of the flesh. But by "fleshly" living, I don't simply mean carousing or drunkenness or sexual immorality. We can do good works in the flesh. We can give good gifts in the flesh. And when we do, not only are we subject to the law of sin, but we cannot hope to please God.

QUESTION

Read: *Romans 8: 1-11*

Under which law are you operating most of the time? Set your mind on the things of the Spirit today.

Who Searches The Heart?

MEMORIZE

*"And He who searches the heart knows what the mind of the Spirit is,
because He intercedes for the saints."*

ROMANS 8:27

Who searches the heart? The Bible says that the Father searches our hearts. In fact, God is searching our hearts right now! Does that make you uncomfortable? Someone might say, "I'm not sure I want God to search my heart. He may not like what He finds there." But the truth is, God searches our minds, our consciences, our hearts, not like a criminal investigator, but like a treasure hunter. He is looking for glimpses of His Spirit, searching for evidence of His own presence in us. And His aim in searching is not to condemn, but to work out the very best in our lives for His honor and glory, and for our joy.

At Christmas time each year, I think long and hard about what gift to give Jo Beth. I want to buy her something that she needs, certainly, but also something that expresses my personality and brings her great joy. To discover that certain something, I try to search her heart and see if there is something special she desires. I look for clues...for things that make her eyes light up, things she lingers over. As much as I love Jo Beth, our heavenly Father loves us even more. He's constantly searching our hearts to bless us, and to make a difference in our lives. So don't be afraid. Ask God to search your heart, and trust Him to deal lovingly and rightly with what He sees.

ACTION

Read: Romans 8:26-27

As God searches your heart, depend on the Holy Spirit to speak what you have no words to express.

The Holy Spirit Interprets

"...but the Spirit Himself intercedes for us with groanings too deep for words."

ROMANS 8:26

When the Christian prays, the Holy Spirit in him speaks to God the Father through Jesus Christ the Son. In other words, the whole Trinity prays with us! Isn't that something? The Holy Spirit is getting more attention these days, but it seems that His role is frequently misunderstood.

Sometime back I was attending a concert by Caedmon's Call—a band that includes my youngest son Cliff and my daughter-in-law Danielle. Before the concert began, I was introduced to a lot of folks, including a young lady who wanted me to meet the members of her Bible study group. I went over and said hello, and they told me they had been studying the Holy Spirit for over a year and a half! "Let me ask you a question," I said. "You've been studying the Holy Spirit all this time...I wonder if you could tell me what the purpose of the Holy Spirit is in your life?" It was not a trick question, but they were not sure. They looked at one another for help. "Do you know? No. You? No. You? No, me neither." Now if you have been studying the Holy Spirit for a year and a half, you might have a clue about His role. But no one wanted to venture a guess.

The Holy Spirit is not here to bring honor or attention to Himself. He is not here to be worshipped. The Holy Spirit intercedes for us and points us to Jesus Christ. That is His primary purpose.

Read: John 14:16-21

 Have you misunderstood the role of the Holy Spirit? Ask Him to intercede to the Father for you, and to make you more like Jesus Christ.

Forgiveness And Justification

MEMORIZE

*"Now that no one is justified by the law before God is evident,
for the righteous man shall live by faith."*

GALATIANS 3:11

There is a distinction between forgiveness and justification. It is subtle, but important. It looks something like this. Let's say there is a young lady who runs up an enormous credit card debt at a local department store. She has charged more than she could ever possibly pay; she knows it, and the store management knows it. Suppose she goes to the store's credit manager and confesses her guilt, then asks for forgiveness. They could write off the debt, or they could press her to pay. Either decision would be within their rights. Say they decided to take her to court. She must plead guilty. She has no option. But before the trial, our young friend meets the son of the department store owner, and they fall in love. He marries her, takes responsibility for her debt, goes to the store and pays every penny of it himself. Then how would she plead? Not guilty. Because the son of the owner—the one to whom the debt is due—has paid her way. There is no more debt. He has covered it.

Forgiveness occurs when I go to Jesus Christ and confess my sin. He forgives me. Justification occurs when God acknowledges the forgiveness that Jesus has extended, and accepts His payment of my debt. You and I plead "not guilty" to the Father because Jesus Christ the Son has paid our debt of sin. We have sinned, but He deals with us as if we were sinless. He treats His Son as the sinner, and us as the righteous, and we become the recipients of the riches of His grace.

REFLECTION

Read: *Galatians* 3: 23-29

*How should a forgiven, justified sinner respond to the grace of God?
Are you thankful for His payment of your debt...and do your actions
demonstrate the thanks?*

The Big Picture

MEMORIZE

*"...God causes all things to work together for good to those who love God,
to those who are called according to His purpose."*

ROMANS 8:28

Romans 8:28 may be the most often quoted and misunderstood verse in all of the New Testament. It must be taken as a whole, not in pieces, for its truth to be rightly applied.

For many Christmases, my wife bought one of those 1,000 piece jigsaw puzzles as a family holiday project. We would get out a little card table, dump the box out, and get to the task of putting that puzzle together. I don't know if any of our boys particularly liked jigsaw puzzles, but we managed to make it into a sort of competition somehow—and they did like that. When you're working a puzzle that size, it helps to find the corners, then fill in the outer edge, then the interior. I can't tell you the number of times one of us said, "There has to be a piece missing. I've touched every piece on this table, and not one of them fits this space."

A lot of us view life like a jigsaw puzzle. It's as if God has handed us the pieces and we struggle to make them fit. But God does not see it that way. In this puzzle we call life, He sees the whole even as we fumble with the pieces, and He causes it all to work together for our good and His glory for those who love Him, and are called according to His purpose.

REFLECTION

Read: *Romans 8:28-31*

 What pieces in your life seem out of place? Which seem to be missing? Thank God that He sees the whole, and is at work in ways that we cannot see or understand.

IN THE EVENING...

The richness of God's creation is so awesome—both to the eye, and to the heart. He is such a bountiful Provider, and His table is so rich with goodness. This painting speaks of new growth, and the many colored blessings of our loving Heavenly Father.

Jo Beth Young

The Power of Words

MEMORIZE

*"Words from the mouth of a wise man are gracious,
while the lips of a fool consume him."*

ECCLESIASTES 10:12

King Solomon recognized the dangers of putting a little person in a big position. Just let a fool talk, he reasoned, and his words will get the better of him. Words are powerful things. Used rightly, they bless, encourage and instruct. Used haphazardly, they can wound, confuse and destroy.

Leaders-in-training at West Point are taught economy with words early in their careers. They begin their freshman year with a severely limited vocabulary. Plebes may answer questions from their superiors in only four ways: Yes, sir; No, sir; No excuse, sir; and Sir, I do not understand. "Yes, sir" and "No, sir" teach the value of being direct. "No excuse, sir" ensures that they learn to think in terms of teamwork and success. "Sir, I do not understand" impresses cadets with the importance of making sure instructions and expectations are crystal clear. It is a rather limited vocabulary—but it works, and any system for developing leaders that has been honed for nearly two centuries probably has as much to teach us ordinary folks as it does future generals.

The bottom line is this: a wise man (or a wise woman) carefully measures his words. Jesus told his followers to "let your yes be yes and your no be no." A fool says too much, and often says it recklessly. Understand the impact and the power of words. I learned many years ago that before I broadcast my profound opinion based on excellent insight, I had better get all the facts that are available and seek the whole truth, not just a piece of it. The fool is indiscreet, but the wise man measures his words.

ACTION

Read: *Ecclesiastes* 10:1-15

When you are tempted to say too much, say nothing until the urge passes. Ask God to guard your tongue and use your words today only to bless.

The Intellectual Hedge

"Professing to be wise, they became fools."

ROMANS 1:22

Have you ever had someone tell you they had "intellectual problems" with Christianity? Although I hear that a lot, I can name on one hand individuals I know who have genuine, intellectual reasons for not believing in God or trusting in Jesus Christ. A friend of mine was talking to such a man and finally said to him, "I want to ask you a question: If I could prove to you with empirical evidence that Jesus Christ physically rose from the dead, would you become a Christian?" The man honestly answered, "No, I would not." My friend rightly said, "Then yours is not an intellectual problem. It's one of two other things. Either you are caught up in pride or immorality."

Pride says, "I'm not going to give up on my life. I'm not going to humble myself and throw myself on someone's mercy." The prideful man or woman cannot say "Lord, I submit my mind, my life, my will, my all to You. You run my life." The immoral man says "I refuse to renounce the sin in my life, and play by your rules, God. I like my sin too much to turn from it."

Aldous Huxley, in his book *Ways and Means*, wrote "I set out to disprove God so I could be free in two areas of my life." Those two areas, according to Huxley, were sex and politics. The intellectual hedge makes fools of men who profess to be wise.

Read: Romans 1:18-25

The next time someone you know hides behind the intellectual hedge, look deeper.

Christian Myths

MEMORIZE

*"You, however, continue in the things you have learned and become convinced of,
knowing from whom you have learned them."*

II TIMOTHY 3:14

There are a lot of myths being perpetrated in Christianity today, and that is why it is so important for every believer to know God's word and measure any strange teaching he might hear against it. One myth I hear often is this: "Christians never doubt." How ridiculous! Christians do doubt…and it does not mean they have lost their faith. In fact, doubts can strengthen our faith, confirming our beliefs by examination. Doubt can be a stimulus to growth and maturity, a goad to get to the truth.

Another popular Christian myth is "Christians are always passive people." The truth is, most Christians I know are passionate people! When I read my Bible I see that many of them considered their faith to be something worth dying for—hardly a passive response! Hebrews 11 tells us that some early believers were actually sawed in two because of their belief! A radio preacher once told a story about a Quaker who was milking his cow. While he milked, the cow kicked over a bucket, and the Quaker turned the bucket upright and started the chore over again. Then the cow stepped on his foot, but the man just leaned into the cow until he moved over. Finally, the cow kicked the Quaker backwards, and when he did, the Quaker said "Thou knowest that I cannot strike thee, but if thou doth not behave, I shall sell thee to a Baptist!" (That would do it, would it not?)

Christians doubt, Christians take action, and Christians even suffer and die. So test these "myths" and make sure you continue in the things you have learned, knowing from whom you have learned them.

QUESTION

Read: II Timothy 3:14-17

What myths about Christianity have misled you in the past? Where can you find the truth?

The Jericho Road

"But a certain Samaritan, who was on a journey, came upon him; and when he saw him, he felt compassion."

LUKE 10:33

In the parable of the Good Samaritan, Jesus tells of a man traveling from Jerusalem to Jericho. I've been on that road, and I can tell you that it is downhill all the way. The distance between Jerusalem and Jericho is 17 miles... and the drop in elevation is 3900 feet. It was (and is) an easy walk downhill, but a dangerous road. Robbers would hide in the rocky crags. No one traveled it alone if they could help it. But this man did. Also the Jericho Road was the route from worship (at the temple in Jerusalem) to the world. Jericho was a place of trade, of commerce...of daily existence.

You may have never traveled to the Holy Land, but I can tell you this: the Jericho Road runs right through your life. You go to Jerusalem—church—and then you go home to Jericho. For some it may even be close to a 17 mile drive. But in that 17 miles (or whatever the distance is) you and I can become as blind as the priest and as hardened as the Levite. We can go past people who are hurting and never look twice. We can close our eyes to the pain and suffering and lost-ness and heartache of our world while we hum our favorite hymn. And many times, we do just that because the Jericho road can break your heart. It can tug at your heart until you feel compassion...and then what? It might require that we love our neighbor. You see, a right relationship with Jesus Christ should overflow to those around us, especially on the Jericho Road.

Read: *Matthew 25:31-46*

 Ask God to open your eyes today to those who are on the Jericho Road...then act on what you see.

Get Involved!

MEMORIZE

"Let love of the brethren continue."

HEBREWS 13:1

We live in a culture that is reluctant to get involved. We leave well enough alone. We steer clear of messy, complicated inter-action with others. We mind our own business, and keep to ourselves—even those of us who go by the name of Christian.

We're like the fellow on the bus who refused to tell another passenger what time it was. After being asked several times, he turned his back, and the young man went on and asked someone else. At the next stop, some-one who had seen the exchange scolded the man, and this was his ratio-nale: "If I had told that young man what time it was, we would have struck up a conversation, and I probably would have liked him. Before long, he would have gotten himself invited to supper, and my beautiful daughter would have met him. The two of them would probably fall in love, and want to get married...but I don't want my daughter marrying a man who can't afford a watch!" We intuitively know that involvement could prove expen-sive...so we shut ourselves off in the name of caution.

The only problem is, we are commanded to love the brethren. In fact, the mark of a Christian is the love we have for one another. It is almost impossible for someone who has experienced the love and grace of God to live in isolation...but some of us do a pretty good job. Instead of hiding, get out of your comfort zone and reach out to those in your circle of influence with the love of Christ. It is dangerous, yes. But the only place outside of heaven where we can be safe from all the dangers of love is hell.

QUESTION

Read: *John* 13:33-35

Who has God placed in your path today that needs to be loved?

The Hammer, The File And The Fire

"All discipline for the moment seems not to be joyful, but sorrowful; yet to those who have been trained by it, afterwards it yields the peaceful fruit of righteousness."

HEBREWS 12:11

The race that you and I run is not a sprint; it's a marathon. The Christian life is a long distance race, and it is not for the faint of heart. Like any marathon, it involves some pain. The hands get heavy. The knees get weak. The lungs fight for air and the heart pumps harder to supply the straining muscles. And the pain itself is reason to be thankful! Samuel Rutherford said it this way: "God, I thank you for the hammer. I thank you for the file. I thank you for the fire."

How could he say this? Because Rutherford knew that the hammer was in the hands of the Carpenter, and the Carpenter takes that hammer and drives the nail in place, so that it can fulfill the purpose for which it was made. Is life beating you on the head? Throwing you around? The good news for those in Christ is that any blows you experience are being administered by the hand of the Carpenter. What about the file? The file smooths the rough edges of a piece, using just the right amount of pressure for a perfect finish. And the fire? It burns off dross, or waste, so that what is left is pure and strong. All of this discomfort is shaping and molding you and me for the purpose for which God made us...and I can think of nothing more tragic than to miss the purpose for which we were created.

QUESTION

Read: *Hebrews* 12:7-11

 Can you thank God for the hammer, the file and the fire in the midst of discipline?

Links In A Chain

MEMORIZE

*"And all these, having gained approval in their faith,
did not receive what was promised..."*

HEBREWS 11:39

Hebrews 11 is a history of men and women who lived (and died) by faith. Some of the names—Abraham, Moses, Noah—are familiar. Others—Barak, Jepthah—are not. And some are not called by name at all, but their stories are recorded in shorthand: men and women who quenched the power of fire, escaped the edge of the sword, became mighty in war, were tortured, stoned, tempted, put to death, even sawed in two! All of these died without receiving the promise, Paul tells us, and the promise is Jesus Christ, the Messiah. But they were all men and women of God, and they are links in a chain of faith that reaches all the way to you and me. They exercised faith by looking forward to the promise. We exercise faith by looking back at it. But we are linked by a common faith.

I don't visit a lot of cemeteries, but when I do, it always means something to me. I think everyone should visit them every now and then, because it reminds us that death is a certainty. There's a spot in Hawaii called the Punch Bowl where soldiers who died in the Pacific in World War II are buried. I am linked to them by our national heritage. They sacrificed for me. In Rome, the catacombs hold the bones of early Christians who were martyred for their faith. I am linked to these who had to worship underground and fight for their beliefs in a pagan culture. And closer to home, in Laurel, Mississippi, there's a little cemetery that holds the bones of people I grew up with, my wife's grandparents, her father, my parents, my grandmother and other relatives. Their faith and their prayers and their generosity are links in a chain that runs all the way to me. From Adam to Edwin and at every point in between, we are linked together by faith to an incredible cloud of witnesses.

REFLECTION

Read: *Hebrews* 11: 1-40

*Consider the links that connect you with great men and women of faith.
What kind of link will your life be?*

Faith That Works

MEMORIZE

"Now faith is the assurance of things hoped for, the conviction of things not seen."

HEBREWS 11:1

Faith is the assurance of things hoped for...the conviction of things not seen. It is confident obedience to the word of God, regardless of circumstances or consequences. Faith is an active thing, not a passive feeling. I wonder how many Christians never really exercise their faith? They've trusted God for their salvation, but cannot (or will not) trust Him in their day to day living. What a waste!

A friend of mine once played the Augusta National Golf Course where the Masters is held each year. His assigned caddie watched his shots for a while so he could help him with club selection on the course, then they were off. My friend said he was playing fairly well when he came to the famous "Amen Corner." At number 13 (a par-5) he hit a booming drive, then asked his caddie what iron he needed to lay up. Knowing that a lot of pros had tried to hit over the creek and on to the green in two—and missed—he never thought of trying it himself. His caddie looked at him and said, "You flew all the way from Oklahoma to play this course?" My friend nodded. "Think you'll ever play here again?" My friend said no, he did not imagine he would be back. "Then mister," the caddie said, "you've come too far to lay up."

God has brought us so far. Too far, in fact, for us to settle back in the safety of the ordinary and not exercise our faith. We've simply come too far to lay up...and we'll never pass this way again.

QUESTION

Read: II Chronicles 20:5-25

 What would you attempt for God today if failure was impossible?

A Faith Worth Imitating

MEMORIZE

*"Remember those who led you, who spoke the word of God to you;
and considering the result of their conduct, imitate their faith."*

HEBREWS 13:7

Does martyrdom appeal to you? How does dying for your faith in Jesus Christ strike you today? If you think the question is outdated, let me remind you that more people have given their lives for the cause of Christ in the twentieth century than in all other centuries combined! When the writer of Hebrews encouraged his readers to imitate the conduct of those who led them, it is very likely he was referring to the martyrs of the early Church. Is that the kind of life you would like to imitate?

A friend of mine returned from Romania after spending some time with spiritual leaders there. One man, Josef Sun, had survived years of communist rule and persecution. My friend asked him why Romania saw so many people come to Christ when freedom finally came. Josef answered this way: "So many have been killed in Romania through the years for believing in Jesus Christ, that when freedom came, these Christians were willing to introduce people to Christ at any cost." My friend then asked Josef about the persecution he endured, and he told him that just before the communist dictator was overthrown, a group of his henchmen came to Josef and said, "If you do not stop talking about Jesus Christ, we will kill you." Josef calmly told the group, "If you take my life, you will sprinkle blood over every pamphlet I have written and every sermon I have preached. Your weapon is killing. Mine is dying. If you use your weapon, I'll be forced to use mine." They did not take his life. They were afraid of the power of his weapon.

ACTION

Read: *Hebrews 6: 9-12*

Read about the lives of twentieth century martyrs, or the leaders of the early Church. Consider the result of their conduct, and imitate their faith.

The Narrow Belt of Truth

"Stand firm, therefore, having girded your loins with truth..."

EPHESIANS 6:14

I saw a famous young actor interviewed on television who shared a philosophy I'm afraid is far too prevalent these days. He said something like this: "The world needs to stop debating what is right and wrong. Everyone must search for their own truth, and live on the basis of what they believe to be true." The key idea here is that truth is debatable. But in fact, truth is very concrete, and very narrow. God has built this world on the basis of absolute truth, not relative truth or perceived truth.

A palm tree down in Florida might say, "You know, I don't like this hot climate and all this sand. I think I'll transplant myself to the Arctic Circle." Do you think the palm tree would survive? A polar bear might decide that he's much too chilly in Antarctica, and decide to live instead in the Bahamas. But he wouldn't live long. You see, we were created to operate within certain spiritual parameters in the same way the palm tree and the polar bear were made for certain physical parameters. So the person who says, "I don't like these rules, I don't believe this truth, I don't choose to submit to this code of morality," is not really going to live. If we are to be successful in this life, we must gird ourselves with the narrow belt of truth. To do anything else is to merely exist.

Read: II Peter 1: 16-21

Are you regularly reading, studying and memorizing the truth contained in God's word? If not, begin today!

It's A Miracle!

"Though your sins are as scarlet, they will be as white as snow;
though they are red like crimson, they will be like wool."

ISAIAH 1:18

What is a miracle? If someone had told Columbus in 1492 that he could view the new world simply by touching a screen in Madrid, he would have probably exclaimed, "It's a miracle!" Lawrence of Arabia brought some Arab chieftans to the West after World War II, and they were astounded by western culture. But what really stopped these desert-dwellers cold was not an automobile, or a rail car, or a telephone. It was the "miracle" of a waterfall. You see, it is the state of our knowledge and the extent of our experience that condition our idea of a miracle.

The word "miracle" is derived from the Latin verb which means "to wonder." First and foremost, a miracle is something that moves us to wonder. And we wonder at that which we can neither understand, nor do ourselves. But that is not the full meaning of a miracle. For example, I do not understand electricity, but I do not consider it a miracle. Some do understand how electricity works, and are able to explain it to others. My television set is not a miracle, either. Although I can operate it, I could not take it apart and put it together again...but a television repairman could. A miracle then, is something that defies human skills to perform, and baffles human wisdom to explain.

The disciples worked many miracles as the New Testament Church was born and built. They healed sickness. Escaped from prison. Even brought the dead back to life. But the greatest miracle of the New Testament (and of our day!) is the miracle of a changed life. There's simply nothing else that even comes close.

Read: Acts 9: 32-43

Do you consider your salvation a miracle? Were you able to humanly perform it? Can you explain it using only worldly wisdom?

Small Miracles

*"Therefore let it be known to you, brethren,
that through Him forgiveness of sins is proclaimed to you."*

ACTS 13:38

Sometimes "small miracles" can have tremendous impact. A physical healing is a dramatic and unarguably miraculous event. But so is an unheralded change of heart. There is just such a miracle in the story of Peter recorded in Acts chapter nine. We are told that Peter, a Jew, was staying in the home of a Gentile man named Simon. And Simon was, by profession, a *tanner*! Tanners handled the hides of dead animals, and were considered unclean by Jewish rabbis. But God was beginning to change Peter's heart, and would soon show him that the Gospel was (and is!) for everyone...not just for good, law-abiding Jews.

Peter's "sleep-over" at Simon's home might seem insignificant...but it was a micro-movement toward a larger goal: the opening of the door of salvation to the Gentiles. A huge transition was taking place, one small miracle at a time.

God can—and does—work in dramatic ways. But He also works in ways that are very nearly invisible until the work is done. If you have experienced a slow change of heart like Peter's, you know this. Don't make the mistake of thinking you have never witnessed a miracle because nothing has happened in your life that would make the nightly news. God's small miracle in Peter's life became the means by which every non-Jew since has come to know Jesus Christ as Savior. Even me.

Read: *Acts* 10: 17-23

 Ask God to make you more aware of the small miracles He does in your life.

This Grace In Which We Stand

MEMORIZE

"...we have obtained our introduction by faith into this grace in which we stand..."

ROMANS 5:2

A lot of us are struggling under legalism even though we speak of living by grace. We're trying hard to keep the rules, assuming that God will reward our good behavior and (hopefully) overlook our mistakes. I've been a dedicated rule-keeper myself. My mom and dad taught me some basic rules, and most of them were excellent—right over the plate. But they're not biblical, and they have nothing to do with my standing before God. They taught me everyone needs a solid eight hours of sleep each night. When you get up in the morning, you brush your teeth. And do the same before going to bed. Before you eat a meal, you wash your hands. Period. And when you pray, you must close your eyes.

Once a visiting pastor spoke in our small church, and when he prayed, he did not close his eyes. (I peeked.) I decided that either he was a phony, or that this particular "eyes-closed" rule might not be of the iron-clad variety. Too often we define Christianity by a list of arbitrary do's and don'ts, reducing a relationship with God through Jesus Christ to an exercise in rule-keeping. But God cannot be put into a box. He's much, much bigger than that. And His grace is super-abundant.

Make no mistake. We stand right before God not on the basis of our ability to keep an exhaustive list of rules, but on the rock-solid reality of the shed blood of Jesus Christ. When we place our faith in Him, His grace "covers" us, and His righteousness becomes our own.

QUESTION

Read: *Romans 5: 1-8*

What rules are you striving to keep so that God will look on you with favor?

What Forgiveness Is...
And Isn't

"...and without the shedding of blood there is no forgiveness."

HEBREWS 9:22

To forgive is a difficult thing. To be forgiven is a terrifying thing. Forgiveness is serious, serious business, because it requires the shedding of blood. Forgiveness is not a cheap, throw-away declaration: "Oh, that's okay...I forgive you." It is a transaction that is bathed in blood every time it takes place.

Many people have the mistaken idea that forgiveness eliminates the fact of our sin. It does not. Sin does not just "disappear" when we say we are sorry. It must be dealt with. Through the blood of Christ, our sin is covered, but it is not magically made to disappear. The prodigal son went to the far country... and every scar he received there he carried home. His sins were forgiven by his father, but they did not go away. Neither does forgiveness eradicate the consequences of sin. The universal laws of cause and effect are not superceded by forgiveness. Sin's consequences remain. The thing that forgiveness does is set up the possibility for restoration of relationship.

We know that forgiveness requires repentance, and we're pretty good repent-ers. But forgiveness, when possible, also involves restitution, so that restoration can be achieved. It costs us to forgive, and it costs us to be forgiven. Anyone who offers or expects easy, cheap forgiveness has yet to come to terms with the seriousness of sin.

Read: *Exodus 34: 6-14*

 If you need forgiveness, demonstrate your heart-felt repentence by trying to make restitution where possible.

I'm Okay...Right?

MEMORIZE

"But wishing to justify himself, he said to Jesus, 'and who is my neighbor?'"

LUKE 10:29

I f there is anything I am good at, it is justifying myself. You would be hard pressed to find anyone as effective at it as I am...unless it is you. "I was short with my wife today, but I'd had a really stressful day..." or "Boy, I never meant to say those words, but I had so much on my mind, they just slipped out." Self-justification. We're experts, are we not? The lawyer who spoke these words to Jesus was seeking to justify himself. He asked a question to which he knew the answer, and then, when he realized he fell short of his own prescription for salvation, he tried to mince words to justify himself. "Well, of course, I'm to love my neighbor, but...who is my neighbor, exactly?"

We do the very same thing. "I used to go to church, but I don't anymore, because old so-and-so really offended me by acting in an un-Christian way." Well, welcome to the world! God is not fooled by our weak attempts at self-justification. Why? Because he knows our hearts—just as he knew this legal eagle's heart. We've become theological politicians, trying to parse words with God to ease our own conscience...but it won't work. In this man's case, Jesus handled his dodge by telling a story—the story of the Good Samaritan. And even though we are not too keen on rules and laws, we can't help but be drawn in to a good story. This one had dramatic conflict (near-dead man by the side of the road).It revealed shocking secrets (a priest and a Levite refuse to give aid). And a surprise ending (he finally receives help from a Samaritan). And it required the listener to provide the obvious answer to the central question: which of these three was a real neighbor? The lawyer was trapped. He answered the only way he could, and then Jesus delivered the crushing directive: "Go and do the same."

Self-justification ends where obedience to truth begins. It's not enough to know what is right and have a very good reason for not doing it. When we know what is right, we must act on it.

QUESTION

Read: *Luke* 10: 30-37

Is there an area in your life for which you've been making excuses to God? Re-examine it today.

What Do You See?

MEMORIZE

"And seeing the multitudes, He felt compassion for them,
because they were distressed and downcast like sheep without a shepherd."

MATTHEW 9:36

Two men were in a nursing home. One bed was by the window, and the other by the door. Every day the man in the bed by the door would ask his roommate, "What do you see out there today?" The man in the bed by the window would say, "Oh, the sun is shining, and it's a beautiful day. I can see a mother playing with her children by the lake." His roommate would ask, "What's on that lake?" And the man with the view would describe what he saw. "Oh, I believe I can see a little duck…yes, there it is. There's a duck." He described the view in the summer time, the fall, the winter, and the spring. Then one day he died.

Now the man by the door had the opportunity to switch beds. So he did. He got his things, made the bed, propped up his pillows, looked outside and saw nothing—nothing but a gray brick wall. From every angle, all he could see was the side of the building next door. He called the nurse in and asked, "When did that wall go up? It's spoiling my view." She said, "Sir, that wall has always been there." The man didn't say much for a few days, then one day he asked the nurse when he would be getting a new roommate. She told him it would be very soon. "That's good," he said. "I can hardly wait for him to come so I can tell him all I see outside our window."

The Samaritan saw a man who needed help by the side of the road. The priest saw filthiness and defilement, and the Levite saw trouble and inconvenience. But the Samaritan saw a man. Same view. Different perspective. What do you see around you?

ACTION

Read: *Matthew 9: 35-38*

 Ask God to help you see with His eyes everywhere you look today.

Do You Love Me?

MEMORIZE

"If you love Me, you will keep My commandments."

JOHN 14:15

I f I could ask every person reading this book "Do you love God?", I would be surprised if anyone said no. I believe everyone would say, "Yes, I love God. I certainly do." But there is a test of sorts that tells us how much we really do love God…and that test is quite simple. It has nothing to do with church attendance, or a daily quiet time, or singing praise songs. It has everything to do with obedience. "If you love me," Jesus said, "you will keep my commandments."

Obedience is God's "love test." And Jesus goes even further. He says not only will we obey His commands, but also, we will not find them burdensome. We will not moan and groan about being obedient to Him…we'll do it joyfully. Gladly. There is probably no area of life where this is more easily demonstrated than the area of stewardship. We are commanded to return a portion of what is God's (called the tithe in the Old Testament) to His storehouse, which is the church or the body of Christ. In the Old Testament, a percentage was allocated for the tithe—10 percent. But the New Testament teaches grace giving…in other words, as God has blessed you, give. Give joyfully, liberally and generously. But we are commanded to give.

Don't be confused. The *amount* we give is not the measure of our love for God. The *way* we give is indicative of how much we love Him. If His command to give is not burdensome to us, we can be confident in our love for Him.

QUESTION

Read: II Samuel 24: 18-24

Are you a grudging giver? Aren't you thankful that God did not begrudge you the gift of His Son Jesus Christ?

The Discipline of Sons

*"For those whom the Lord loves He disciplines,
and He scourges every son whom He receives."*

HEBREWS 12:6

Would you like to have genuine character? To be the kind of person that others respect and admire? What if I told you the only way to develop true character was to suffer and endure discipline? Would you change your mind? Many do. You see, we don't like the rod. We don't like pain or discomfort, even if it's temporary. But it is through discipline that we develop the fruit of righteousness, and discipline is required course work in God's university.

The finest professor I had in seminary was Dr. Mark Loveless. Dr. Loveless lectured with a pool cue, and without looking he could point on a map to Qumran, Beersheba, Masada, or the Dead Sea. He knew German, Latin, Greek, Hebrew and Arabic, and it was work for us students simply to keep up with his lectures. I worked harder in his class than I ever have before or since. In one of his courses, we did not have a test the entire semester. On the day of the final exam, he walked to the blackboard and wrote one word: WRITE. I did. For everything I was worth. Dr. Loveless' classes were nothing but struggle for me, but his exacting ways made me a real student. Every other class I took was easy. He stretched me. But when it was all said and done, I was disciplined in a way I had never been before.

God's discipline is proof of His love. If we are His, He has promised to discipline us for our good and for His glory. When discipline comes, see it as a loving touch from a Father too good to leave us "well enough alone."

Read: *Proverbs* 19: 20-27

 The next time you experience the discipline of God, thank Him for loving you as a son or daughter, and for the fruit of righteousness that will result.

Surprised By Joy

MEMORIZE

*"These things I have spoken to you, that My joy may be in you,
and that your joy may be made full."*

JOHN 15:11

I saw some good news on television recently. A newscaster reported on a 29-year old policeman in Los Angeles who pulled over a driver for having an expired license plate, only to discover that the man was his father! The two had been separated shortly after the young man's birth. His father had re-married, had another family, and never located his son. Father and son were re-united against almost unbelievable odds, and were glad to find each other. (No ticket was issued, just a warning, and an invitation for dinner.) What a joyful surprise!

We need a lot of things in this world. We need wisdom. We need love. We need insight. We need commitment. But I think more than anything else, our world might just need an overwhelming dose of joy. Mother Teresa was asked once what it took to do the work she did, and she simply smiled and said "A willingness to work hard, and a spirit of joy." Joy. It is not the same as happiness. It is not "circumstantial goosebumps." It is not the absence of pain or suffering. It is another domain entirely.

When C. S. Lewis became a Christian, he described the experience as being "surprised by joy." Lewis, one of the most brilliant apologists who ever lived, did not "think" his way to Christ. He fell into a joy so deep that he recognized it as true. Jesus is the only way to true joy. And His desire, His prayer, for you and me is that His joy would become our own.

QUESTION

Read: *Deuteronomy* 30: 8-16

Look in the mirror. Do you see joy?

Joy Killers

"Rejoice in the Lord always; again I will say, rejoice!"
PHILIPPIANS 4:4

Two men who hadn't seen one another for 20 years met up at a high school reunion. One looked at the other and said, "What have you been doing with yourself all these years?" The second man replied, "Well, I own a ranch." Not knowing much about ranching, his friend said, "How interesting. What's the name of your ranch?" He said, "My ranch is called the Greater Los Alamos Santa Gertrudis, Charolais, Black Angus, Quarter Horse Ranch of North America." His friend was impressed. "My goodness. That sounds like some ranch. How many head do you have on that spread?" The rancher shook his head. "Not as many as you might think. The branding kills most of 'em."

Do you know what kills our joy? It's when the world puts its brand on us. When the world brands us, we're encumbered by worry and people and circumstances and situations that wear us down and rob us of the joy of Christ. The best way I know to combat the joy killers of the world is to say these simple words: "Thy will be done." When we say "Thy will be done" in response to the worries and concerns of the world, we die to selfishness, and as we die to selfishness, God gives joy. As we seek His will for our lives, He will kill out the boredom, wickedness, greed, lust and striving in our hearts. As we desire His will, we receive His joy.

Read: *Philippians* 4: 4-9

 Can you identify any joy killers in your life? Pray over each one, and say "Thy will be done."

Building Blocks

"Train up a child in the way he should go,
even when he is old he will not depart from it."

PROVERBS 22:6

A good self-image is one of the most important things we can build into our children. I believe there are at least ten building blocks to establish a child's self image, enabling them to see themselves as God sees them.

First, we must express love to our children. That sounds so basic, but many children never hear their parents say "I love you." You can't say it too much. Second, be predictable. Children need stability, not capriciousness. Be predictable in your discipline, your standards, your love. Third, communicate clearly with your children. Do not expect them to read your mind. Remember that children are quite literal and do not understand nuance or subtlety as adults do. Fourth, try to understand the source of behavior problems, instead of dealing only with the symptoms. Fifth, catch your children doing good! That's right—catch them doing the right thing, and praise them for it. Sixth, provide a safe environment, emotionally and physically. Make your home a safe place for your child. Seventh, set reasonable limits based on your child's age and development. Eighth, teach your child problem-solving skills. Don't do everything for them. Ninth, don't overreact. Ninety-nine percent of the things we parents loose our cool over are not life-altering. Finally, be patient. Parenting is a long-term effort, and you cannot achieve all that you hope for in a day.

If you remember these things and strive each day to do them...with a word, a look, a touch...your child will have the foundation he needs to grow strong.

Read: II Peter 1: 2-8

If you are a parent, keep this list of building blocks close by, and strive to
combine several of them each day for the benefit of your child.

Love's Finest Hour

MEMORIZE

"For Thou didst form my inward parts; Thou didst weave me in my mother's womb."

PSALM 139:13

We call them exceptional children. Special needs children. Disabled. Handicapped. Whatever the term, the challenge is enormous for a parent gifted with such a child. But this much is clear: every child is perfectly made by God. God is sovereign over all the earth, including the womb. He has superintended our very conception and existence, and every child born is fearfully and wonderfully crafted by Him.

Scripture is actually filled with those who are physically handicapped. Jacob walked with a limp for the rest of his life after his midnight wrestling match with an angel. Mephibosheth's body was hopelessly twisted and crippled. King Jereboam had a withered hand. Namaan was a leper. Even Paul suffered from an unnamed "thorn" in his flesh. In addition to their challenges, all of these had something else in common: not one of them was miraculously healed. So many times we gravitate toward the miracles of the Bible, and there were many. But there were many more who lived day to day with all kinds of indignities, pains and disabilities. A lot of people live without a miracle. But who is to say that the power of God cannot be even more dramatically displayed in the life of one who struggles, but remains steadfast...who seeks to make sense of what appears as nonsense?

I believe the power of God is displayed all around us, in the lives of exceptional people who never experience a life-changing miracle. They are not changed. They change us.

ACTION

Read: II Corinthians 4: 7-8; 10-14

 Thank God for the exceptional people in your life. If you are the parent of such a child, ask Him to display His power in your precious loved one's weakness.

When God Seems Far Away

*"My God, my God, why hast Thou forsaken me?
Far from my deliverance are the words of my groaning."*

PSALM 22:1

Elie Wiesel was 15 years old when he was captured by Nazis and sent to Auschwitz concentration camp. Wiesel, a Jew, and another man, a Dutchman, were caught with a cache of arms and sentenced to be hanged. Also implicated in the crime was the Dutchman's young servant. When this boy refused to cooperate with the Nazi's, he too,was sentenced to be hanged. Wiesel tells the story of this child in his own words: "Three victims in chains. One of them they called little boy, the Angel, the Sad-eyed Angel. The head of the camp read the verdict. All eyes were on the child. He was liquidly pale, almost calm. Three victims together were mounted on the chairs. Three necks were placed in the same moment within the nooses. "Where is God? Where is He?" someone asked behind me. At a sign from the head of the camp, the chairs were pushed over. Total silence throughout the camp. The two adults were no longer alive...but the third rope was still moving. Being so light, the child was still alive. For more than half an hour he stayed there struggling between life and death, dying in slow agony under our eyes. Behind me I heard the same man asking, "Where is God now?" And I heard a voice within me answer him, "Where is He? He is here. He is hanging here on this gallows."

In every dark night of the soul, God is present. For every son and every daughter, He is there. Through His death on the cross, Jesus forever identified with the anguish of all mankind, and provided a way through when life bottoms out.

Read: *Psalm 36: 5-9*

 When darkness covers your soul, remember God's presence. He will never leave or forsake you.

Fighting Fire With Fire

"For the Lord your God is a consuming fire; a jealous God."
DEUTERONOMY 4:24

We have all heard the expression "the way to fight fire is with fire." I've heard it all my life, but it came alive for me in a new way when I heard a story told by Norman McLean about a Montana smoke jumper who did just that. Wag Dodge was one of 15 smoke jumpers who were sent to battle a forest fire in August of 1949. Shortly after their jump, these tenacious, well-trained, young men were surrounded by an inferno. As the wind shifted 180 degrees and picked up velocity, what had been a manageable fire became what is known as a blow out. The only way to safety was to race 200 yards to the top of a ridge—quite literally, to out-run the fire. When Dodge realized the fire would overtake them, he screamed to his men to stop and gather around him. Most did not hear, and were overcome. Then, with fire racing toward him, Wag Dodge lit a fire of his own and followed it, then circled back and laid down in the grass it had burned. When he did, the flames went around what had already been scorched, leaving him safe on the ground. He fought fire...with fire.

We are surrounded on every side by the super-heated flames of our culture. How do we fight them? The way this young smoke jumper did. We set our own fire. And as the fire of our devotion to Christ begins to burn, our God who is a consuming fire, burns brighter and stronger than the flames of this fallen world. We fight fire with fire!

Read: James 4: 1-8

 How are you doing in the fires of our pagan culture? Are the flames gaining on you?

Identified With God

"And I will bless those who bless you, and the one who curses you I will curse."

GENESIS 12:3

When a person steps out in faith to follow Jesus Christ, he becomes identified with Christ. Abram's faith and obedience caused him to be forever identified with God—to the degree that God's enemies became Abram's enemies, and God's friends became Abram's friends. A Christian soon discovers that those who would curse God do not hesitate to curse him, and those who would bless God, bless him, too. It's a family thing.

While I was away for a short while from the church where I pastor, my son Ben preached in my place. A woman who had never visited our church before but had watched our services on television attended for the first time. At the end of Ben's message, this woman came forward to receive Christ, and she told the counselor she spoke with afterwards, "You know, the pastor looks so much younger in person than he does on television...someone should see if they can touch up the tape!" The counselor laughed and said, "That wasn't the pastor—that was his son!" Like it or not, my boys are often identified with me. There is a definite family resemblance.

The fact that people identify me with my sons has always been a pleasure to me. I am proud of them. They are fine men. But I wonder if God is always so proud of our family resemblance? Do my actions as a son bring Him honor? I pray they do.

Read: *James 1: 21-27*

Would anyone be surprised to learn that you are a son or daughter of God?

A Radical Change

MEMORIZE

"Go forth from your country, and from your relatives and from your father's house, to the land which I will show you."

GENESIS 12:1

Abram was called by God to leave the land he'd lived in all his life. When God calls you and me, it is usually a call just like the one Abram received: a call to radical change. We don't generally like to leave what we know, even when it's bad. We especially don't like to leave what is known for what is unknown. Abram left his culture. His friends and relatives. His father's house. His old routine. His old agenda. His old nature.

A few years ago the cover of *Time* magazine announced that "Infidelity May Be Genetic." I remember reading it and thinking, "this world has gone nuts! Now they're trying to excuse adultery by saying it's in our genes." Then I thought more about it and realized they were right! There's a fallacy about these days that man is inherently good, but he is not. He is inherently sinful. It's our nature. It may not be in our physical DNA, but it's definitely in our spiritual make-up. We are all born with a bent toward sin. So when God calls us, He says we are to leave our old nature behind and make a radical change in lifestyle. The good news is, the change takes place from the inside out. Not only does God call us, He transforms us. He replaces our old heart of stone with a new heart of flesh, and He gives us the power we need to obey Him.

REFLECTION

Read II Corinthians 5: 14-21

 Reflect on your salvation experience. Was there a radical change in your life after you received Christ? Has there been a radical change since that time?

Partial Obedience

"How long will you hesitate between two opinions? if the Lord is God, follow Him..."

I KINGS 18:21

Abram did not go directly from the land of Ur into Canaan. He made a 15-year detour in a place called Haran. Haran was not a bad place, but it was not the place God was calling him to remain. Haran is a symbol of compromise, of partial obedience. And it is a place with which most of us are quite familiar.

How many of us have joined a church, gone through the motions of repentence and commitment, and stopped short of God's destination for us? We're living in Haran—not Canaan—and we may be satisfied, but God is not. We've exercised enough faith to make a start, but we are seriously lacking in follow-through. Maybe you are in Haran right now. You've made a break from an ungodly relationship, moved out of your cultural comfort zone—maybe even cleaned up your language or your lifestyle...but you are still in Haran. You've broken a few worldly habits, but you are still sold out to the world's agenda.

I have a personal theory that those who leave Ur and stop in Haran are more miserable than those who never left at all. How tragic to hear the call of God and obey it only partially! Compromise is the saddest place in the world to live, because it yields neither the fleeting pleasures of sin, nor the full-weighted blessing of complete obedience.

Read: I Kings 18: 21-39

Is there an area of your life that is stalled in Haran? Give God your complete obedience and move on.

No Ordinary Book

"The precepts of the Lord are right, rejoicing the heart..."
PSALM 19:8

My earliest remembrances of my childhood in Laurel, Mississippi, are of nightly Bible reading. Every night, without fail, my mother would open the Bible with my brother and me, she would read from scripture, and we would pray. My dad did not participate in this time of family altar until years later when he became a Christian, but mother was not deterred. I discovered early on that when the Bible is being read, something important—something supernatural—takes place. God's Word has a way of breaking down barriers, crumbling defenses, melting hearts. The Bible is no ordinary book.

The Bible is unique in its distribution. There are more copies of it in print today than any other book. Year in and year out, the Bible is a bestseller. It is also unique in its translation. The Bible has been translated more than any other book in history. It has been translated more than 1,280 times, and new translations in many dialects are constantly being completed. The Bible is unique, too, in its accuracy. In the manuscript world, the number of copies extant verifies the accuracy of a book. There are over 20,000 copies of Bible manuscripts. Other classical writings with less than 50 copies are considered highly accurate. Not surprisingly, the Bible is unique in its infiltration. It is truly amazing where Bibles can be found. When Christians were banned from China fifty years ago, there were nearly 25 million Chinese believers. Today that number is eight times greater. How could that be if there were no preachers, no missionaries? There were Bibles—and they were treasured and shared and read and memorized. There is quite simply no book like this book. It is living, and it contains the power to change lives.

Read: *Psalm 19: 7-14*

 What is your view of the Bible? Do you see it as just another book?

The Shadow of Death

"O death, where is your victory? O death, where is your sting?"

I CORINTHIANS 15:55

Emperor Philip of Macedon was awakened every morning by a slave who spoke these words: "By His divine decree, by His imperial order, Philip, you too will die." Every morning Philip faced the certainty of his death. He wanted to be reminded that he would not live forever, and that he should do what he could do now—because tomorrow was not guaranteed.

Death is a sure thing. Unless Jesus Christ returns in our lifetime, all of us will die. One day the obituaries will contain our name, and we will not wake again. Death is sure...but it is not a comfortable subject. No one really likes to talk about it. I was an adult before I ever attended a funeral service...and I was the pastor officiating! Death is sure...but for the Christian it is not threatening. For those who believe in Christ, the sting of death has been removed.

A mother died, leaving her husband and daughter. After the funeral, the little girl asked her dad, "Daddy, why did Mother die?" The father did not answer right away. He was struggling to find the right words. A short time later, the two were walking together when they were passed by a large truck. As the truck came close, it cast a shadow over the two of them, and the father saw his answer. "Do you remember asking me about Mom, and what happened to her?" The daughter nodded. "Well, let me ask you a question. When that truck came by just now, did it hit us?" The girl shook her head. "But something did hit us, didn't it? Something dark?" Her eyes lit up. "Yes, Daddy," she said, "the truck's shadow hit us." Her dad said, "That's what happened to your mother. Death did not run over your mother. Only its shadow did. And shadows don't hurt. I don't know why it happened, but I know that she's okay."

Read: I Corinthians 15:50-57

Is death a threat to you? Are you living with the end in mind?

Making Wise Choices

"So Lot chose for himself all the valley of the Jordan; and Lot journeyed eastward..."

GENESIS 13:11

When the time came for Abram and Lot to part company, Abram gave Lot his choice of land in which to dwell. He gave Lot "first pick" so there would be no animosity between them. But Lot did not choose well. He decided to homestead in a place called Sodom...a place that would become synonymous with sin and disaster.

How could Lot have made such a poor choice? Easy. Lot looked with his eyes. He saw a lovely, well-watered valley. He saw prosperity and riches and ease. Because generally speaking, we see what we love. When I go to another town, I see churches. I look at their steeples, their grounds, their doors and windows. That's my love. I love the church. I have a good friend who sees cleaning businesses because that is his love. He'll drive through a small town and say, "Gosh, look at that, they've got a dry- cleaning operation." I wouldn't see it...but he does. Lot loved the easy life...and he saw a glimpse of it in Sodom. So he chose the valley. But in so choosing, he lost everything.

When we choose with only ourselves in mind, we mix together the deep drink of selfishness and godlessness with disregard for future consequences. And the combination—as Lot discovered—can be deadly.

Read: *Galatians 5: 16-25*

On what basis do you make choices in life? Do you simply choose what looks good to you?

Exam Time

*"Take now your son, your only son, whom you love, Isaac,
and go to the land of Moriah; and offer him there as a burnt offering..."*

GENESIS 22:2

At 11:30 a.m. on the thirtieth of May, 1953, Sir Edmund Hillary ascended to the top of the highest mountain in the world, Mt. Everest. At the summit he planted the Union Jack of the British Empire, culminating years of planning and preparation, and days of agonizing effort. No man will ever climb higher than Hillary did that day at 29,002 feet above sea level. He had reached the pinnacle.

But Genesis 22 records a climb that was in some ways much more difficult than Hillary's ascent of Everest. When Abraham climbed Mt. Moriah with his promised son Isaac, he faced the ultimate test of faith and endurance...the final exam to end all final exams. It represented the pinnacle of sacrifice for Abraham, and the pinnacle of submission for Isaac. What made the climb so agonizing was not the terrain, but the assignment that was to be carried out at the top. God asked Abraham to offer his own son as a sacrifice—the son who was the very promise of God Himself. It was inexplicable. Inconceivable. But through this test, God was saying to Abraham: "I think you've matured to a new level of faith. I believe I can test you, and that you will prove faithful." And in a single afternoon, Abraham's hope was put to the test, his faith was put to the test, and his love was put to the test. God will have nothing less than all of us, and Abraham offered God all that he had.

REFLECTION

Read: *Matthew 16: 19-24*

What is it in your life that you treasure most? Are you ready to give it up entirely to God?

My Way or Yahweh?

*"Oh, the depth of the riches both of the wisdom and knowledge of God!
How unsearchable are His judgments and unfathomable His ways!"*

ROMANS 11:33

D o you ever look around you and wonder if God knows what He's doing? When His promises seem a long time in coming, do you wonder if He will make good on them at all? If you answered "no," I wonder if you are human. If you answered "yes," you are in good company. Even Abraham, the father of the Jews, wavered in his faith. When he and Sarah were still childless a decade after God promised them descendants, he did what we do many times. He began to rationalize and second-guess God. Then he tried to "help." He had sexual relations with his wife's maid Hagar, and she bore him a child. Needless to say, it was not what God had in mind.

It is easy to see how Abraham could have made such a poor decision. But what we need to understand is how he could have made a better one. What do we do when we are faced with a dilemma? How do we make difficult decisions, especially those related to faith? Here are a few suggestions. First, we need to listen to Godly counsel. Abraham did not. He listened to Sarah, who thought the surrogate mother program might be a solution. Second, we must exercise patience. Patience. Wait on the Lord. Finally, take the long look. Short-term solutions are not always best. Look far into the future, and try to imagine the long-term ramifications of the choice you are making. (I doubt that either Abraham or Sarah imagined their choice would affect Jewish-Arab relations several centuries later!) Nearly every choice you and I face is a choice between our way, or God's way. "My way—or Yahweh." Which will it be?

Read: Psalm 92: 4-8

 If you are facing a major decision today, carefully consider these three aspects of sound decision-making.

A Severe Mercy

MEMORIZE

"The outcry of Sodom and Gomorrah is indeed great, and their sin is exceedingly grave."

GENESIS 18:20

God detests sin. It is an affront to His holiness. He cannot abide it. The sin of the two cities of Sodom and Gomorrah was an out-cry to Him, and He resolved to destroy them. Now some may say, "What is this all about? How can a God of love destroy whole cities?" When God revealed His plan of destruction to Abraham, Abraham interceded for the inhabitants of these cities. God even agreed to spare Sodom if ten right-eous men could be found in it, but they could not. So the God of grace, for-giveness and love destroyed this ancient city. And that destruction was a severe mercy...an act of love toward the unborn generations that would have borne the consequences of the Sodomites' sins.

Suppose in New York City there was an entire city block of people addicted to crack cocaine. And suppose they were having crack addicted babies. How much of a godly remnant could be expected to counteract the results of their sin? What would it take to give these unborn children a chance at a drug-free life? When evil becomes so prevalent that any decent remnant is consumed, destruction is mercy. God brought judgment on the cities of Sodom and Gomorrah for immorality, lustfulness, decadence, and godlessness. Someone has said that if God does not judge New York or Los Angeles or San Francisco or Houston in the same way, He will owe Sodom and Gomorrah an apology! Every day that God does not bring down His arm in judgment is an act of mercy. And when He does, we can be sure that, too, is mercy.

QUESTION

Read: II *Corinthians* 6:14 - 7:1

What about you? Would you be considered a part of the godly remnant in your city?

Dung

"But whatever things were gain to me, those things I have counted as loss
for the sake of Christ."

PHILIPPIANS 3:7

At the risk of being considered indelicate, Paul used the strongest Greek word he could think of to say what all his worldly attributes meant to him...and the word he used was *dung*. Maybe your translation says something more delicate, like "rubbish," or "refuse," but it is exactly what you think it is. And Paul was a guy who had a lot going for him in a worldly sense. He was a Jew's Jew...a learned man, a lawkeeper, zealous, righteous—he had it all. And he called it dung.

Now, he didn't call his credits dung to be clever or provocative. He called them dung in *comparison* to the one thing he believed had real value in life: gaining Christ, being found in Him, and knowing Him. That, Paul decided, was the great work of his life. Everything else paled in comparison to the privilege of honoring and glorifying Christ, of knowing Him and making Him known.

Paul knew a secret. In order to live, you have to die. We must die to self, to ego, to power, to control, to applause, to achievement. We must count it all dung, waste, garbage, if it stands in the way of knowing Christ. Are you ready to do that? Are you interested in that kind of all-out surrender? If so, you will gain Christ...and He, as Paul well knew, is everything.

Read: *Luke* 14: 25-35

 What things in your life stand in the way of knowing Christ? Are you ready to call them what they are?

Never Alone

"For consider Him who has endured...so that you may not grow weary and lose heart."
HEBREWS 12:3

In the race of life, Jesus Christ is running with us. He is not only the starter of our race, He is our pacesetter, our encourager, and our partner. We live the Christian life not by our own effort, but by His strength. In Him, we are never alone. Without Him, we are easily discouraged, and tempted every day to quit.

When I was a boy, I took piano lessons...but not by choice. My mother made me take them, and I quit as soon as I could. (Maybe you did, too.) But I remember a story about another boy who had real talent. His mother encouraged him to keep on playing when the scales got boring and the work was hard. When a world-renowned pianist came to their city, this mother took her son to see him play. She thought it would inspire him to continue. As the crowd gathered in the concert hall awaiting the performance, the boy wandered up to the stage to see the great, shiny, grand piano. Quietly, he made his way up to it, and very quietly started to play...chopsticks. The murmuring crowd quickly hushed, then began to protest. "Get that kid down. What is he doing up there?" The great pianist heard the commotion, and entered from the wings of the stage, putting his arms around the boy's from behind. First, he joined in the boy's simple song, then he began playing beautiful music, fabulous chords, part of a concerto...and it was wonderful. The whole time he played he whispered in the child's ear, "Don't stop, keep playing, never quit."

When you want to quit, remember, the Lord Jesus has His arms around you, and He is whispering in your ear: "Don't stop, keep on, I believe in you."

Read: Matthew 11: 25 - 30

Are you discouraged? Listen for the voice of Jesus, encouraging you to endure.

Superfluous Weight

"...let us also lay aside every encumbrance, and the sin which so easily entangles us..."

HEBREWS 12:1

The successful runner knows he must strip down to run his best. At any track meet, you'll see plenty of runners preparing for their races in warm-ups, but they take them off to run. Some athletes even train carrying weights...but they never compete with them. When the writer of Hebrews says to lay aside every "encumbrance," he uses a Greek word that means...*superfluous weight*. If we are to run with endurance, we must lay aside any superfluous weight!

Now, in the race of life, what constitutes extra weight? It may be that our excess weight includes some good things, like hobbies, recreational pursuits, or even charitable works. But if we get so caught up in these good things that we lose sight of what is best...they must be laid aside. Other, not-so-good things can be extra weight in our lives. Besetting sin can slow us down. Ignorance can slow us down. So can a victim mentality that excuses us from taking responsibility for our own actions and choices. Procrastination can be extra weight as well. Tomorrow I'll get right with God. Tomorrow I'll seek His will. Tomorrow I'll study His word. And then tomorrow becomes today, and today becomes yesterday, and you've missed the race of life!

We are to run our race—the one God has set before us—and run it with endurance. Don't join the throngs of whiners and quitters who have been worn down by extra weight. For the glory of God in Jesus Christ, run the race!

REFLECTION

Read: *Philippians 3: 12-14*

What are the encumbrances of your life? Resolve to set them aside and run your race.

A Cloud of Witnesses

MEMORIZE

*"Therefore, since we have so great a cloud of witnesses surrounding us,
let us...run with endurance the race that is set before us."*

HEBREWS 12:1

Anybody remember Derek Raymond? His is not a household name, but few could forget the injured runner in the Barcelona Olympics who was helped around the track by his father as he struggled to finish the race. No medals are given for bravery and love, but if they were, Derek Raymond and his father would have won the gold.

The writer of Hebrews evokes just this sort of imagery when he describes the great "cloud of witnesses" that surrounds the Christian as he strives to finish the race of life. Who are these witnesses? They're those believers who have gone before us, having completed the race. They're heavenly witnesses. Abel is there, saying, "Nothing but the blood. You can make it." Moses, staff in hand, is saying, "You may feel cornered, but God's power will see you through impossible situations." Gideon is saying, "You may be outnumbered, but keep running, stay in your lane." Samson is saying, "Even if you've been caught in sin and scarred, God can still use you. Keep on." David is saying, "Murder...adultery...God's seen it all before. Seek His face again, and run your race."

When we go to an athletic event today, we see 22 men on the field, surrounded by 70,000 armchair athletes who desperately need exercise. Not these witnesses. They're the real thing, not plastic saints. They've run the race the same way we will...by grace. And they're cheering us home.

REFLECTION

Read: Exodus 14: 13-31

 Consider the lives of those who have run the race before you, and be encouraged.

Christianity vs. Religion

"He is the stone which was rejected by you, the builders, but which became the very cornerstone."

ACTS 4:11

The number-one enemy of Christianity today is religion, not unrepentant sinners. It was so from the very beginning. Jesus did not offend sinners…he offended the religious men of His day. He was the cornerstone rejected not by the passers-by, but by the builders themselves. In the person of Jesus, religion and Christianity tackled head-on.

How can you distinguish religion from authentic Christianity? Here are a few clues. First, religion loves ritual. Religion delights in the status quo. Change makes it uncomfortable. Religion is a commitment to a system of beliefs, attitudes and practices. Second, religion responds to challenge with intimidation. Challenge religion, and it will attempt to intimidate you into submission. What does an attorney do when he suspects that truth may not be on his side? He buys time, attacks procedure and assassinates character. Religion is defended the same way.

What about Christianity? Well, Christianity loves the truth. Aristotle defined the truth as "saying of what is that it is, and of what is not that it is not." In other words, truth has a standard, and is not relative. Also, Christianity responds to challenge with boldness. Why? Because knowing the truth and embracing it gives us courage.

When religion and Christianity clash, what happens? Many times, people come to know Christ. When Peter and John were arrested for the first time, five thousand people were saved! Don't be afraid when your faith is challenged by religion. When this happens, the stage is set for blessing, not for defeat.

Read: Acts 4: 5-22

 Do you really believe in Jesus Christ, or are you practicing religion?

Motivation

MEMORIZE

*"What shall we say then? Are we to continue in sin that grace might increase?
May it never be!"*

ROMANS 6:1-2

What motivates you? What compels you to follow Christ in obedience, choosing His commands over the world's temptations? Is it fear? Pride? Guilt? Motivation is so important.

There was a fellow who was an over-the-hill linebacker, several years out of college and far, far over his playing weight. He had tried every diet, every program, with no success. One day a good friend approached him and said, "I can help you lose weight. I've got a diet that's never failed." So his buddy gave him these instructions: "Take this letter, jog over to this address tomorrow morning, and ring the bell. When the door opens, read this letter. You'll know what to do." It sounded strange, but he agreed to give it a try.

The next day he got dressed, jogged over to the the address he was given, and rang the bell. He was surprised to see a beautiful woman in jogging clothes answer the door. He ripped opened the letter and read, "You can have her if you can catch her." She took off, and he ran after her. But he was in no shape to keep her pace. So he began to eat right and train, and each day he would get a little closer to her in the chase. Finally, he was within an arm's length of the woman. He knew tomorrow would be the day. The next morning he arrived at her door, rang the bell, and the door opened to a girl who weighed almost 400 pounds. She was holding a letter that read, "If you catch him, you can have him." And he took off without looking back.

It's a question of motivation, isn't it? And grace should motivate the Christian to live a God-honoring life. The grace that you have received should inspire you to grace-living.

ACTION

Read: *Galatians* 3: 13-16

Meditate on the grace of God today, and let it motivate you to joyful obedience.

Kissed And Tucked In

MEMORIZE

"He will not allow your foot to slip; He who keeps you will not slumber."

PSALM 121:3

B ob McAllister met Rusty Wellborn on death row. Bob was the Assistant to the Governor of South Carolina; Rusty was an inmate. Bob was a Christian man who routinely visited death row to talk to prisoners. And Rusty was one of the worst. He had been physically and emotionally abused, and had never known a loving home. He had been on death row for ten years for a brutal crime spree that involved four murders. The first few times Bob visited, Rusty never spoke. He lay curled up on the floor, broken, filthy and unresponsive. Gradually, Bob got him to talk, and eventually, to read the Bible with him. Weeks and months passed, but finally God broke through—and Rusty Wellborn received Jesus Christ. When all appeals for Rusty's life were exhausted, an execution day was set. Bob visited him the night before, and Rusty asked him to read from the Bible until he fell asleep. When Rusty's breathing was even and his eyes closed, Bob closed the Bible, crept over to Rusty's bunk, pulled up the blanket and gently kissed him on the cheek. The next day as he was led to his death, Rusty turned to the guard who was escorting him, and said, "It's sad, isn't it, that a man has to wait until his last night on earth to be kissed and tucked in?"

When we receive Jesus Christ, it is as if we are kissed and tucked in each night by the Holy Spirit. He watches over us, and makes our sleep sweet. But we are also to "kiss and tuck in" one another—as Bob did for Rusty. To show the love and compassion of Christ at every opportunity. Rusty was right: no one should have to wait until his last night on earth to be kissed and tucked in.

QUESTION

Read: *Psalm 121: 1-8*

 Are you kissed and tucked in? How can you do the same for those you love?

Socrates, Patton And Dear Abby

MEMORIZE

"And these words, which I am commanding you today, shall be on your heart; and you shall teach them diligently to your sons..."

DEUTERONOMY 6:6-7

Genetic engineering is only about 20 years old, but someday soon, it may bring us cures for cystic fibrosis or cancer, or enable us to avoid various birth defects. Some say the field will one day allow parents to determine the genetic make-up of their children with sort of a catalog approach: "We'd like a dark-haired, blue-eyed artist," or "We'll take a well-muscled, strong athlete." So genetic engineering has an upside medically that is promising, but also a potential downside that is frightening.

Personally, I believe genetic engineering works the wrong side of the equation. We don't need to think about engineering children—we need to worry about how to re-engineer parents! If there were a catalog for parenting skills, I know what I'd choose. I'd like to have the intelligence of Socrates, the discipline of General George Patton, and the practicality of Dear Abby. But what if we could be re-engineered by God's grace into better parents? And what if our "catalog" was the Bible? Then I would want the ability to give my child a good self-image. To see himself the way God sees him, not as the world sees. Also, I would want the insight to weave my child's special strengths into a feeling of competence. To give him confidence that he can get on in this world. Finally, I would want the emotional stability to teach him good relationship skills. (By the way, none of these— I believe—are mastered by watching television!)

How do we do this? We do it by being teachers. By constantly teaching and living out and demonstrating the precepts of God's word. When we do this consistently, our children are better equipped for life than any catalog of engineered traits could ever hope to make them.

REFLECTION

Read: I Samuel 1: 19-28

 If you are a parent, what do you want to give your child? Ask God to help you teach these things by your words, your actions and your own life.

Study Your Children!

"Thou dost scrutinize my path and my lying down,
and art intimately acquainted with all my ways."

PSALM 139:3

Did you know that God studies His children? He does! He is a student of your ways and my ways, and He is intimately acquainted with everything about us. Just as God studies His children, we parents should study ours. We should become "intimately acquainted with all their ways," because every child is different. For that reason, we must learn to give our children the kind of love they need. We may be great at telling our child that we love him, but what he'd really respond to is a hug. If we haven't studied that child and observed his particular bent, we won't know.

Parenting is not easy. It's not for cowards. But when we study and discern the uniqueness of our children, they are honored and affirmed in who they are. When the writer of Proverbs instructed parents to "train up a child in the way he should go," he did not mean the way *we think* he should go, but in the way he is already bent. You don't try to make an artistic child athletic, or vice versa. You don't try to force a shy child into public speaking. You discern the natural, God-given bent of your child and do all you can to encourage growth in that direction.

It is impossible to do this kind of training in scheduled, five or ten minute "sessions." Intense, focused "quality time" is a child-rearing myth. Quality time is a result of quantity time. The high moments of parenting are unscheduled and fleeting. We must be present when they happen to participate. Given a choice between "quality time" and "quantity time," a child will choose quantity every time. Be there. Study your child. Encourage his growth in the bent that you see.

Read: Psalm 139: 1-5

If you are a parent, what have you learned by studying your child this week?

Terminal Words

MEMORIZE

*"Let no unwholesome word proceed from your mouth,
but only such a word as is good for edification..."*

EPHESIANS 4:29

I f our children do not know how to forge healthy relationships with others, it is because we have failed as parents to provide them with the
model they need. We must model and teach the things that will equip
our children for the future. Unfortunately, too many parents are failing in
this area. Too often we speak "terminal words" that neither edify nor support. They tear down. Let me suggest ten things we should never say to our
children, and encourage you to avoid them at all cost.

No child needs to hear the words "Why can't you be more like...". Every
child is unique, and God has created them just as they are. Don't say "act
your age." What does that mean? Children do act their age! They act like
children. They will be adults soon enough. Don't ridicule a child for being
a child. Don't say "Is that the best you can do?" Whether you are questioning their appearance or their performance, these words are never helpful.
Don't label your children with words like "You're the cute one," or "You're
the smart one." Children allow such words to define and limit them. Never
say "How could you be so stupid?" Stupid is a terminal word, and a degrad-
ing one. Never—not even in a moment of exasperation or fatigue say "I wish
I'd never had you." Never. Don't tell your children to "shut up." There are
other ways to contain inappropriate outbursts. Also, don't say "Do it, or
else!" Or else what? These words are an invitation to a child to test your
limits. Finally, never threaten to leave your child for any reason, for any
length of time. Threats are ineffective discipline.

Replace the terminal words in your parenting vocabulary with life-giving words; words that build up rather than tear down.

ACTION

Read: James 3: 2-12

 *No parent has avoided these mistakes, but study this list and resolve today
to retire your "favorite" terminal words.*

Many Counselors

MEMORIZE

*"Where there is no guidance, the people will fall,
but in an abundance of counselors there is victory."*

PROVERBS 11:14

Only a fool is afraid to listen to the counsel of others. Are you threatened by an "abundance of counselors?" You need not be. Some will never believe this, but the input of two or three or four sharp counselors will put any decision maker way ahead of the game.

William G. Pagonis, the lieutenant general and logistics wizard responsible for moving the equivalent of the population of Alaska (and their personal belongings) to the other side of the world in Operation Desert Storm, formed a team of advisors he called the "log cell." Members of the log cell reported directly to Pagonis and acted as an ad-hoc "think tank," communicating honestly to their superior when asked for advice. They were expected to provide fast, no-nonsense feedback and were given the freedom to point out what they deemed to be any ill-advised plans.

Every leader needs to create an atmosphere where trusted advisors can speak the truth in love. Sound decisions generally flourish where there is free and open dialogue and a healthy sense of give and take. The leader who is inexperienced, but insists on doing it alone, is making a self-indulgent (and serious) mistake.

ACTION

Read: *Proverbs* 15: 21-29

 Are you facing an important decision? Seek the wisdom of one or two counselors whose insight you trust before making up your mind.

Credit Where Credit Is Due

MEMORIZE

*"Men of Israel, why do you marvel at this…as if by our own power or piety
we had made him walk?"*

ACTS 3:12

The apostle Peter was the kind of guy who had no trouble finding the front of a parade. He was drum major material! But when Peter and John performed their first miracle, healing a lame beggar at the temple gate, even Peter knew better than to take credit. Peter called on the name of Jesus to perform the healing ("In the name of Jesus Christ the Nazarene—walk!"), and he credited Jesus afterward ("by the name of Jesus Christ the Nazarene…this man stands before you in good health").

When the Holy Spirit empowers us to serve, do we give credit where credit is due? When God uses you to teach a Bible study or comfort a friend, or lead another person to Christ, does your drum major syndrome kick in? Do you shrug and assume an air of mock humility ("Oh, really, I uh, it was nothing…"), or do you name the name of Jesus Christ? Never allow yourself to imagine that you had anything to do with the results when you are used by God. The works He does through our lives have no basis in our limited resources. Peter and John didn't have the stuff to make a lame man walk, and they knew it. They weren't about to pretend that it was their doing. When the Spirit works through you and me, the miraculous things He may do are only half of His agenda. The other half is seeing Jesus Christ exalted as a result. Don't get in front of the parade when the band begins to play. Give credit where credit is due.

REFLECTION

Read: *Revelation 15: 3-4*

Have you seen the Holy Spirit's supernatural work in your life as an opportunity to exalt Jesus Christ?

The Prison of Unforgiveness

"...Lord, how often shall my brother sin against me and I forgive him?
Up to seven times?"

MATTHEW 18:21

The Isle of Pelicans is its official name...but you would probably know it as Alcatraz. For thirty years—from 1933 to 1963—it housed the very toughest of federal prisoners. During that time, 26 tried to escape...but only five succeeded. Alcatraz, surrounded by the chilly waters of the San Francisco Bay, was considered the finest maximum security prison of its time. But there is a prison more secure than Alcatraz, or any other prison on the face of the earth. It is the prison of the human heart that refuses to forgive.

We like forgiveness most when we are in a position to receive it. When we've sinned, we want to hear about God's amazing grace. (Incidentally, I've heard the hymn Amazing Grace sung at the funerals of some of the meanest scoundrels who ever lived!) It is when you and I are in a position to extend forgiveness that we become quite a bit more stingy. But did you know that we are forgiven in the exact same proportion with which we forgive others? That's right. To the degree that I forgive, the forgiveness of God is made available to me. Peter wanted to make sure he understood forgiveness when he asked Jesus how many times he should forgive a brother who sinned against him...and he thought seven was a generous estimate. Imagine his shock when Jesus multiplied that number by 70! What He was really saying was that we should only limit our forgiveness to others if we want God to limit the forgiveness He offers us. Simply put, if unlimited forgiveness is what we desire, unlimited forgiveness is what we should be willing to give.

Read: *Matthew 18: 21-35*

Is there someone in your life you feel like you've "forgiven enough?"
Have you received all the forgiveness you'll ever need?

Get A Life!

MEMORIZE

*"The thief comes only to steal, and kill and destroy; I came that they might have life,
and might have it abundantly."*

JOHN 10:10

Man has a hunger for life built into his very being. We want to live, and live fully, not merely exist. This instinctive desire to live is illustrated by an old story about a man who decided to commit suicide. He was intent on taking his life, and planned to combine every possible method so that no cause of death could be determined. To that end, he got a boat and pushed it out into a lake. He carried a rope, gun, some poison, kerosene and matches. With all of his paraphernalia ready, the man stood on the seat of the boat, flung the rope over a limb, put the noose around his neck, swallowed the poison, doused himself with kerosene and lit a match. Then he took the gun and cocked its trigger, but as he did, he slipped on the boat seat, shot the rope in two, fell into the lake and put out the fire, then swallowed water and threw up the poison. Later he said, "I was fortunate. If I had not been such a good swimmer, I might have drowned."

When Jesus said that He came to give life, He struck a deep chord in the hearts of men. They knew His words held power and promise...and that He was offering something they desperately craved. Not just a home in heaven after this life was over, but a full, rich, abundant life that begins here and now. Someone has said, "I have never known a lost person who did not know something was missing in his life...something they deeply longed for." That something is *life*...and only Jesus gives it. He said "I am the way, the truth and the *life*, and no man comes to the Father but by Me."

QUESTION

Read: John 10: 7-15

*Your salvation was meant to be the entrance into a full, abundant life. Are
you missing something?*

Free Indeed

MEMORIZE

"If therefore the Son shall make you free, you shall be free indeed."

JOHN 8:36

When our boys were growing up, they frequently asked me to take them to various parks around our city where they could play pick-up basketball. One evening I took one of them to a lighted court a few minutes from our house, and settled in to watch two half-court games. On one end of the court it was a free-for-all. I think the game was basketball, but I couldn't be sure. It looked like a combination of football, rugby and wrestling. No rules. No regulations. No whistles. No fouls. And from the looks of it, no fun.

On the other end of the court, a smooth, sharp game was in progress. These guys were players. They handled the ball like you would not believe. The knew what a foul was, and even called a few on themselves! With the talent and discipline they exhibited, these guys were going somewhere...and their high-flying, above-the-rim kind of game was a thrill to watch.

If you were a real player, the second game would be the game for you. The game with no rules and no skill would only frustrate (and might kill) you. But at the other end of the court, you could shine. The game with no rules would inhibit your freedom to excel, but the disciplined game would allow you all the freedom you need to play well. The truest freedom you and I can experience is the freedom that most closely conforms with our God-breathed, God-designed nature. He knows best how we are to function, and His parameters give us the freedom to really live.

QUESTION

Read: I Peter 2: 11-16

 Are you straining against God's commands in any area of your life? Say "yes" to a higher freedom by obeying Him.

The Humble Man

MEMORIZE

*"Take My yoke upon you and learn from Me, for I am gentle and humble in heart;
and you shall find rest for your souls."*

MATTHEW 11:29

Humility is not thinking poorly of yourself. Humility is not thinking of yourself at all. Humility is the one grace that, as soon as you declare you have it, you've lost it. Jesus Christ, the Son of God, the Savior, the King of Kings, was a humble man. "He was a man of no reputation," it was said. Nothing about His appearance or manner suggested divinity. The apostle Paul wrote to the Philippians that it would please him (and God as well) if the Philippians would become humble men and women, in imitation of Jesus Himself.

Modern man is chiefly concerned with working his way up. Up the corporate ladder. Up the office pecking order. Up the social register. Jesus worked his way down. Jesus started at the top. Paul said, "He existed in the form of God." But He didn't cling to that position. "He did not regard equality with God a thing to be grasped." Not only did He not cling to His top spot, He emptied Himself. He cashed it in. Walked away from it all. We're stunned when we see people at the top walk away, aren't we? But Jesus left it all and became not only human in form—He adopted the role of a servant. Do you see it? He worked His way down. And finally, He died the death of a desperate, wicked criminal. Then God brought Him back to life, and brought Him back home to glory. Jesus emptied Himself...and God exalted Him. Can you imagine the applause in Heaven over Jesus' return? Humility is a key to true joy. Jesus didn't just say it...He proved it.

QUESTION

Read: Philippians 2:1-11

What are you working your way toward? Is your goal in conflict with a humble heart?

Mission Accomplished!

*"I glorified Thee on the earth, having accomplished the work
which Thou hast given Me to do."*

JOHN 17:4

Near the end of his life, pastor Robert S. McArthur was speaking in Baltimore, Maryland. He began his message with these words: "As you can tell, I've just about finished the course. I hope that when I come to the end, I'm as thorough in the accomplishment of my life's purpose as three boys I saw in Birmingham, Alabama, many years ago." Then Dr. McArthur told a story about preaching in a Birmingham church and watching three teenage boys acting up in the balcony. It seems a gentleman on the lower floor had fallen asleep with his mouth open and his head back, and these boys spent most of the sermon trying to toss spitballs into this man's mouth. "I couldn't keep my eyes off of them," he said. "They tossed spitball after spitball until I heard a cough and a gurgle, and the man sat up with a start. I knew then they had accomplished their mission! After that they were satisfied, and leaned back and listened to the rest of my sermon."

Mission accomplished. What a thrill to be able to say those words at the end of life. Jesus did. He knew he had accomplished the work set before Him by the Father. Paul said them, too. "I have fought the good fight. I have run the race." Those who can say "mission accomplished" live every moment of every day with their mission in mind. They are focused. They are single-minded. They are compelled by a higher call. Are you living in such a way that when the end comes, you, too, can say "mission accomplished?"

Read: John 17: 1-8

 Are you seeking to do the things that the Father has set aside for you to do, or are you living by your own agenda?

What Matters Most

MEMORIZE

"You blind guides who strain out a gnat and swallow a camel!"

MATTHEW 23:24

I t is easy to get so caught up in the details of life that you lose sight of the big picture. Jesus took to task the Pharisees of His day for their pious attention to the minutiae of the law while ignoring the heart and spirit of the commandments. They were so focused they couldn't see what mattered most.

The great Greek orator, Demosthenes, was speaking to a large crowd of people and noticed that some were actually falling asleep. He was dealing with great truths, and his audience was catnapping! He became so bothered by this that he interrupted the point of his address with a story. "Once there was a man with a burden on his back," he said. "He had to travel over a high mountain, and the load was heavy, so he rented another man's donkey to carry the load. He had gone about half-way up the mountain when the sun became unbearably hot, and he grew weary. Looking for shade and finding none, he settled down to rest in the shadow of his donkey. Soon the owner of the donkey came by...also hot and tired. He spied his animal, and insisted the "renter" move over and allow him to rest in the donkey's shade. An argument ensued over whose right it was to rest in the shadow of the donkey. And the two debated until..." then Demosthenes walked away. By this time, his audience was wide awake, on the edge of their seats awaiting the verdict. "Wait, Demosthenes," they shouted. "Come back! We must know how the story ends."

So he returned and said, "Just as I thought. You are more interested in who owns the shadow of a donkey than you are in the great issues of life and death." And aren't we, too, at times?

REFLECTION

Read: *Matthew 23: 23-33*

Have you allowed the details of life to crowd out what matters most? Make today a day of re-establishing priorities.

Held Hostage By Sin

"For I know my transgressions, and my sin is ever before me."

PSALM 51:3

D avid succinctly describes in Psalm 51 the prison of every secret sinner: "My sin is ever before me." As long as sin is secret and unconfessed, it can hold us hostage. Even children know this. Susie and Johnny were two city kids who loved to visit their grandparents' farm. On one extended visit, Grandpa made Johnny a slingshot. Johnny shot at everything he could see, but he never hit much until he hit his grand-mother's pet duck as it strutted through the yard. One shot to the neck— bam!—and it was, in fact, a dead duck. Susie saw the whole thing, and decided quickly that she could use her brother's misfortune to her advan-tage. "Johnny," she said, "if you'll do my chores this weekend, I won't tell Grandma how you killed her duck. Otherwise, I'm telling right now."

So all weekend long, Susie played and Johnny worked. She rode horses. He washed dishes. She fished. He swept the porch. All Susie had to say when Johnny got tired was "Remember the...". Johnny remembered. Finally, he'd had all he could take. He went to his grandmother in tears and told all. "I didn't mean to, Grandma, but I shot your duck and killed it. Then I buried it off in the woods and did all the chores so Susie wouldn't tell." His grandmother took him in her arms and said, "You know Johnny, I was watch-ing out the window when you hit the duck. I was just wondering how long you'd do all your work and Susie's, too, before you decided to tell me."

Isn't that the way we operate? We try to hide our sin until the hiding becomes unbearable, then we resort to the truth. But until we confess, we're hostages.

Read: II *Samuel* 11: 1-27

Is there something in your life you haven't dealt with before God? Tell Him about it.

A Leader's Humility

*"Though you build high like the eagle, though you set your nest among the stars,
from there I will bring you down, declares the Lord."*

OBADIAH 1:4

The finest illustration of leadership that I know does not come from the pages of the Harvard Business Review, but from the pages of the Bible. Jesus Christ was the ultimate servant-leader. "The Son of Man," He said, "did not come to be served, but to serve, and to give His life a ransom for many." The servant-leader is quite willing to live in obscurity, but he seldom does. A leader "wanna-be" is likely to fall in love with his own image, and to believe in his own good press.

I am reminded of the humorous story of a visit by the President of the United States to a nursing home. The President entered the facility with his entourage and was received with delight by the elderly residents. As he went from person to person in the living area, he noticed a woman in a wheelchair who seemed rather disinterested in all that was going on. Years of campaigning had taught him how to work a room, and he did not want to offend someone who might be around for the next election. He approached her, smiled, patted her shoulder and gently squeezed her frail hand. She smiled back, but said nothing. "Do you know who I am?" the President finally asked. "No," she replied, "but if you'll ask the lady at the nurses' station over there, she'll tell you." So much for self-importance!

Humility is that trait which, when you're sure you've got it, you can be sure that you don't. The true essence of great leadership is servanthood.

Read: Mark 10: 35-45

*If you are a leader, are you also a servant? How would those whom you
lead rate your service?*

A Hill Worth Dying For

"If it be so, our God whom we serve is able to deliver us from the furnace of blazing fire; and He will deliver us out of your hand."

DANIEL 3:17

The sergeant has received his orders. "At any cost, take that hill." He turns to his men and says, "Check your rifles...affix your bayonets. At my signal we charge and take the hill!" The men in his company have been in the trenches for days. They've seen other men try to take the hill and fail. They know the enemy is heavily entrenched and determined to hold their ground. And each man, as he waits for the command from his sergeant, is asking himself one question: "Is this a hill worth dying for?"

Those of us who have never been to war cannot completely understand the anguish of such a moment where life hangs in the balance, but we have asked the same question in different, if less threatening, terms. "Is this principle worth risking my job?" Or, "Is this argument worth the damage it might cause in my marriage?" On what basis do we choose which hills are "worth dying for?" I believe if we have made the right life commitments, the question answers itself when it arises. Our problem is we don't nail down the big questions at the outset, and so we waver on the smaller ones. The book of Daniel records the story of four young men who were kidnapped and carried into a foreign land. As the prevailing powers in this new country tried to "assimilate" them, they received a shock! These young men had made up their minds not to defile themselves or turn their back on their God, so when the questions of diet and prayer practices came up, their decisions were already made. When we nail down the big choices, the other decisions fall more readily into place.

Read: *Daniel* 3: 17-30

One of the key questions of life is this: Whom will you serve? How you answer this question will help you answer a host of other, smaller questions.

And The Winner Is...

MEMORIZE

"Thus the last shall be first, and the first last."

MATTHEW 20:16

We live in a day where first is first and last is last...and where it is deemed far better to be first. But Jesus taught that God's scorecard is often a mirror image of our own. Why? Because He does not look only at the "bottom line," He examines the heart. In the parable of the vineyard laborers, those who "signed on" at day's end were paid just as much as those who worked a full day—a fact that angered many of the full-day workers. But God looks at each man's heart, and judges accordingly.

A father had three sons, all of whom worked for a furrier. The father of these boys was a friend of the owner, and he was aware that all three boys had the same job, but were paid differently. When he casually asked the owner about the discrepancy, the man invited this dad to spend a day at his warehouse observing the three boys. When the father arrived, the owner picked up the phone and called the first son, who made about $100 a week. He said, "There's a ship at the dock from Ontario with some hides on board; go down to the dock and see what they've got." The son said he would check it out, and called back in three minutes. "I called down to the dock," he said, "and they have 1500 seal pelts aboard." The owner said thank you and called son number two, who made $200 a week. He made the same request: "There's a ship from Ontario on the dock with some hides. Go take a look and let me know what they've got." An hour later he reported in: "I checked on the ship and they have 1500 seal hides on board. They look good." Again, the owner thanked the boy. Then he called son number three, who made $500 a week. Same instructions. Four hours passed, but at the end of that time, the third son had this to say: "I went down and looked at the pelts, and bought 500 seal for $5 apiece, then sold them for $7 to one of our customers. They also had 500 red fox pelts, which we don't handle, but I know someone who does, and was able to sell them to him for a $4,000 profit. There were 39 minks on board, too. I know you like to examine those yourself, so I optioned them for an hour until you can take a look." The president of the company said, "Thank you very much," then looked at the father. "Do you understand now?" he asked him. "Yes," the dad said, "I certainly do."

What kind of worker are you in the kingdom of God? Have you given him everything you have?

REFLECTION

Read: *Matthew 25: 14-30*

Stop worrying about what others are doing and how they are being rewarded. Examine your own heart and say, "Is God getting my all?"

Are You A "Big God-er?"

"He only is my rock and my salvation, my stronghold; I shall not be greatly shaken."

PSALM 62:6

D r. Robert Wilson was a Princeton Theological Seminary professor and Hebrew scholar. Dr. Wilson made it a practice to hear every one of his students when they preached at Millard Chapel, but he would hear them only one time. Someone asked him, "Dr. Wilson, when you go back to hear your students, what are you looking for? What are you listening for?" Dr. Wilson's answer was unusual: "I'm just trying to determine whether they are a little God-er or a big God-er. I only need to hear them once to know." He went on to explain, "If they are little God-ers, I know their ministry won't go far, and they'll probably always be struggling. But if they are big God-ers, I know God will work through them in a wonderful way."

The man asked him how he could make the distinction between little God-ers and big God-ers. "A little God-er," he said, "will begin with a series of problems, and he'll have a low view of scripture. He won't perceive God as One who is actively involved in the lives of people, and will consider Him a force to be manipulated rather than a Person to be worshipped. A big God-er, he went on to say, "talks about the God who is moving in history, and he speaks of the relevance and authority of God's timeless word."

Are you a little God-er or a big God-er? You don't have to be a preacher to know. Are your circumstances bigger than God, or is He bigger than your circumstances? What worries occupy your mind? What passions drive you? If the minutiae of life overwhelm you, your God is too small!

Read: Psalm 62: 5-8

 If you are a little God-er, resolve today to enlarge your view of the Almighty.

A Sensitive Subject

*"Flee immorality. Every other sin that a man commits is outside the body,
but the immoral man sins against his own body."*

I CORINTHIANS 6:18

Sex is sensitive because it is inherently, undeniably personal. It involves our body and our soul. We are not, and can never be, comfortably distanced from it. That makes sexual sin especially complex. There is, of course, no hierarchy of sin. There is no sin that is more acceptable to God than another, because no sin at all is acceptable to Him. But because sexual sin is a sin not only against God, but against our very own bodies, its consequences can be more devastating to us than those of other sins.

When Hitler was systematically attacking the continent of Europe during World War II, allied forces joined in a united defense. American soldiers fought and died on foreign soil, and the conflict certainly took its toll on our country—but we sustained nowhere near the damage that Britain or Austria or Poland suffered. Why? Because the war was not fought on our own soil. By contrast, battles over sexual sin are always fought at home. They take place "on our own soil," on and within our physical bodies. There is no escaping the shrapnel of sexual sin. Sex outside of God's established parameters impoverishes a man or woman the way a war at home impoverishes a nation. You will be affected—physically, mentally, emotionally and spiritually, because sex is a personal thing. You can't get away from it. It is within you and within me.

Read: *Psalm 119: 9-16*

*Have you received God's forgiveness for any sexual sin in your life? Ask
for it. It's yours.*

Standing Close To The Edge

MEMORIZE

"Flee from youthful lusts, and pursue righteousness, faith, love and peace, with those who call upon the Lord from a pure heart."

II TIMOTHY 2:22

Anytime God's parameters for sexual expression are taught, someone inevitably asks a question like, "Well, if unmarried persons are not to have sexual intercourse, what can they do with one another and still be within bounds?" That's just like human nature, isn't it? We want to know just how close to danger we can lurk without inviting disaster. The answer to the question lies in God's prohibition of pornea, or lustful activity between the unmarried. Bluntly speaking, any activity that is sexually provocative to the parties involved should be avoided.

When my son Ed attended Florida State University on a basketball scholarship, he discovered how tough it is to prepare physically, mentally and emotionally for a game you may not play. As a freshman, Ed spent a lot of time on the bench, even though he suited up, made practice shots, stretched, dribbled and shot free throws before every game. When the time for tip-off came, Ed would have worked up a sweat. Then the starting line-ups were announced, and Ed—loose, warmed up and ready to play—would take his seat at the end of the bench. He was trained, prepared and disciplined, but he didn't get into the game. It wasn't his time. If you are unmarried, the time for you to enjoy the expression of your sexuality through intercourse has not arrived. Don't choose to make yourself miserable and frustrated by constantly "warming up" for a game you are not yet slated to play.

ACTION

Read: *Colossians* 3: 1-10

If you are single and have not done so, determine today—regardless of your past—to reserve the total, physical expression of sexual intercourse for the commitment of marriage.

Say "Yes" To A Higher Love

MEMORIZE

*"When I was a child, I used to speak as a child, think as a child, reason as a child;
when I became a man, I did away with childish things."*

I CORINTHIANS 13:11

Have you ever seen Michelangelo's famous David? It stands in a modest rotunda in a Florence, Italy, museum, beautifully elevated and bathed in natural light. It is impressive from any angle, but almost no one comments on the tree stump that the artist carved to support his sculpture's right leg. The stump is not ornamental—it is an essential balance to the entire work of art. Without the half-hidden stump, Michelangelo's masterpiece would have toppled over centuries ago, because the David as he stands could not bear his own weight.

You see, Michelangelo knew his craft. In David, he created something that was not only breathtakingly beautiful, but would stand the test of time. It would last. He knew the raw material—the marble—and what it could and could not do. Real, relational intimacy is the foundation for pure sex. Sex without relational intimacy is like a fragment of a masterpiece.

If you are among the majority of unmarried adults who are sexually active, I encourage you to "just say yes" to building a solid foundation of relational intimacy—not sexual intimacy—in your relationships with the opposite sex. Pure sex—the kind of sex God intends for a husband and wife—is simply too heavy to support with no foundation. It needs a solid, relational base to bear its weight.

REFLECTION

Read: *Ephesians 4: 14-24*

 Instead of thinking what you might be missing by saying no to premarital sex, think what you could be gaining by saying yes to a higher love.

The Anatomy of An Affair

*"But each one is tempted when he is carried away and enticed by his own lust.
Then when lust has conceived, it gives birth to sin..."*

JAMES 1:14-15

I f it had happened today, in our time and culture, the headlines would read something like this: AFFAIR OF ISRAELI KING RESULTS IN ILLEGITIMATE HEIR, MURDER! Following would be a lurid description of the rooftop bath that set things in motion, and perhaps an account of David and Bathsheba's tryst from a servant who pressed her ear to the wall of the king's bedchamber that day. Unnamed hospital sources would report the baby's birth (if it were allowed to be born at all), and secret military sources would describe doomed Uriah's last moments on the battlefield. We would know exactly how these events took place, but we would not know why.

The real story behind David's dangerous liaison (and of any affair) is even more significant than the details of the act itself. Writer Walter Wangerin says, "adultery is never a sudden, spontaneous, totally unexpected act. It is always preceded by a longer drama, at the beginning of which *you are not helpless*." David's affair began long before it culminated in his well-documented one night stand. It began with a host of small concessions, many of them only mental, and ended when he was finally carried away by his own lust. The time to check lust is before it has conceived. Once it does, birth is inevitable.

Read: James 1: 13-17

No one is immune to unfaithfulness. Examine your thoughts and small actions today to detect any trace of concession to lust.

A Home Security System

MEMORIZE

"For every house is built by someone, but the builder of all things is God."

HEBREWS 3:4

Like many of our friends and neighbors, we have a security system in our home. When I open the door, I hear a little beep that reminds me to enter a code to temporarily deactivate the system. When we are in for the night, I enter the same code again so an alarm will sound if an intruder enters. Why do people install security systems? So they can feel safe in their homes and protect their loved ones and their property from those seeking to cause harm.

While every home may not need a security system, every marriage does! It takes a security system around every husband and every wife to ensure that a marriage remains intact, safe from those persons or forces that would harm it. Even if only one partner puts such a system in place, the odds of adultery occurring decrease by 50 percent! What are the components of such a system?

First, be controlled by the love of God. Let His love dictate your thoughts and actions. Second, be wise in the fear of God. Understand that He is just and settles His accounts. Third, be certain of the judgment of God. One day each of us will stand before Him and be held accountable for every thought and deed. Fourth, be identified with the cause of God. Fly your flag for Him, and fly it high. Fifth, be accountable to the people of God. Allow those close to you to examine your life. Finally, be your mate's best option for companionship, love, lovemaking and nurture. Don't be fooled into thinking your marriage is "burglar-proof." Set up your security system today.

QUESTION

Read: I Corinthians 10: 1-12

Do you have the components of a good marital security system? What is lacking?

Headline News

"If two of you agree on earth about anything that they ask,
it shall be done for them by My Father who is in Heaven."

MATTHEW 18:19

We live in a news-saturated culture, with easy access to a wider menu of media options than any generation in history. There's Headline News. CNN. Dateline. Nightline. Add to these a whole host of news "journals" and commentaries, both written and broadcast. If that's not immediate enough, there's the Internet...with myriad up-to-the minute sources for the latest breaking stories. But who determines what is news? Who decides what makes the headlines?

The first century church was, to my mind, a source of winning news stories. Peter preaches. Two thousand saved. Christians pray. Peter released from prison. Paul shipwrecked. Safe at Malta. But more than likely, these were not the "big stories" circulating among the general public. If you were living in the first century A. D., you might have heard of Stephen's execution, but not Saul's conversion. You might be familiar with Herod's death, but not an Ethiopian's second birth.

There is no "scoop" bigger than the story of God's involvement in the lives of His people, and the growth of His church, one believer at a time. Move the calendar ahead a hundred, two hundred, three hundred years from now, and the things we see in today's headlines will be forgotten. But in the Lamb's book of life, no turning, no answered prayer, no sacrifice, no new beginning will be forgotten. And they won't be footnotes. They'll be headline news...every single one of them.

Read: Acts 12: 1-29

 What news-worthy thing has God done for you today? Why not broadcast it so that others can rejoice?

DAY
153

Learn To Pray By Praying!

"...you do not have because you do not ask."

JAMES 4:2

D
o you know who prayer intimidates the most? Christians! A lost person who wants to be saved can pray a prayer of repentance and forgiveness without giving much thought to form or style. He or she simply cries out to God, and asks for what is needed. Many Christians do not have because they do not ask. They do not know how to pray because they do not pray.

George Beverly Shea told me he had a dream one night that he was in Heaven. As the Lord was showing him around, Bev says they came to a large room filled with seemingly endless compartments, each one bearing a person's name. Bev asked what the compartments were, and God replied, "These belong to every person who has ever lived and been my servant." Bev asked the Father to show him his own compartment, and God did so. As they opened it and looked through its contents together, Bev was over- whelmed. It was full of wonderful things. Fabulous things. It was literally a treasure chest of blessings. "I don't understand," Bev said. "These things are fantastic, but are you sure they're mine? I don't remember having any of them." God nodded in agreement. "You didn't have them, Bev. But I would have given them to you if you had only asked."

We do not have because we do not ask. And we do not ask because we do not know how to ask. In other words, we don't know how to pray. But the secret to prayer is this: we learn to pray by praying. When Jesus' disci- ples asked Him to teach them how to pray, He did not give them a step-by- step, how-to list. He said to them, *"Pray, then, in this way..."*. How do we learn to pray? By praying. Begin today. Begin now. Ask.

Read: *Matthew 6: 5-13*

Ask God today for what you need. Order your prayer to Him, and eager- ly watch for His answer.

As Jesus Would Pray

"But when He, the Spirit of truth comes, He will guide you into all the truth..."

JOHN 16:13

We learn to pray by praying. And we are helped in prayer by the Holy Spirit, who "tunes" our prayers to the very heart of Christ, teaching us to pray as Jesus would. How does this work? Just imagine Jesus praying for you. Then listen in. What would He say to the Father on your behalf? How would He plead for you? I try to picture Him and say, "Lord Jesus, I know You are interceding for me right now. What are You praying for?" Then I listen in, under the leading of the Holy Spirit. Since I have begun to do this, it has changed my prayer life. By listening to Him, I know how to pray for myself.

Also, I listen to how Jesus would pray for those I love. I say, "Lord, what are You praying for my wife? What does Jo Beth need? What are you praying, Jesus, for my children, my grandchildren, my church, my friends?" I listen, and I order my prayers as the Spirit leads, seeking to pray as Jesus would pray.

Do you wonder how Jesus might pray for you? Let me give you a hint. Look through the window of John chapter 17, and see what Jesus prayed for you and for me on the last night of His life. He interceded on our behalf to the Father, asking that we might be one with Him and with God the Father, and that on the basis of that unity, the world might believe that Jesus Christ is the Son of God. He also prayed that we would know we are loved by God with the same love which He has for His only Son. Listen to the heart of Jesus as He prays.

ACTION

Read: John 17: 15-24

 Hold your loved ones up before the Father, and ask, "Lord Jesus, how would you pray?"

Seeing As God Sees

MEMORIZE

"...are you not fleshly, and are you not walking like mere men?"

I CORINTHIANS 3:3

We walk in the flesh. Any debate there? You and I are flesh and blood; we're protoplasm and water and salt and albumin. In other words, we're human. But we do not war in the flesh. Our spiritual battles are not fleshly battles. They are fought in another realm. You face a river you cannot cross. A mountain you can't scale or tunnel through. How do you handle it? If you rely on your own ability, your own power, your own skill, you will most certainly fail. When we war in the flesh, we lose. Our human ingenuity, talent, giftedness, education...will not serve us well as weapons in spiritual warfare. We need something else. Something other-worldly.

The apostle Paul says that the weapons of our warfare are not of the flesh. Many of us operate as if they were. When the bottom falls out of life, our first impulse is to say "What can I do? How can I work this out? What solution can I bring to bear on this dilemma?" But that is not how battles are won against the fortresses, the strongholds that we wage war against.

If you are in prison today in your soul, if you are depressed, broken, confused or disturbed, no amount of skill or determination will set you free. Don't battle in the flesh. Battle in the Spirit. Pray. When we pray, we begin to see things as God sees them. And when we gain His perspective, the victory is as good as won.

REFLECTION

Read: II Corinthians 10: 3-7

 Do you face a seemingly insurmountable battle? Ask God for His perspective, and pray and act accordingly.

You Can't Stay Where You Are

"Therefore if any man is in Christ he is a new creature; the old things have passed away; behold, new things have come."

II CORINTHIANS 5:17

There is one place that God will never let you stay...and that is the place where you are. Once God touches our life, we can be certain that we will never be the same. He will move us; He will change things; He will shake us up to get us where He wants us to go. For the Christian, there is simply no such thing as status quo.

Change was the hallmark of the early church, but many churches today resist change. Someone has said that the seven last words of the church are: "We've never done it that way before." When God revealed His plan to spread the Gospel to the Gentiles, the Jewish Christians were faced with the need for radical change. Old beliefs and attitudes had to die so that new ones could take their place. The Christians at Jerusalem were content to be a Jews-only brotherhood, but God had other plans. Change was in order.

There is a chorus I have sung with thousands of teenagers over the years on beach retreats. I never get tired of it. It challenges me as much as it does them: *"Will you stay where you are, or will you reach for a star? Play the game? Be a fraud? Or die to self and live to God? This could be victory's hour, claim His grace, claim His power. Will you stay where you are, or reach for a star?"*

Read: *I Corinthians* 10: 1-12

Where is God calling you today? Will you follow?

The Truth About Prejudice

MEMORIZE

"What God has cleansed, no longer consider unholy."

ACTS 10:15

Prejudice is not a twentieth century phenomenon. Why were the Jewish Christians so slow in reaching the "uttermost parts" of their world with the gospel? I can give you the answer in one word: prejudice. The Jews hated the Samaritans. They had no dealings with the Gentiles. But God intended that the way of salvation be made available to all men, regardless of their heritage.

Do you know what lies at the root of all prejudice? It's pride. And pride is something that God absolutely abhors. Many in our world today are prejudiced against those of a different heritage...whose skin is a different color, or whose language is not their own. But we are all sons of Adam, made from the dust of the ground. There is no skin color that is better than another; no country of origin that is favored over the rest.

When I was growing up in the rural south, I had many occasions to witness prejudice, but I remember one instance where it was confronted, and overcome. The pastor of my home church in Laurel, Mississippi, invited a young woman with an incredible voice to sing for our congregation. The entire church rose up against him because of it, and he survived with his job by the skin of his teeth. Why the opposition? Because this teenaged woman was black. But the invitation stood, and she sang...and the most famous thing about my home church today is that once, years ago, one of the greatest sopranos in all of history sang there. Her name was Leontyne Price.

REFLECTION

Read: Acts 10: 1-23

 Examine your own prejudices in light of God's word. Are you condemning anything (or anyone) that He has accepted?

Dirty Laundry

"...yet God has shown me that I should not call any man unholy or unclean."

ACTS 10:28

I am thankful that segregation is a thing of the past in America. But I am not so foolish as to think that the prejudice behind it has been eradicated. A film called "Once Upon a Time When We Were Colored" movingly depicted those not-so-distant days of segregation and their impact.

A young, black boy raised by his grandparents was promised his first trip to town with granddad. He cleaned up, put on his best clothes and climbed into the car for his journey. On the way, his granddad stopped for gas. The boy needed to use the restroom, and was halfway there when he was called down by the white gas station owner. "Boy, you can't go in there. There's no place for you here." His grandfather quickly got him back in the car, paid for his gas, and left. Once they were back on the road, he explained to his grandson that they would stop somewhere else for a bathroom break, and that he would let him know when and where. Then he took an old paper bag, and drew a big "C" on one side, and a big "W" on the other. "Now boy," he said, "this "w" is for other people, not for us." He turned the sack over. "But this "c," is for us. When you see a "c", it's okay to go in, or get a drink, or whatever. But if you see a "w", you keep away. Understand?" The boy nodded yes, and took the bag. Every few miles he would turn it over and back again.

When they got to town, the old man got groceries, and the boy began to look for something to buy with the coins in his pocket. Soon he was thirsty, and spied a water fountain. Approaching it carefully, he pulled the paper sack out of his back pocket. He looked at the "c" and the "w" for a long time, then drank from the fountain whose sign said "Colored." As he ran back to his granddad he said, "How'd I do grandpa?" The granddad shook his head with tears in his eyes and said, "You did good, boy. You did good."

Read: Acts 10: 10-16; 24-33

What prejudices are you still carrying that are out-of-date and displeasing to God?

Are You A Legalist?

MEMORIZE

"I also please all men in all things, not seeking my own profit, but the profit of the many..."

I CORINTHIANS 10:33

Alegalist says, "I've never done anything like that, and I never will." Legalists make lists of things they will and will not do, and hold strictly to their own self-imposed version of righteousness. When Peter was shown in a dream that it was fine for him to eat the flesh of animals on his "don't eat" list, he protested. "No, Lord, for I have never eaten anything unholy or unclean." But those are the words of a legalist.

God told Peter, "Kill and eat," but Peter told God "No, Lord, by no means...". Let me suggest that the word "Lord" presupposes that the only appropriate answer is "yes, by all means." To say "No, Lord" is contradictory. If He is Lord, we cannot say "no." But Peter, like all of us, had a list of "no's" to which God would say "yes." When Jesus said He would be crucified, Peter said "no." A crucified Savior was not on his list. When Jesus told Peter that all of the disciples would turn away from Him in His hour of need, Peter said "no." Cowardice was not on his list. Peter had a habit of saying "No, Lord," when God had already said "yes!"

A legalist says, "Look at what a great guy I am. Here's my long list of things I don't do, and I stick to it!" He mistakenly believes that God applauds and says "Oh, you're right. Look what a good boy you are!" All the "no's" in the world will not get a legalist into heaven. But one "yes" to the Lord Jesus Christ and His cleansing sacrifice will.

QUESTION

Read: *Matthew* 15: 7-14

What lists of "do's and don'ts" do you need to tear up? Will you do so today?

Absolutes And Negotiables

"What God has cleansed, no longer consider unholy."

ACTS 11:9

In every group of people, every institution, every organization, there are people who are opposed to change, people who are ready to change, and people who just want to wait and see. Studies have shown that ten percent of any given group are innovators. They're ready to try new things and risk change. But eighty percent are "show me" types. They might change, but you must first prove to their satisfaction that change is advantageous. The final ten percent are nay-say-ers, against any change at all, regardless of the advantages.

I know of a church where a near-riot took place over a movie projector. Someone brought a projector into the church and showed a film (with biblical content, of course), and a meeting of the church leadership was called to debate it. "We can't have this," some said. Others argued that a movie projector was no big deal: "We bring in missionaries who show slides. What's wrong with a movie that talks about the Lord?" The nay-say-ers quickly took the matter in hand: "If the pictures stand still, it's all right. But if they move, it's sin."

There are absolutes, and there are negotiables. Don't confuse the two. What is clearly taught in God's word is not up for debate. But what is not addressed specifically is not worth clearing the house over. In the absolutes: obedience. In the negotiables: liberty. In all things: love.

Read: I Corinthians 10: 15-24

What are the absolutes of the Christian faith? Are you confusing some "negotiables" with these absolutes?

Whose Values?

MEMORIZE

"In those days there was no king in Israel; every man did what was right in his own eyes."

JUDGES 17:6

We have veered off course as a civilization, as a society, for two reasons: we have refused as a people to look to a transcendent, authoritative God for moral absolutes, and we have depended instead on our own depraved determination of what is right and wrong. God said this same thing to the nation of Israel thousands of years ago: *"My people have committed two evils: They have forsaken Me, the fountain of living waters, to hew for themselves cisterns, broken cisterns, that can hold no water."* (Jeremiah 2:13)

Think about it. A hundred and thirty-five thousand students go to school with weapons every day in America. Twenty-one percent of students say they do not go into restrooms in their schools because they are afraid of being molested or attacked. Forty percent of teenage women in America will have been pregnant at least once by the time they are nineteen. Suicide among teenagers has increased three hundred percent in the last thirty years. One third of all teachers are contemplating retirement or career change next year because the conditions under which they must teach are so threatening. Simply put, the evil of our day is so pervasive we cannot live without it touching us somehow, somewhere.

What is the answer? Men and women everywhere must look to God and say, "Yes. There are absolutes and immutable laws at work in this world. You have established them. And if we are going to live successfully, we must obey them." When this happens, America will come to its collective senses. Revival will replace relativism, and we will have hope once again.

QUESTION

Read: *Jeremiah* 2: 4-13

 Does your life reflect your belief in a transcendent, authoritative God of the universe?

Celebration's Prerequisite

MEMORIZE

"This is the Lord for whom we have waited; let us rejoice and be glad in His salvation."

ISAIAH 25:9

Have you ever felt emptiness in the midst of a celebration? As if the party were going on around you, but you couldn't join in with true abandon? A secret cheater, for example, is miserable at an awards banquet in his honor. A researcher who falsifies data to win a grant is never sure his efforts are worthy. An employee who misrepresents his performance for an incentive competition is curiously dissatisfied with the prize. Each could attend a celebration...but none could fully enjoy it.

Oddly enough, it is obedience that frees us to experience real celebration. When we live by God's precepts, we are ready at any moment to celebrate life, and to participate fully in joy. Someone has said that the greatest lie of Satan is that obedience can never bring happiness. A quick reading of Jesus' Sermon on the Mount verifies that assessment. The real joy, the real blessing, the real celebration lies in obedience. It is impossible to celebrate what God has done when we have not been a part of it through our own obedience.

Only when we give our all to a cause and follow God completely does joy burst forth when the time for celebration arrives. Holiness during the week yields joy at the worship celebration. Sacrifice over time yields joy when the challenge is ultimately met. Obedience insures we will never feel empty when the party begins!

REFLECTION

Read: *Matthew 5: 2-12*

What is keeping you from true celebration? Is there any area of your life where you are refusing to follow God completely?

Where is Joy?

"In Thy presence is fulness of joy; in Thy right hand there are pleasures forever."

PSALM 16:11

We long to experience the soul-delighting, abundant life that Jesus spoke of in John chapter 10. Many of us catch glimpses of it, but they do not satisfy. Instead they only whet our appetite for more. When joy surprises us, it comes as almost an ache—a sharp realization that there is more to life than we are experiencing, more than we have yet laid hold of.

Richard Foster says that hurry, noise and crowds are the tools of the Enemy, who is out to rob us of joy and destroy our souls. But God stands ever ready to offer us that for which our hearts long. The psalmist wrote that joy is found in God's presence. Meditation on God and His goodness is our answer to the Enemy's onslaught. Someone has described meditation as a cup of tea. We are the hot water. God's word is the tea bag. Hearing the word through a sermon or Bible study lesson is like dipping the tea bag in water. But taking time to read, study and memorize scripture is like immersing the tea bag in water and letting it steep for an extended period of time.

When we consistently combine God's word with time and a teachable heart, His truth permeates our very lives. Like sponges, our hearts absorb more and more of Him, and we are transformed in the process.

Read: *Psalm 119: 103-106*

 When was the last time you experienced fullness of joy? Have you neglected being in His presence?

Where is Truth?

"Sanctify them in the truth; Thy word is truth."

JOHN 17:17

The truth is found in God's word, and in His Son, Jesus Christ. And there is freedom in knowing the truth.

The film *Amistad* depicted the story of a ship of African slaves who fought for their freedom through the U. S. legal system. Three times their case came to trial, and each trial yielded the same result: three decisions for freedom. In both the factual evidence presented and in the climactic argument before the Supreme Court, one crucial element operated in the Africans' favor: truth.

When falsehood triumphs in our lives, we remain enslaved. Besetting sins, addictions and disobedience wreak their tragic consequences. We yearn for freedom, but only God's truth has the power to set us free. The truth we need to release us from our chains comes from the disciplined study of scripture. Truth about God, ourselves, and the awesome power of the gospel often lies just below a surface reading. Only deep exploration and submission to God's word yields the truth that explodes falsehoods and frees us from our chains.

Read: *John 8: 31-36*

 Pray that neither pride nor laziness nor apathy will keep you from apprehending the truth of God.

The Romance of Fasting

MEMORIZE

*"Man shall not live on bread alone, but on every word that proceeds
out of the mouth of God."*

MATTHEW 4:4

Have you ever been separated from a special loved one for a long period of time—or what seemed like a long period of time? Do you recall how it "hurt so good" to get a letter or a call during that time of separation? For a few precious moments it seemed as if your special someone was near, and that you were together once more. Then the letter or the call concluded, and the long wait to reconnect with your loved one began again.

Although we belong to Jesus Christ; though He is our beloved and we are His, we are "separated" from Him by sin, by neglect, and by the cares of this world. We are "homesick" for Him in a way that is difficult to describe. John Piper calls fasting the "hunger of homesickness for God." Fasting is a discipline that woos us back into the romance of faith with our soon-to-return Bridegroom Jesus Christ.

When we fast, competing suitors for the jealous love of Christ are revealed and destroyed. By abstaining from food for a period of time, the desire for it re-ignites our deeper hunger for the Bread of Life whose name is Jesus.

ACTION

Read: *Matthew 4: 1-11*

Skip a meal or two today. When you hunger, turn your thoughts to Christ and His return.

Becoming What We Adore

MEMORIZE

"Worthy art thou, our Lord and our God, to receive glory and honor and power..."

REVELATION 4:11

Successful men and women attract a following. Have you noticed? It seems we believe that success breeds success, and if we associate with successful people, we too might become successful. The truth is, very often people do become like the object of their focus.

We are to worship God because He alone is worthy of our worship. Over and over again in the book of Revelation we see the phrase "Worthy art Thou." And He is. But His worthiness is not the sole reason we worship God the Father. We also desire to become like the One we adore.

Henry Scougal, the English Puritan, writes, "The worth or excellency of a soul is to be measured by the object of its love." Think about that! If we love lowly things, our soul will be lowly. But if we love glorious things, worthy things, our soul is exalted, or carried higher. God is the most glorious Being of all, and if we adore Him, our souls will become excellent. Worshipping God helps us to become like Him. "Oh, come, let us adore Him!"

QUESTION

Read: *Revelation 4: 5-11*

 How is the glory of God transforming you?

A "Yes" Face

*"When he saw Peter and John about to go into the temple,
he began asking to receive alms."*

ACTS 3:3

A man was trying to get across a river on foot with little or no success. He spied a man on horseback, took one look at him, and said "Please let me ride over with you on the back of your horse. I need to cross this river." Sure enough, the rider lifted him up and took him across the river. The man on the horse was named Abraham Lincoln. When they reached the other side, those gathered on the bank who had witnessed this act of kindness said, "You wanted the President to take you across, didn't you? The rest of us weren't good enough." But the man shook his head and said, "No, I didn't recognize Mr. Lincoln. I didn't know it was him." His answer was met with disbelief. "Then why did you single him out, and ask him instead of all the other riders who crossed before him?" Without hesitating, the man replied, "That's easy. He had a 'yes' face, and I saw it right away."

Do you have a "yes" face? Are you approachable? Do strangers ever ask you for directions? Do friends ask you for help? Peter and John must have had "yes" faces, because the lame beggar at the Beautiful Gate of the temple singled them out to ask for alms. But he got more than he bargained for. Peter and John were willing to help, but not in the way this beggar envisioned. Peter told him he had no gold or silver, but he was willing to give what he did have: healing. "In the name of Jesus Christ the Nazarene," he said, "walk!"

The truth is, the beggar at the gate had more gold than either Peter or John. But they had something he needed more than money. Jesus has a "yes" face. He is willing to help when we call on Him. But He knows better than we do what our true needs are. The question is, are we willing to call on Him, and to receive what He deems best for us?

Read: *Acts 3:1-10*

 Imagine yourself looking into the face of Jesus. What do you need? Will you ask for it, willing for Him to answer as He discerns?

Good Guilt!

MEMORIZE

"For whoever keeps the whole law and yet stumbles at one point,
he has become guilty of all."

JAMES 2:10

Does "good guilt" seem like an oxymoron? It is not. Good guilt is the guilt we feel when we truly are guilty! We feel good guilt when we have broken God's laws, and our conscience is pricked. Good guilt is a sign that the Holy Spirit is at work in our hearts, convicting us of sin. The trouble is, many of us stop with feeling guilt, and do not move forward to repentance and forgiveness.

Peter may not have made a lot of friends when he preached his second sermon recorded in the book of Acts, but the Holy Spirit used his words to stir up good guilt. He told those who had witnessed the healing of a lame man, "The God of Abraham, Isaac and Jacob, the God of our fathers, has glorified His servant, Jesus, the one whom you delivered up, and disowned in the presence of Pilate when he had decided to release Him. But you disowned the Holy and Righteous One, and asked for a murderer to be granted to you, but put to death the Prince of life...". Pretty direct, is it not?

When Peter finished preaching, he called for his audience to repent, and the Bible records that "many of those who had heard the message believed; and the number of the men came to be about five thousand." (Acts 4: 4) Are you experiencing any good guilt today? What are you going to do about it?

QUESTION

Read: Acts 3: 12-19

Do you need to repent and seek forgiveness in response to the good guilt you feel? Will you?

Something About That Name

"That at the name of Jesus every knee should bow, of those who are in heaven, and on earth, and under the earth..."

PHILIPPIANS 2:10

There's just something about the name of Jesus. When the disciples healed in the name of Jesus, it was not their faith in healing that restored health; it was their faith in the name of Jesus. They simply claimed the promise Jesus had made to them: "Whatever you ask in my name, that will I do, that the Father may be glorified in the Son." (John 14:13)

Have you had the experience of asking in someone else's name for what you could not receive on your name alone? It's a humbling thing to say, "Mr. So-and-So suggested I call you," or "Ms. What's-Her-Name said you would have those tickets for me." You ask and receive, not because you are worthy, but because you are asking in a name that is more powerful than your own.

The name of Jesus has amazing impact. You can go on television and talk about Christ, and no one gets upset. You can run ads that talk about the Messiah or the Lord, and never raise an eyebrow. You can say Redeemer, Savior, Master, Teacher or Friend, but call the name of Jesus, and watch what happens. By naming His name you are drawing a clear line, because there is no other name on earth by which men may be saved. There is power in His name.

QUESTION

Read: John 14: 8-13

Do you hesitate to name the name of Jesus Christ? One day every tongue will confess Him. Don't wait until then to call on Him.

The Results of Repentance

"If we confess our sins, He is faithful and righteous to forgive us our sins and to cleanse us from all unrighteousness."

I JOHN 1:9

To repent means to change your direction, to change your mind, to change your lifestyle, your habits, your relationships. Unless these changes have taken place in your life, you have never really come to know Jesus Christ. Repentance, true repentance, yields forth changed lives. It's a radical thing.

When we experience this true repentance, three things happen. First, our sins are wiped away. I never get over that. When we confess, God is able and just to forgive that which we have confessed. Our sins are erased, and God sees them no more. Also, when we repent we experience a time of refreshing from the presence of the Lord. The picture of this refreshing is one of catching your breath. When sin delivers a sucker punch, the breath is knocked out of us. But when we repent, a time of refreshing comes. Also this refreshing is like finding a cool stream of water in a hot desert. It's taking the Nestea plunge...receiving just the pick-me-up we need. Finally, when we repent, the Jesus who seemed out of place in our lives before because of sin now fits perfectly. He's the appointed one whose presence is just right. He fits exactly inside of you and inside of me.

Have you experienced the results of repentance?

Read: Acts 3: 19-26

Would you say that you have experienced true repentance evidenced by these three things?

It's Easy And It's Hard

"For the good that I wish, I do not do; but I practice the very evil that I do not wish."
ROMANS 7:19

I don't know about you, but when I became a Christian I said, "This is the easiest thing in the world. What a deal!" I walked down the aisle of our country church, said "I believe in Jesus," was baptized, and hence, my Christian life began. I somehow had the idea that I could live just as I had been living, and when (not if!) I did something wrong, I could ask God to forgive me, and all would be well. If I died prematurely, as a member of God's family, I would most certainly go right to heaven. I had this Christianity thing licked!

But then a Bible study teacher named Mr. Alexander exploded my ease. He taught the Bible to us straight and clear. He ran a shoe store, but he was an anointed teacher who made me realize that receiving Christ was easy, but living the Christian life was not. In fact, many times it was downright hard. Finally, as I began to study the word on my own, I came to the conclusion that the Christian life was not hard…it was impossible! I could completely identify with Paul when he said he did what he did not wish to do, and did not do what he wished to do! If Paul struggled, what hope was there for me?

Then I discovered I could not live the Christian life under my own power any more than I could get right with God on my own merit. I began to understand the work of the third person of the Trinity, the Holy Spirit. As He fills my life, He enables me to live and walk in victory. So I came full circle. The Christian life is easy. The Christian life is hard. The Christian life is impossible. The empowered Christian life is exciting…and that power comes from the Holy Spirit Himself.

Read: Acts 1: 4-8; 2: 1-4

 Have you discovered the secret of living a Spirit-empowered life?

Divine Guidance

MEMORIZE

"The fear of the Lord is the beginning of wisdom,
and the knowledge of the Holy One is understanding."

PROVERBS 9:10

Picture Forty-second Street and Broadway, New York City. It's peak traffic time. Buses, cars, trucks, taxis, delivery vans...all are zipping by at a dull roar. On the curb is a mother cat with a kitten in her mouth. She is trying to carry her baby across the street at one of the busiest intersections on earth. She starts out. She darts back in. She darts out a little farther and is almost run over. She tries a third time with no success. Finally, an old Irish cop with a heart as big as the city itself sees her dilemma, and takes the situation in hand. Whistle blowing and hand raised, he steps out into the intersection of 42nd and Broadway and stops traffic cold. The mother cat sees her opportunity and scampers across safely. All the power and energy of New York City was held at bay by that policeman's right hand, but the mother cat never knew it.

I wonder how many times in your life and my life the sovereignty of God has prevailed at critical junctures? How many times has He enabled us to move safely through a moment of difficult decision? You see, there is a moral guidance system by which we humans operate, and that system helps us determine the will and the purpose of God. We can sense it, but it is difficult to explain. Would God leave His children with no way to determine His will for their lives? Never. He has given us our own built-in reason, intelligence, giftedness and inclinations. Best of all, He has left us His own "inner voice" that speaks to us when we get still enough, and leads us in the right way.

Don't lean solely on your own understanding. Acknowledge Him, and He will direct your path.

QUESTION

Read: *Proverbs 3: 5-6*

What decision are you facing today? Will you listen for God's voice as it speaks to your heart about what you should do?

Doing Something With Nothing

MEMORIZE

"Trust in the Lord with all your heart, and do not lean on your own understanding."

PROVERBS 3:5

W henever I am asked to sign a book for someone, I frequently write the notation "Proverbs 3:5-6" next to it. It is one of my favorite passages of scripture. *"Trust in the Lord with all your heart, and do not lean on your own understanding. In all your ways acknowledge* Him, *and He will make your paths straight."* In all your ways acknowledge Him. Don't lean on your own understanding. How does that work? What does it mean?

It works like this. I am nothing. That's right. I am nothing, and so are you. Is your ego smarting? It shouldn't be. God wants you and me to become nothing. Then we will understand that He is everything. Dr. William Newell was teaching the Bible at a mission in China, and was leaving to return to America. He spoke with the director of the mission and said in a very pious voice, "Oh, please pray that I shall become nothing." The director of the China inland mission laughed and said, "Newell, you are nothing. Take it by faith."

The secret to being sure you are in the middle of God's will is to understand that you are nothing. You came from dust, and in a little while you will be nothing more than a vapor. With this understanding, you can empty your life of self-importance and pride, and simply say, "Lord Jesus, fill me with your Holy Spirit. I have no agenda of my own." Then God can take your nothing-ness and my nothing-ness, and make something beautiful of it that He can use and bless. God makes somethings out of nothings!

REFLECTION

Read: *Philippians* 1: 12-20

Is your agenda getting in the way of God's will for your life? What would it take for you to become nothing?

The Beautiful Bride

"The marriage of the Lamb has come and His bride has made herself ready."
REVELATION 19:7

There's something about the beauty and purity and magnetism of a bride. I've attended and officiated at a lot of weddings, and I don't think I've ever seen a bride who was not beautiful. Paul says the church is to be the bride of Christ. God said to Israel, "You are my bride," and that same symbolism is used of the church in the New Testament. But if we, the church, are the bride of Christ, I wonder…how do we look?

Most brides are irresistible, but are we? Are non-believers attracted to the bride of Christ? We can introduce people to Jesus Christ in many ways, but however it is done, the church should be a winsome, caring, loving bride that draws wanderers near. The primary way we do this as a body, as a church, is through friendship, or relational evangelism. That means a man or a woman must sense the music of the gospel in your life before they ever really want to hear the words. There must be music before the words can be received and understood. And the music of the gospel is this: the relationship those who are in Christ have with Him, and with one another.

Also if the church is to be a beautiful bride, she must have not only "music," but a high view of the word of God. A reverence for the word of God and a belief in its inerrant truth are the "words" of the gospel. When this high view of scripture is undergirded by a rich melody of love, the bride of Christ is the most compelling force on the planet! So the question for you and for me is this: do we make a beautiful bride?

Read: 1 John 4: 7-16

 Does your love for Christ and for others radiate? Do you make the bride of Christ more beautiful?

A Reason To Boast

MEMORIZE

"I can do all things through Him who strengthens me."

PHILIPPIANS 4:13

It's no secret that I'm a Michael Jordan fan. I don't believe there's ever been a better, more complete player in the game. But some time back, I saw a television commercial that made me appreciate his accomplishments even more. He said, "I've taken almost 9,000 shots…and missed. I've played in almost 300 games…and lost. My coach and my team have asked me to take the final shot that would have won the game twenty-six times…and I missed. I have failed in life many, many times," and then he added, "and that's the reason I'm a success." I like it!

The apostle Paul is another hero of mine. I believe he could have made a similar commercial, perhaps even more dramatic. Can you imagine it? "I've been beaten more times than I can count. I've been in two shipwrecks. I've been run out of town, lowered over a wall in a basket, stoned and left for dead, and whipped within an inch of my life. I've been in more jails and dungeons in more towns than almost anybody on the planet…and that's the reason I'm a success!" Paul was a priest—a Christian under the new covenant—he was a preacher, and he was a pioneer. But he never boasted of those things. Instead, he boasted of the power of Christ as it was displayed in his own weakness! Imagine—boasting in weakness!

Paul knew better than to boast about his accomplishments. He would speak of nothing but what Jesus Christ did through him. He knew Jesus did not say, "Without Me you can do very little," but "Without Me you can do *nothing*." Paul was not displaying false humility. He was just stating the facts! All that he had ever done was through the power of Christ alone, and he knew it.

ACTION

Read: II *Corinthians* 11: 18-23

Write your own "failure commercial." Then give God praise for what He has done through you..

The God of All Comfort

*"For just as the sufferings of Christ are ours in abundance,
so also our comfort is abundant through Christ."*

II CORINTHIANS 1:5

G od's outlook on suffering is so different from our own. He sees not just the instance of suffering, but its end result. Not just the pain involved, but the refinement that is certain. Someone has said that from the perspective of eternity, the worst suffering this life could hold would look like "one night in a bad hotel." I believe that. But even though God's view of suffering is higher and longer than ours, He is always there to comfort us in our pain.

One of the most encouraging things about suffering is to see how God uses it not only in our lives, but in the lives of others. Two individuals in our church family have beautifully illustrated this. Blaine is a grade school student whose leg was amputated just below the knee due to cancer. Shortly after Blaine's surgery, Ted, a high school teacher, was involved in a four-wheeler accident that left him paralyzed from the waist down. While Ted was working hard in rehab, he received this letter from Blaine, who had heard about his accident: *"Dear Coach "T": My name is Blaine. You may have heard about me, but I have cancer. I'm going through chemo and I know I'm going to lose my leg, so I know what you're going through. I bet it's hard knowing that you may not walk again, but keep praying for God to give you peace over this. He has given me peace. Never give up on God and keep on praying for a miracle, and never stop because he is always in the miracle business. Remember I'm praying for you. Love, Blaine H."* And then as a P.S. he added: *"For I know the plans I have for you, declares the Lord; plans to prosper you and not to harm you, plans to give you a hope and a future."* One last afterthought, scribbled at the bottom of the page, read: *"Remember, God always has the BEST plans for you."*

Read: II Corinthians 1: 2-7

 How could you use your own personal suffering to minister hope and help to someone else?

My Brother's Keeper

"Am I my brother's keeper?"

GENESIS 4:9

D r. Donald Gray Barnhouse, one of the great godly pastors of our day, was speaking to a large assembly of people. After his message, two elderly ladies approached him and said in a whisper: "Dr. Barnhouse. Did you know that some of the young ladies here are not wearing stockings?" He realized they wanted him to condemn this obvious affront to God and Christianity...but he did not. "That's quite interesting," he said. "You know, the virgin Mary did not wear stockings, either." They weren't quite sure what to do with this piece of news. "That's right," Dr. Barnhouse continued. "In fact, the first reference to any woman wearing stockings was in the 15th century, when some Italian prostitutes began to wear hosiery." Now he was in dangerous waters. "Then," he said, "women of royal blood in the Victorian era introduced the practice and all upper class women complied, until at the end of that period, stockings became the attire of a prude." (I don't believe the ladies had another question for the good Doctor.)

Certainly there are absolutes in our Christian faith. But the truth is, there are more "gray" areas where the Bible does not speak to a particular practice. This creates problems in the church today, as it created problems in the first century church. While we deal with things like drinking alcohol or dancing, the early Christians wrangled over eating meat that had been sacrificed to the idols of the day, or keeping certain Jewish practices as a prerequisite to Christianity.

How do we know what to do in such instances? I believe we employ a few basic principles. First, we must get out of the judgment business. That's not our role. Second, we must be sure to do nothing that might cause another brother or sister in Christ to stumble. Third, we must not do that which would cause us to stumble. Finally, we must realize that we owe to other believers a debt of love...and in the area of Christian liberty we really are our brother's keeper.

Read: I *Corinthians* 10: 23-31

Are there any gray areas in your life that you need to examine in light of this principle?

The Hour is Late

"It is already the hour for you to awaken from sleep;
for now salvation is nearer to us than when we believed."

ROMANS 13:11

What time is it? I'll tell you. The hour is late. Our nation is, in the words of one cultural observer, "slouching towards Sodom and Gomorrah." We can no longer sit back comfortably and say, "There's always been a crisis in the world. Today is no different. Our society will go on, and our country is basically strong." Those who do so are only kidding themselves.

A friend of mine said that as a young man he had a twelve o'clock curfew. His father told him, "Jerry, you be in by midnight. If not, your hide is mine." Jerry said he got out with the guys one night and before he knew it, it was almost two in the morning. He said he flew home, quietly unlocked the front door, took off his shoes (I know none of you have ever done this) and began to climb the stairs to his room. As he took his first few steps, his dad's voice called out, "Jerry, is that you?" He said "Yes, sir, it's me." About that time, the cuckoo clock in the hallway began to chime. "Cuckoo! Cuckoo!" Two o'clock. And Jerry said he froze in the hallway and as clearly as he could, he "cuckoo-ed" ten more times!

Ladies and gentlemen, we are at a late hour in our history. We are nearer to the coming of our Lord than we have ever been before. His return is the last great event yet to come before the curtain of time is brought down. In this world of darkness, we are to be a light to those around us. God is not fooled about the hour, and His return is certain and irreversible.

Read: *1 Thessalonians 5: 1-11*

How would considering Christ's return as an event that could take place today change your plans?

Put On Christ

MEMORIZE

"Put on the Lord Jesus Christ..."
ROMANS 13:14

"Clothes make the man," the old saying goes, and there may be a lit-tle truth to that. If clothes don't entirely make the man, they can at least identify him to a degree. What a person chooses to put on can tell you a lot about him or her. What they value. How they see them-selves. What their priorities are.

When you and I "put on the Lord Jesus Christ," we are saying something. We put on the Lord, meaning we recognize His lordship over us. He is Lord of all. He controls our life. His word is the last word, and He is the one to whom we must answer. We are saying that He is supreme. He is omnipo-tent. He is the audience of one to whom my life is played. We put on Jesus, too—the humanity of the incarnation. To put on Jesus is to put on love. Jesus gives us the capacity to love our neighbor and love our enemies and love the unlovely. With Jesus, we put on the ability to love. And finally, we put on Christ—the Messiah or Anointed One. When we put on Christ, we affirm the resurrection power that He gives to sustain and deliver us. It's quite a wardrobe, is it not? We put on the Lord, and He is supreme. We put on Jesus and His capacity to love. And we put on Christ, Who gives us the power to live this life.

You see, when we put on the Lord Jesus Christ, there is a whole new agenda in place. We think differently. We act differently. Our old desires are replaced by a new desire to be holy and pleasing to God. That's what His love does for us, and that is what our love, in Him, is to do for others. So, let me ask you a question. What are you wearing today?

ACTION

Read: *Romans 15: 1-6*

Consciously think today about what it means to put on the Lord Jesus Christ.

What Kind of Saint Are You?

"...you are fellow citizens with the saints, and are of God's household."

EPHESIANS 2:19

W hen we think of saints, we think of people like Mother Teresa, or Billy Graham, or, in our church, our dear graduated sister Jane Elder. Definitely "saint material," all. But did you know that you are a saint? That I am a saint? That's right. Paul called saved sinners "saints" in his letters to the churches. If you were a Christian, to Paul's way of thinking, you were a "saint." He used the term no less than sixty times in the New Testament!

So, Christian: what kind of saint are you? Basically, saints in the church fall in one of three categories. First, there are those we call the real saints, or the "saintly saints." They are committed to the Lord Jesus Christ, have a deep personal relationship with Him, are led by the Holy Spirit, rooted in God's Word, and available to be used by God in the Body of Christ. Then there are the "side-tracked saints," or the lukewarm saints. They're not hot, but they're not cold either. They're for what God is doing as long as it makes them comfortable. They sit on the sidelines saying, "feed me, help me, nurture me, love me." When these sidetracked saints are asked to do something, they have plenty of reasons why they shouldn't—most of them selfish. (The Bible says this kind of saint makes Jesus nauseated.) Finally, there are the "pseudo-saints," or the phony saints. They have their name on the church role, and know a bit of religious lingo. They pass through worship every Easter or Christmas or Mother's Day and nod at God as they go. But they don't have a clue about what it means for Jesus to be Savior, let alone Lord. The pseudo-saints.

It matters what kind of saint you are. Because if there is ever to be a hope of revival and renewal in our culture, we need the side-tracked saints to come alive and the pseudo saints to get a clue. That's the only hope we have. So what kind of saint are you?

Read: *Ephesians* 2: 13-22

 Ask yourself what kind of saint you are. If you are dissatisfied with your answer, do something to change it.

How Do You Smell?

*"For we are a fragrance of Christ to God among those
who are being saved and among those who are perishing."*

II CORINTHIANS 2:15

Maybe you read the title of this devotional and thought, "I'll just skip this one. This guy's getting a little too personal." Well, this is personal. So I'm asking: how do you smell? When Christians use their gifts in the Body of Christ, their service is a pleasing aroma to God. When someone writes a note and says "I missed you at church," or "I'm praying for you in this difficult time," or when someone makes a phone call or cooks a meal or teaches a class or checks a roll, that act of service is worship to God. A sweet-smelling aroma goes up from that sacrifice to the throne of God, and He says, "That's worship! That smells good. That gives Me pleasure."

Often I'll put in praise tapes as a part of my time with God. If I'm in the office or running or in the car, I might have praise music on. I've even been known to break out in song if I'm alone, and sing praises to God at the top of my voice—and when I do, the place I'm in becomes a sanctuary where God is worshipped. I believe God likes it when I do that. My private worship is a pleasing aroma to Him, too.

Also, our relationships with others can be an act of worship. When we are in right relationship with others and we're speaking and sharing and having the right kind of chemistry with people, our interactions are God-honoring and God-glorifying. That's worship, too. The aroma of it pleases God, and He says, "That makes Me feel good. That is a blessing to Me." What kind of aroma are you to God in your service, your praise and your personal relationships? In other words, how do you smell?

Read: II Corinthians 2: 14-17

Is there any area of your life that is a stench to God? What will you do to make it a pleasing aroma instead?

Third-Rate Causes

MEMORIZE

*"You look for much, but behold, it comes to little;
when you bring it home, I blow it away."*

HAGGAI 1:9

When Nikita Khrushchev made his first visit to America, he was escorted to a football game between the Washington Redskins and the Dallas Cowboys. Khrushchev didn't know a thing about football, but he took his seat in the stands and watched the entire game. When it was over, he was asked, "Mr. Khrushchev, what did you think of this great American pastime?" He truthfully responded, "Never have I seen such first-class passion and energy wasted on a third-rate cause."

We spend so much energy, so much passion, so much emotion on third-rate causes. They're not bad things. They're just not the best things. Sports. Recreation. Entertainment. Travel. Furnishing our homes. Improving our appearance. What if we took a fraction of that energy and transferred it to diligent study of God's Word or witnessing or teaching or discipling or serving in the Body of Christ, the church? What if our passion for souls exceeded our passion for self? What if we were as excited about what God is doing as about what we are acquiring?

Anytime we choose activity over relationship, we are probably not choosing well. God values our devotion to Him more than service to a cause or accomplishments for the good of society. When Mary and Martha welcomed Jesus into their home, Martha was too busy with her homemaking preparations to delight in His presence...but Mary "chose the good part," and was content to sit at the feet of Jesus for as long as He would tarry.

QUESTION

Read: *Luke* 10: 38-42

Is there a third-rate cause that is consuming a disproportionate amount of your time and energy? Identify it, and determine today what you will re-channel those efforts toward.

IN THE DARKNESS...

This painting was a wedding gift to our youngest son and his wife. Each item has a story behind it, just as each family has its own legacy of stories, memories and milestones. Edwin and I are thankful for our family's legacy of faith, and pray that it extends through the generations yet to come.

Jo Beth Young

Shadows And Sunshine

MEMORIZE

*"Even though I walk through the valley of the shadow of death, I fear no evil;
for Thou art with me."*

PSALM 23:4

The kinds of sermons you see are infinitely better than the ones you hear. God invited Jeremiah to "see" a sermon one day by directing him to the house of the town potter. So Jeremiah went down to the potter's house, and watched. He saw the potter spinning his wheel, molding a vessel, then destroying it and molding it again...better, stronger, more flawless. Over and over again, the potter took the spoiled vessels—cups, bowls, pitchers—and remade them "as it pleased the potter to make." All around there was evidence of the potter's handiwork: strong, sturdy pieces of earthenware, shaped to perfection by his hands. And also there were broken pieces, too hardened to reshape and left on the shop floor as castaways.

Do you see an application there? I do. In my life, I want perfection, not pain. I want sunshine, not shadows. If today is a beautiful day, I want tomorrow to be just like it. I want to be healthy, happy, joyful. I want my wife and children to be well, my friends to be faithful, and my days to be filled with excitement and wonder. I don't want clouds—-and I certainly don't want thunderstorms. Just give me sunshine and beauty, thank you. But life is not like that, is it? A life that has only sunshine is not a life that is being shaped and formed by God's design. Because He is aiming for perfection—for Christ-likeness—He'll use sunshine and shadow to shape His masterpiece.

QUESTION

Read: Psalm 23: 1-6

 Is this a shadow time for you? God isn't done with His handiwork yet.

Broken Things

*"For I consider that the sufferings of this present time are not worthy
to be compared with the glory that is to be revealed to us."*

ROMANS 8:18

Part of the maturing process of the Christian life involves suffering. We learn more through brokenness than we can ever learn in times of ease and blessing. I don't know about you, but if suffering were an elective, I would never take the course. I don't rejoice when suffering comes, I rejoice when it leaves. Whether it is a health issue, a financial difficulty, a relationship problem—whatever—tough times are no fun. We don't like them! But Paul says if we have identified ourselves with Jesus Christ, we will experience brokenness. He did...and so will we.

A.W. Tozer once said, "I doubt God ever uses any greatly until they have been seriously hurt." Brokenness before blessing. This is an immutable principle. For a tree to be used, it must be cut down. For a rock to become the foundation of a skyscraper, it must be broken. If soil is not turned over with a plow, no seed can be planted, and therefore, no harvest gathered. The Bible says that unless a grain of wheat falls to the ground and dies, it cannot bear fruit.

In Genesis, fellowship was broken with God, so that man would turn to Him for grace. In Exodus, the commandments were broken, establishing our need for salvation. In Samuel, a man with a broken back was seated at the king's table. In Psalms, we read again and again that God honors a broken and contrite heart. In the New Testament, bread was broken, and an alabaster box shattered to pieces, tiles of a roof were broken to lower a broken man for healing, and a net was broken by the weight of many fish. Then finally, in the upper room, our Savior said, "This is my body, *broken* for you." We see brokenness as a tragedy, but God sees it differently.

Read: Psalm 27: 7-14

If there is brokenness in your life today, do not despair. Hope, and rejoice!

Groaning Before Glory

MEMORIZE

*"For we know that the whole creation groans and suffers
the pains of childbirth together until now."*

ROMANS 8:22

Do you groan a lot? I do...especially when I get sick. A few years back we took our Schnauzer Sonny to get his ears clipped. The vet taped them upright and gave him medicine...but Sonny was in bad shape. That same day I came home with the flu. I wasn't feeling so great myself. As I lay I bed, sick at my stomach, feverish, groaning, I heard Jo Beth talking sweetly to Sonny. "Oh, you're a sweet boy," she said. Jo Beth had put a little bell by my bed in case I needed something, so I began to ring it. "Joby, I need aspirin," I wheezed. "Can you bring it?" Then, "Joby, I need some water. I'm thirsty."

For two days straight as Jo Beth nursed Sonny, I rang my bell. The next day some friends came over—to check on Sonny. My fever was up, I was having chills, and the whole neighborhood was worried about Sonny's ears! So I decided to give him a run for his money. I took some tissues from the nightstand and carefully wrapped my ears in them, ringing my bell for all it was worth. When Jo Beth came in, I told her I thought my ears were begin-ning to hurt, too, and she shook her head (and laughed a little) as she said, "Oh, Edwin."

In this life, we groan. Things are not as they should be...not as they will be. But Paul said he considered the sufferings of this present world "not worthy to be compared to the glory that is to be revealed." Did you get the order? Groaning before glory. But glory is a promise from God Himself!

QUESTION

Read: *Luke 17: 11-21*

Are you groaning right now? Remind yourself that the story is not over...and that glory is ahead.

A *Prelude* To Glory

MEMORIZE

"But in all things we overwhelmingly conquer through Him who loved us."

ROMANS 8:37

An author tells the story of her mother's battle with lung cancer, and how the doctors fought to save her life. "When they came to drain the fluid off of her lungs," this daughter wrote, "I would hold mom's hands and look into her eyes with my own. She was in agony. There may be a treatment that is more painful, but I doubt it." She said her mother tried to smile through the pain, but kept asking, "Is it over? Are they almost through?" As the doctors shook their heads, she would reassure: "Almost, Mom. Just a little bit more."

Then her mother's face brightened. "Joyce," she asked her daughter, "honey, would you sing for me?" Without looking up the daughter could see the doctor's gaze. She was about to tell her mother she had no voice at all when the doctor interrupted and said, "Mrs. Miller, Joyce has been here seven days a week around the clock. She's tired. She probably can't sing. Don't ask her to." At that, the mother's patience snapped and she fixed her eyes on the doctor. "Listen, sonny. If you paid for as many voice lessons as I have, you'd know that when I say 'sing,' my daughter sings."

And there beside her mother's bed, she sang the song her mother requested: *The Sound of Music.* She sang the whole thing while her mom clasped her hand. Near the end of the song, her mother turned her face to the window, straining to feel the sunlight. And she sang the last four lines with her daughter: *"I go to the hills when my heart is lonely. I know I will hear what I've heard before. My heart will be blessed with the sound of music. And I will sing once more."* This dying woman didn't need the assurance of a hymn or gospel song. No wonder she wanted *The Sound of Music.* She wanted a song that would be a prelude to her homecoming...an earthly overture for the great heavenly concert that was about to begin for her.

REFLECTION

Read: *Revelation* 15: 1-8

All of this life, even the pain, is but a prelude to glory for the man or woman in Christ.

Life Without God

"For they exchanged the truth of God for a lie, and worshipped and served the creature, rather than the Creator."

ROMANS 1:25

An innovative church erected a large sign on Peachtree Street in Atlanta, Georgia. It read, "IF YOU ARE TIRED OF SIN, CALL 438-8282." Several months passed before someone climbed up on the billboard and embellished it with these additional words, painted in red: "IF NOT, CALL 846-7721."

What about the idea that we could be tired of sin? Do we ever get tired of sin? I'll tell you, if you sin persistently, if sin becomes your agenda, eventually you'll get tired of sin. Paul came to his friends in Rome with good news. But before he shared with them his good news, he had bad news. Before the powerful impact of good news can be felt, often there is bad news. Before someone can come to a knowledge of Jesus Christ and be reconciled with God, they must understand the sickness and the deadliness of sin. The amazing thing is that people who really are sick of sin still reject the way out that Christ provides. For the pagan, self-imposed ignorance keeps him from receiving the good news. For the moral person, a sense of self-righteousness numbs him to the good news. For the religious person, "relative justification" overshadows the true way out. ("I know I'm not perfect, but I'm better than a lot of other people who say they believe.")

But no matter why someone rejects the good news, their sin problem doesn't go away. They exist on a slippery slope, and no one can predict the day they will reach the point of no return.

Read: *Romans* 1: 21-32

Are you tired of sin? How tired? Tired enough to embrace the good news of salvation in Christ?

Too Much Rope

*"Therefore God gave them over in the lusts of their hearts to impurity,
that their bodies might be dishonored among them."*

ROMANS 1:24

The words "God gave them over" are among the most frightening in all of scripture. When Paul uses them, he means that God eventually allows men to pursue their desires with no interference from Him. The rebellious heart becomes so seared by sin that God's kindness and mercy can no longer be felt.

The Niagara River is somewhat placid upstream. But as the river moves toward the falls, there is fast, rough water, then white water, then the deadly rush toward the brink. Just imagine for a moment that four teenage boys are in a fishing boat. They're way upstream on Niagara, and the boat is held by a strong rope. Holding the other end of that rope is God.

As the boys drift downstream, God says, "Well, they're young. I'll just go with them, and let out a little more rope." They continue to float with the current, and God gives them more rope. Finally, they get to faster waters, and God tightens His hold on the rope with a warning: "Guys, it's getting dangerous." But they resist. "Hey, loosen up. We're just having fun." Then they come upon the white water, and God is still holding on. He knows the danger. "As long as I hold this rope," He says, "there's hope for you. I can pull you to safety before it's too late." But they refuse, and then curse God, insisting that He let go and get out of their way. "This is fast," they say. "It's thrilling! We don't need your kind of help." Then the inevitable happens. God begins to let the rope out little by little, more and more, until it sings through His hands and follows them over the falls. "God gave them over. God gave them over. God gave them over." It's a terrifying proposition, is it not?

Read: *Genesis* 19: 1-26

Where are you with God? Can you hear the waters rushing yet? Is the rope slack, or taut?

Has God Forgotten Me?

MEMORIZE

"Now faith is the assurance of things hoped for, the conviction of things not seen."

HEBREWS 11:1

Ever felt like God has forgotten you? Joseph must have. He was far from home, given up for dead by his family, framed for a crime he would rather have died than commit, and left to languish in prison. He must have wondered when God would ever rescue him. You see, it's one thing to believe God knows our circumstances, but it's another thing entirely to believe steadfastly that He will act on our behalf. The first involves faith in who He is. The second requires hope in what He will do. The apostle Paul said that hope in God is a choice that will not disappoint (Romans 5:3-5). It is an absolutely reasonable choice no matter what our circumstances because it is based on who He is. Because God is righteous and holy, His actions will always be an expression of His character.

There is an acronym used in the computer industry that is easy to spell and hard to say: WYSIWYG. It simply means "what you see is what you get." Just so with God. He is not capricious or arbitrary; He is faithful and true. The turning point in Joseph's dungeon experience came when he ceased to wait anxiously on the system and began to wait expectantly on God. His belief that God would act on his behalf was based on Joseph's experiential knowledge. He knew that God had spared him from death at the hands of his brothers; that He had placed him in a position of influence in Potiphar's household; that He had given him dreams as a child...and he trusted that the same care would continue. It was just a matter of time. The faithfulness in question is not His—it is ours! Will we wait expectantly and trust Him?

QUESTION

Read: *Genesis 39: 19-23*

Are you thinking that God has never acted on your behalf before? Read Romans 5:6-8.

Facing Temptation

MEMORIZE

"No temptation has overtaken you but such as is common to man; and God is faithful, who will not allow you to be tempted beyond what you are able..."

I CORINTHIANS 10:13

Regardless of the trends, sexual temptations have always been with us, and they are here to stay. In Homer's *The Odyssey*, the sirens were mythical, evil creatures, half-bird and half-woman, who lived on an island surrounded by submerged, jagged rocks. As ships approached the island, the sirens would sing their beautiful, seductive songs, luring sailors to their death. When Odysseus' ship approached the island, he ordered his crew to fill their ears with wax to muffle the sirens' songs. This done, he commanded them to bind him to the mast as they passed the island so that he could not change his orders. On another occasion, the ship of Orpheus sailed by, and Orpheus sang a song of his own so beautiful that his sailors did not even listen to the sirens' music.

The destructive siren song of sexual temptation can be overcome, but not by ignoring it. As the stories of Odysseus and Orpheus illustrate, we must be more proactive than reactive. We must understand that such temptation is common, and have a plan to deal with it. No matter what we choose to call it, sin is sin, and God is not confused about it, although too often, we are. We live in a moral universe, and one in which sin has consequences. Four hundred years before the law that reads "You shall not commit adultery" was given to Moses on Sinai, Joseph told Potiphar's wife that to have sex with her would be a sin against God. Joseph's parameters were in place long before Potiphar's wife propositioned him. He knew his answer before he ever heard the question. God was more real to Joseph than anything else in his life, and it was this undeniable reality that enabled him to live a life of sexual purity.

ACTION

Read: *Genesis 39: 3-9*

Temptation is common. It will come. But it is not indefensible. Determine now what your response will be when you are tempted sexually.

Confidence In God

"His work is perfect; for all His ways are just;
a God of faithfulness and without injustice; righteous and upright is He."

DEUTERONOMY 32:4

D o your circumstances ever cause your confidence in God to waver? I think of Joseph, wrongly jailed in Egypt and forgotten by his freed cell mate. Every time he heard the rattle of keys or the creak of a cell door, he must have thought, "This is it! They're finally coming for me! The butler has worked out my release at last!" But the days turned to weeks, the weeks to months, and eventually the months became years. It began to look as though he might never be released, but Joseph still rested in the faithfulness of God.

Francis Schaeffer said that when we lack proper contentment, either we have ceased to believe that God is God, or we have failed to be submissive to Him. Believing that God is God requires believing that He is faithful and just, because those are essential aspects of His character. Our confidence in God is much like that of the little girl who crawled up into her father's lap while he was reading and told him how much she wanted him to build her a dollhouse. She didn't climb down until her daddy promised to do just that, although he was somewhat distracted, and agreed mostly because he wanted to get back to reading his paper. In fact, he forgot his promise entirely until he walked into her room one evening and saw all her dolls and doll furniture were packed to move into the new dollhouse. When he questioned her about it, she simply told him she knew he would be building it (even though he hadn't yet begun!) because he promised that he would. His word was good enough for her.

Our God is a God who keeps His promises. Because He is changeless, we know He is still in the business of keeping them today. We can rest in His faithfulness even when uncertainty is all around us.

Read: *Deuteronomy 32: 1-14*

Thank God for His perfect work; even that which we cannot yet see with our eyes but believe in faith.

The Secret of Suffering

*"Consider it all joy, my brethren, when you encounter various trials,
knowing that the testing of your faith produces endurance."*

JAMES 1:2-3

We're all familiar with the cliché "When the going gets tough, the tough get going." But for many of us that phrase is incomplete. It should continue, "the tough get going in the opposite direction!" So often we retreat from the tough times and question the plan of a God who would allow us to experience pain. But He is neither a wasteful Father, nor a cruel one. Suffering presents us with a personal challenge: we can either use our suffering as a bridge in building relationships with others, or we can view it as a wall that separates us from those around us. The choice is ours.

James writes that suffering is actually productive. It produces endurance in us by stretching our faith. Paul adds that it makes us useful to others, because the God of all comfort "comforts us in all our tribulation, that we may be able to comfort those who are in any trouble, with the comfort with which we ourselves are comforted by God." (II Corinthians 1:4)

Maybe like Joseph, you are in the pit. Maybe you're waiting in a dark, windowless place of suffering. Perhaps your personal "pit" is so deep and dark that it has caused you to question the very existence of God. If so, take heart in this basic, biblical principle: *those whom God would greatly use and bless will always experience a time of suffering.* It is not possible to be used significantly by God in any area of endeavor without suffering. You don't have to consider the suffering itself joy...but joy will be the end of what God will do with it if you trust Him.

Read: *Genesis 37: 18-25*

Ask God to use your suffering to make you more like Jesus, and to comfort you so that you may comfort others.

It's A Rough Ride!

"He has also set eternity in their heart, yet so that man will not find out the work which God has done from the beginning even to the end."

ECCLESIASTES 3:11

Mark Twain once asked a baggage handler on a passenger train if the man thought his briefcase was strong enough to be placed in the baggage compartment. The baggage handler shrugged, took Twain's case, and promptly hurled it to the pavement. "That, sir," he said, "is what she'll get in Philadelphia." Then he picked it up and struck it four or five times against the side of the train. "And that," he continued, "is what she'll get in Chicago." Finally he threw the case to the ground and stomped on it vigorously until the author's books and papers spilled out, saying, "And that's what she'll get in Sioux City." As Twain watched slack-jawed, the handler nodded at his now mangled case and advised, "If you're going any farther than Sioux City, sir, I'd suggest you carry it on yourself!"

In a sense, Twain was lucky. He saw before he boarded the train what the journey ahead would entail. But the best most of us can hope to do is observe the journey of life from our fast-moving train and attempt—while the scenery whizzes past us—to make some half-ordered sense of it all.

Life is full of contrasts and ripe with paradox. It contains full measures of trouble and triumph, of sadness and joy. But at its heart, there is a divine order. Although we long to see it in full and understand it completely, we cannot. We can only trust that God knows the journey, and that His view is bigger and more complete than our own.

Read: *Ecclesiastes* 3: 1-10

Are you learning to live with the tension between what you see from your "window" on life, and who you know God to be?

Defining Moments

"The Lord is my strength and my song, and He has become my salvation."

EXODUS 15:2

Ever heard of Roy Riegel? He picked up a fumble during the 1929 Rose Bowl game and ran as fast as he could...toward the other team's end zone. His mistake set up the winning touchdown for the opposition. A defining moment. Ralph Branca may not be a household name, but many will never forget the pitch he threw in the last game of the 1951 National League playoffs. Bobby Thompson eyed the pitch and pelted "the shot heard round the world," a home run that won his team the pennant and probably the most famous homer in baseball history. Chris Webber's defining moment came when the young basketball star called time out during the 1993 NCAA finals, only to discover his team had no time outs remaining.

What happened to Roy Riegel? I don't know. Perhaps he forgot his blunder, or went on to use it somehow to his advantage. But Ralph Branca turned his defining moment into a turning point. Today he is a major force in an organization called BAT, dedicated to assisting old ballplayers "who have suffered tragedies more permanent than dealing the wrong pitch at the wrong moment." Chris Webber established Time Out Inc., a non-profit agency to "help kids who need a time out to get going again."

Life is ripe with defining moments...moments that can make us or break us, depending on our perspective. For the Christian there is the assurance that God's plans for us are good, regardless of the difficulty of our present circumstances.

Read: *Exodus* 14: 5-12

 Have you recently experienced a "defining moment?" Ask God to make it a turning point in your life.

The Sound of Many Voices

MEMORIZE

"My sheep hear My voice, and I know them, and they follow Me."

JOHN 10:27

A seasoned news commentator took a much needed vacation to a working ranch in a western state. He learned to ride, rope, mend fences and herd cattle. During his stay, a ranch hand's horse was injured, and turned out to pasture to heal. Wild horses entered the pasture one night, and the stallion ran away with them. The newsman asked to tag along the next day when the hand went to try to catch his horse—and it was an experience he said he'd never forget.

They found the horse running with the wild herd, and the ranch hand wasted no time trying to woo him back. He got close enough for the horse to hear him, and began to whistle softly and call his name. When he did this, the wild horses bolted and headed for a canyon, leaving the young stallion torn between two desires. He would trot toward the canyon, then move back toward the young man. He was caught in a crosspull: he wanted to follow his master, but the lure of the wild herd was strong. Neither man could tell which way the horse would go until he finally lowered his head and began walking toward his master.

"As I watched this drama," the newsman said, "I realized I was like this stallion. I hear the voices of the world, and I sometimes long to run with them, but the voice of my Master, Jesus Christ, never fades away." What he had witnessed strengthened his resolve to resist the pull of the world. "I prayed that day that I would never lose my sensitivity to that still, small voice of God." How about you? Have you felt the crosspull? Whose voice will you follow?

ACTION

Read: *I Peter 2: 1-10*

 Identify areas of your life where the crosspull is strong. Resolve to hear and obey your Master's voice.

Just Say No!

MEMORIZE

"How then could I do this great evil and sin against God?"

GENESIS 39:9

Negativity has gotten a bad rap. Sometimes a negative word is just what's needed. A traveling salesman went into a local diner one morning and ordered breakfast. He was feeling a little lonely, so he said to the waitress, "Bring me a poached egg on toast and a good word." She came back a few minutes later with his plate, set it down and began to walk away. "Wait a minute," he said. "What about that good word?" She leaned down to his ear and whispered, "Don't eat the egg!"

It's important to observe some negatives in life. When Joseph was serving in Potiphar's household, he experienced some serious sexual harassment from Mrs. Potiphar. Day after day she propositioned him, and it would have been easy to say "yes." But Joseph said, "no." And he kept saying "no" until Potiphar's wife grabbed him and he fled. He literally left his cloak in her hands and ran!

When temptation comes to us (and it will!), we need to learn the power of "no." We are not victims of circumstance or passion. We can choose to obey God and say "no" to Satan, and the best way to become good at it is to practice! We must take it a step further, however, and not only to say "no" to temptation, but to say "yes" to greater things: righteousness, faith, love and peace. Will you practice your yes's and no's today?

QUESTION

Read: *Genesis 39: 10-18*

What area of temptation in your life needs to hear a resounding "no"?

Pagans Who Preach

"How is it that you are sleeping? Get up, call upon your God..."

JONAH 1:6

The most meaningful words I've ever heard in my own personal life were spoken to me by an atheist. I've heard every kind of preacher there is, but no sermon ever touched my life like this one. I was a freshman at the University of Alabama, far from home for the first time and unsure of myself and my place in the world. One of the guys in my dormitory was Walter Carroll. Walter had been in the Navy, and was the only guy in our dorm with a car—and he had a four-wheel-drive personality to match. He had seen and done it all. One afternoon we were sitting in Walter's room and he looked at me and said, "Edwin, do you believe in God?" I said, "Sure, I believe in God." Walter nodded, then said, "You know, I don't believe in God. I've studied all the major religions, and I just don't buy it. I guess I'm an atheist." He looked at me again and said, "But you really believe in God?" I said, "Yeah, Walter, I really do." Then the sermon...short and powerful: "You sure don't live like it. If I believed in God, I'd live different."

Walter was right, and I knew it. If I believed in God (and I did), then getting to know Him and living in harmony with His commands should be my number one assignment. Jonah knew God, but ran from God's assignment. When his get-away ship was about to be dashed on the rocks, the pagans onboard begged him to get up and pray! "If you have a God," they cried, "call on Him now!" Make no mistake. Pagans can preach. They can arouse a servant of God to action in a moment...and many times do. How about you? Do you believe in God? Does your life verify it?

Read: *Jonah* 1: 1-16

Would your neighbors or co-workers suspect your belief in God, or be surprised by it?

Can't Find God?

"Where can I go from Thy Spirit? Or where can I flee from Thy presence?"

PSALM 139:7

D o you know what eventually happens to every person who runs from God? He runs into God! That's because there is no place we can go away from His presence. When Jonah ran from God, he found that God will use anything—the wind, the waves, a storm, a fish—to declare His presence and His intent to restore.

Years ago, a student at the University of South Carolina came to see me and told me he couldn't find God. I'm no counselor, but I have learned that the stated problem is often not the root problem. "Tell me about it," I invited him. And he did. He told me he grew up in a wonderful Christian home with great parents. Then when he arrived at school, he turned his back on his upbringing and began to live as he pleased. He started seeing a girl with a bad reputation because he wanted to experiment sexually. "We spent the night together," he said, "and I thought it would be a night of pleasure and ecstasy, but it was the most horrible, empty experience I've ever had. Since then I haven't been able to find God. He's just not there." I thought for a minute, then I asked him to take my Bible and read Psalm 139:7-8. When he finished I said, "Your problem is not that you can't find God. It's that you can't get away from Him."

Are you running from God? You'll never get away from Him. You'll only run right into Him at every turn because He is pursuing you with a love that will never end. Why not stop running and let yourself be caught?

Read: *Psalm 139: 7-12*

When God seems far away, ask yourself who moved.

Paying The Fare For Sin

"But Jonah rose up to flee to Tarshish, from the presence of the Lord..."

JONAH 1:2

Do you know Jonah's story? He was told by God to go to Nineveh, and to speak a word of warning there. But he didn't want to go to Nineveh, or to speak of judgment to the Ninevites. So he went in the opposite direction. He was running from God. The rest of this verse says that he got to Joppa, and paid the fare for a boat to Tarshish. When we sin—insist on living life on our terms—there is always a fare to be paid. It costs us something to run from God.

I know a married woman who fell in love with another man. She left her husband, and went off with this man for three weeks. At the end of that time, she could not bear her guilt any longer, and she came home to her husband and daughter. Her husband, like a modern-day Hosea, took his wayward wife back and forgave her. But she is still struggling in her relationship with the daughter she abandoned. "I've lost her," she said. "She's angry and rebellious, and she won't listen to a word I say. I'm afraid my sin has cost me my daughter."

It's expensive to live life on our own terms, with no regard for God and His commands. He will forgive us when we repent, and remember our sin no more, but He does not erase the consequences. It costs something to run from God, and sometimes the price tag is higher than we ever could have imagined.

Read: *Jonah* 1:17 – 2:10

Are you running from God? Consider the cost of your rebellion, and return to Him.

Losing Your Life To Save It

"For whoever wishes to save his life shall lose it;
but whoever loses his life for My sake shall find it."

MATTHEW 16:25

So many of our Savior's teachings seem paradoxical on the surface, but underneath they are brilliantly true. How can life be saved by losing it? How can life be lost by striving to keep it? These deepest truths are proved out, not in the classroom or the lecture hall, but in the very minutes, hours and days of our lives.

A missionary doctor was killed in the Second World War, leaving behind a young and shattered widow. Departing India to return home, she boarded a ship not wanting to live herself. She spoke to no one on the journey, and stayed alone as much as possible. Also on board the ship was a boy whose missionary parents had been killed in Burma. He too, was returning home alone. The boy approached her one day and said, "You know, we are the only two people on this ship who speak English. Maybe we could be friends." The widow was too absorbed in her grief to respond. They parted in silence. But that night, the ship was torpedoed, and began to sink. The widow felt no fear, only relief. She did not fight death. But in the chaos of the hour, she saw the boy alone, clinging to the rail and weeping. In pity, she put her arms around him and held him close as the ship went down. Two days later, the two were rescued from the South Atlantic, and rescuers said they could not tell who had saved whom!

Read: *Matthew 16: 24-28*

Over what areas of life are you striving to maintain control? Will you let them go?

Have You Lost Your Song?

MEMORIZE

*"I would have despaired unless I had believed that I would see the goodness
of the Lord in the land of the living."*

PSALM 27:13

I n musicals, anybody is likely to burst spontaneously into song. That's why they're called musicals. But life is different. Have you noticed? Not everybody sings. In fact, many people have lost their song altogether. Maybe you know someone who's lost their song. Their life used to sing and sparkle, but now there is only discord and static and unrest. Maybe that someone is you.

The Israelites lived this kind of tuneless existence during their Babylonian exile. The psalmist tells us they hung their harps on willows, and explained they couldn't possibly sing God's song in their present circumstances. But the Christian doesn't depend on his or her circumstances for musical inspiration.

A little girl whose family often traveled the Pennsylvania Turnpike used to be terribly afraid of tunnels. When they approached one, she would bury her face in her mother's shoulder until they passed through to the other side. But after traveling the turnpike hundreds of times, she actually began not only to keep her eyes open, but also to look forward to the tunnels. When her parents asked her why, she said with a grin, "Well, it may be dark in the middle, but there's light at both ends of the tunnel." The longer we walk with Jesus, the more we come to trust His presence, and the less we fear our circumstances. With Him, every day, every hour, is ripe for singing!

ACTION

Read: *Psalm* 137: 1-6

If you've lost your song, try focusing on Christ instead of your present circumstances.

Breaking Through on The Graveyard Shift

"He is not here for He has risen, just as He said."

MATTHEW 28:6

I worked in a tunnel once, and I can't say it was fun. It was dark and damp, and daylight was well out of reach. I was on one of two teams of men whose job was to tunnel through opposite ends of a mountain, meet in the middle, and then lay a pipe. Every day our crew would go in and blast with dynamite, then measure our progress. The other crew did the same. After many days, we began to speculate among ourselves when our two tunnels would meet. We knew we were close, but no one was sure how close. "When do you think it will be?" we asked one another. "Could it be today?"

One morning I was greeted by a jubilant band of co-workers. "Last night they broke through," they told me. "When?" I asked. "One a.m.," a guy said. "They broke through on the graveyard shift."

That is what our Lord Jesus Christ did on Easter Sunday. He broke through on the graveyard shift. His followers must have felt like they were trapped in a tunnel of disappointment and despair, but Jesus broke the bonds of sin and death. His resurrection gave rock-solid validity to His earlier promise: "I go to prepare a place for you, and I will come again to receive you to myself, that where I am, you may be also." He is risen! He is risen indeed!

Read: *Matthew 28: 1-7*

 Spend time today praising God for His Son's victory over death.

Just Your Luck?

MEMORIZE

"I saw again…that the race is not to the swift…and neither is bread to the wise."
ECCLESIASTES 9:11

How many times have you heard someone explain their good fortune by saying, "Just lucky, I guess," or shake their head at some misfortune saying, "Just my luck?" Although I've heard both responses given, I do not believe in luck. Instead, I believe in the sovereignty of Almighty God. While we assume the races of life *will* be won by the swift, or that bread (or gain) *will* go to the wise, this is not always the case. Unlikely people end up accomplishing great things as often as truly gifted people fail. God is sovereign, but He is not predictable! He elevates some and humbles others for no visible reason, but you can be sure that, whatever the circumstance, He is in control.

Who would have thought that Wilma Rudolph—a woman who wore leg braces through her childhood—would grow up to be one of the most famous female athletes of her day? Or that eccentric tinkerer, William Sloan, Sr.—a man whose neighbors laughed at his "foolish" inventions—would become a millionaire by inventing a valve that would make toilets flush? Who would have predicted that Bob Love—a former NBA great with the Chicago Bulls—would overcome a speech impediment that rendered him virtually unemployable to become the head of community relations for his former team, making speeches all over the country? Chance? Happenstance? Luck? Or something else?

Could anything but the hand of God elevate a tiny, impoverished Albanian nun who left her country with nothing more than a pail, a toothbrush and a change of clothes, to a Nobel Prize recipient? Mother Teresa wasn't lucky—she was chosen by God to become one of the most important champions for the disenfranchised this world has ever known. Little is much when God is in it, and the poorest, frailest, weakest one of us, under the sovereignty of God, can move mountains.

QUESTION

Read: *Ecclesiastes* 9: 10-18

What in your life have you attributed to luck that was actually the hand of God? Praise Him for it today.

Nothing To Look At

MEMORIZE

"He had no stately form or majesty that we should look upon Him..."
ISAIAH 53:2

Appearances can be deceiving. Sometimes the true qualities and character of a man or woman are not readily obvious to the watching world. Kenny Walker, for example, wasn't a likely candidate to become a star athlete. He was struck with meningitis as a two-year-old and rendered totally deaf, and did not begin to play sports until he was a high school sophomore. In Kenny's senior year, he was All-State in football and basketball, and received a football scholarship to the University of Nebraska. There he was voted all-American two years in a row, and graduated with a 3.2 grade point average in Art History. When Kenny took the field for his last game as a Nebraska Cornhusker, 76,000 fans in the stands rose in a standing ovation—but they did not applaud this deaf student athlete with audible clapping—they applauded him in sign language, as a tribute to his remarkable achievements. Kenny Walker went on to become the only non-hearing person to play professional football, and no doubt a role model for generations of other "unlikely" athletes who would follow him.

Jesus Christ was not a "likely" Savior. He did not look the part, according to the prophet Isaiah. He was not the kind of Messiah central casting would have ordered, nor was He the kind that His own people were expecting. But in the fullness time, he came to die for the unlovely and the outcast—and He became the perfect sacrifice for the sins of men. Ultimately, He will receive His due praise. One day, every human being on earth, in heaven and in hell, will honor Him...not with a standing ovation, but by kneeling and bowing low in recognition of His awesome magnificence. Every man will call Him by His true title—Lord—to the glory of God the Father.

Don't be fooled by appearances. Truth is often wrapped in paradox, and revealed only to the man or woman who is willing to look with more than a glance. If you have not looked intently into the claims of Jesus Christ, do so today.

ACTION

Read: Isaiah 53: 1-5

Ask God to give you eyes that see beyond the surface and refuse to take things at "face value."

The Joy of Youth

MEMORIZE

*"Rejoice...during your childhood... and follow the impulses of your heart
and the desires of your eyes."*

ECCLESIASTES 11:9

How wise is it to tell a young person to follow his or her heart? I think it is very wise! I would say to children and young people, live it up! Enjoy life! I worry about adults who say to the young, "I wish you would grow up; I wish you would be more mature." Why? Youth is the perfect time of life to have fun, to explore, to laugh, to be carefree. If this kind of thinking bothers you, let me suggest you spend the day with a child. If you don't have one, borrow one, and do your best to see life through their eyes. They are sharp, creative, perceptive, uncomplicated. They'll make you think by asking questions you've never even thought of! We're only children for a little while, so why rush the inevitable maturing process? Let the young enjoy being young. Not irresponsible, not disrespectful—but young.

Someone has said that childhood is for fun and middle age is for work and old age is for God. Nothing could be farther from the truth. Although we do gain certain responsibilities as we age, we should never lose our passion for life; our sense of wonder at God's world. There can be joy in maturity, just as there can be a hunger for God in childhood.

Why not throw out a few self-imposed "should's" and "don'ts" today and follow your heart? Surprise your child with a cookie-cutter shaped sandwich, or your mate with a passionate kiss. Skip the nightly news and watch the sunset instead. Jim Elliot said, "Be all there. Live to the hilt every situation you believe to be the will of God." Don't quit living before it's time to die.

REFLECTION

Read: *Ecclesiastes* 11: 7-10

 In what ways have you "quit living?" How could you regain the wonder of childhood today?

Remember Him

"Remember also your Creator in the days of your youth."

ECCLESIASTES 12:1

Sometimes I have trouble remembering things. Do you? Jo Beth will ask me stop on the way home from work and pick something up, and I'll forget. Or I'll intend to make a phone call or send a note to someone right away, but it will slip my mind for a day or so. Some folks have little tricks that help them remember things—and some just have top-notch people around them who make them look good by remembering what they forget!

When King Solomon advises his reader to "remember God," he isn't talking about making a note on your daily calendar that says "Remember God," or writing on your mirror in lipstick: "Don't forget the Father." The Hebrew word he uses for "remember" doesn't just mean to call something or someone to mind, it means to *act decisively*. When Hannah prayed for a child, we are told that "God remembered her." But He didn't just think of her and recognize her plight. He gave her a child! So to remember our Creator is to act on our knowledge of Him. Remember God in your youth—and act decisively.

Solomon had a great beginning. He had wisdom. Discernment. The favor of God. But as a young man he failed to act decisively on his knowledge of God, and the end of his life reflected that failure. Instead of his life being a testimony of devotion to God, it became a testimony of spiritual erosion. He didn't know it at the time, of course. But in hindsight, he could see it. Don't become a victim of spiritual erosion. Remember God.

QUESTION

Read: *Ecclesiastes* 12: 1-8

Are you acting decisively on your knowledge of God the Father, remembering Him in your youth?

Rationalization

*"And Solomon did what was evil in the sight of the Lord,
and did not follow the Lord fully..."*

I KINGS 11:6

The process of spiritual erosion—of allowing the things of God to degenerate in importance—is one that begins with rationalization. King Solomon's spiritual erosion began in just this way. He married an unbelieving wife to gain a trade advantage for Israel, saying, "It would really help God's kingdom and His people if we could be at peace with Egypt. Besides, we once lived in Egypt...and what's one little marriage, anyway?"

How can you tell whether or not you are guilty of rationalization? First, you begin to feel a need to explain your actions to yourself, to others, and to God. Then you rope off areas of your life that you believe are beyond God's authority. Solomon roped off his family life, then he roped off his worship. In spite of God's commands to the contrary, Solomon began to worship on pagan altars. "What's a little incense burned here and there," he must have reasoned. "It smells nice...and it makes my wife happy. Besides—God knows I really love Him."

Then we move from rationalization to justification...and from justification to overindulgence. Eventually, Solomon had so many horses and chariots he felt the need to build an entire city to house them all! If this sounds frighteningly familiar, let me share a secret with you: God never blesses you or me so we can hoard his gifts. He blesses us so we can share them. Don't allow spiritual erosion to begin in your life. It's easier to avoid it altogether than it is to stop it once it has begun!

Read: I Kings 11: 1-13

Has the process of spiritual erosion begun in your life? Are you rationalizing any ungodly behavior?

The One Minute Myth

"And Jesus kept increasing in wisdom and stature, and in favor with God and men."
LUKE 2:52

We have instant-everything. Instant coffee. Instant tea. Instant grits. Instant oatmeal. But there is no such thing as an instant Mom or an instant Dad. Parenting takes time. A while back, a pithy little book called *The One Minute Manager* made it on to the bestseller lists. I liked *The One Minute Manager*. It's principles helped me organize things, and move my work day along at a faster clip. But then the author of *The One Minute Manager* made so much money on his book that he began to churn out sequels, like *The One Minute Father* and *The One Minute Mother*. The only problem is—the idea that you or I can be a "one minute" parent is a myth!

To be an effective, godly parent takes time. We don't need more super-efficient "super moms" and "super dads," we need more *servant* moms and *servant* dads. We need lovers and listeners who model consistently over time what they desire their children to become. When our sons became teenagers, they did not necessarily do what I told them to do—they began to do what I did! I saw them act impatiently, and realized they had seen me act impatiently over time. I saw them get silent when things did not go their way, and realized they had watched me do the same! Before long, every parent begins to see in their children not the values or lessons they tried to teach in a minute—but the behavior they modeled over a lifetime!

We are told that Jesus grew up well. He grew in wisdom and stature, and in favor with God and men. He grew up to be like His Father. His time with God the Father shaped His life. He grew wiser. Stronger. He learned to communicate, to trust and to obey. One thing is certain: our children will bear a strong resemblance to us. Our job is to make certain it is a healthy one, and that will take time, time and more time.

Read: *Luke 2: 41-52*

How long has it been since you spent an afternoon or a day with your children, with no agenda other than to be together?

Solitude And Replenishment

"And He said to them, 'Come away by yourselves to a lonely place and rest awhile.'"

MARK 6:31

S ome people never really rest. They are so busy with the activities of life that they appear to be a blur: always on the way to somewhere; never slowing down. Jesus did not have that problem. He purposely sought solitude for spiritual replenishment. He seemed to know just how important such times were for "re-charging" His spiritual battery, and He took advantage of them at every opportunity. What about you? How long has it been since you were quiet and still in the presence of God, with no agenda other than a desire to sit at His feet? Many view solitude as a negative prospect, and are alone only if, and when, it is absolutely necessary. But solitude rightly pursued and experienced energizes our interaction with others, and nurtures our soul.

When Iowans Bobbi and Kenny McCaughey became the parents of septuplets (that's seven babies, folks!) they were exponentially overwhelmed with the responsibilities faced by every new mom and dad. Seven to rock, seven to feed, seven to change, seven to bathe and cuddle and hold...what a challenge! But this young, Christian couple said, while they appreciated the outpouring of help they received, they looked forward to the time they could be "alone" with their young family for an entire evening. Once, after bringing the babies home, this husband and wife reported that they got in their car, drove to a nearby grain silo, parked behind it, and cried and prayed together. They instinctively knew that stepping out of the fray for a few stolen moments away would strengthen them for the task at hand.

All of us have demands on our time and become weary of life's grind. Time alone with God without phones, pagers, prayer partners, portable cd players or other human or technological distractions, is critical for allowing His Spirit to fill us. In solitude, we can receive from God His life-giving breath, emerging with renewed sensitivity and compassion for others, and intensified love for Him. This is true replenishment from the source of all strength and truth.

Read: *Mark* 6: 30-32

 Steal away to a "lonely place" today for a few moments of rest with God.

The Sound of Silence

"My soul waits in silence for God only; from Him is my salvation."

PSALM 62:1

S olitude and silence are inseparable partners. In them, our souls stand on tip-toe, expectant, and ready to see and hear God. How at ease are you with silence? Can you imagine going a day without speaking, or driving to work with no radio or stereo accompaniment? What about going home in the evening and ignoring the television, perhaps sitting down for some time one-on-one with your mate, or cooking a meal in a quiet kitchen? Sometimes in the presence of one you love, and one who loves and treasures you, words are unnecessary. In fact, they can even become a distraction. The temptation to use them to manipulate or control is always with us, isn't it?

But the discipline of solitude, paired with silence, teaches us the enormously difficult task of relinquishing control. We feel helpless and defenseless in silence...and before God, we are. When Job experienced his terrible suffering, he refused to curse or question God. His friends pontificated for days about what might be causing Job's troubles, but Job said nothing. Then when his friends had finished talking, God spoke...and His words put the other speakers to shame. When He had finished, Job had this response: "Behold, I am insignificant; what can I reply to Thee?"

Silence and solitude enable us to surrender control (or the illusion of it), and learn instead to trust our Heavenly Father, who sees and knows all.

Read: *Job 38:1-11; 40:1-5*

 Spend 10-15 minutes alone today with no agenda but to wait on God in silence.

An Independent Audit

MEMORIZE

"Search me, O God, and know my heart; try me and know my anxious thoughts..."

PSALM 139:23

Corporations have long recognized the value of the independent audit. In such an objective accounting, any financial wrong-doing is brought to light, and all assets and liabilities are clearly identified. This kind of honest, rigorous assessment makes positive change possible. In the same way, through the process of confession, our soul is "independently audited" by God Himself. When our wrong-doing is revealed, we are pierced to the heart with our sin, and keenly conscious of our need for forgiveness in specific areas.

Why not ask God today to audit your life and show you the results? If you are unsure about where to begin, read the Ten Commandments, asking the Holy Spirit to convict you of specific sins. Or consider what theologians have called "the seven deadly sins"—laziness, gluttony, greed, lust, envy, anger and pride—and ask God to show you how you have allowed them to take root in your heart. When the audit is complete, agree with God concerning your sin. Just as the Israelites would place their hands on the head of their animal sacrifices as if to "own" their sin, "own" yours, saying, "Yes, Lord, this is mine."

Audits are useless to the firms that commission them unless wrong actions are rectified, and steps are put in place to prevent them from happening again. Don't stop short in your audit. Follow the process through by confession and repentance, owning up to and turning away from the sin that God reveals.

ACTION

Read: II Samuel 12: 1-15

 Conduct an "independent audit" today by asking God to reveal specific sin to you.

Are You Snake-Proof?

"Do you wish to get well?"

JOHN 5:6

Do you know the number one enemy of the hunting dog? Snakes! A hunting dog will catch the scent of a snake and track it to its hiding place, only to be bitten and die. But it is possible to snake-proof a good hunting dog, and this is how it's done: Put the dog in an electric collar—one that can deliver a low-voltage shock. De-fang a rattlesnake and place it in a bush up-wind from the dog. Allow the dog to catch the snake's scent on the wind, and hear its rattle. At the moment the dog presses his nose into the bush and the de-fanged snake strikes, deliver a small shock to the dog. Repeat this a few times, until the dog passes up the snake in favor of other, more comfortable prey.

What does this have to do with you and me? We've all been bitten by the original "snake," whose name is Satan. We have a sin nature from birth. But through the death and resurrection of Jesus Christ, God has de-fanged the snake. When we place our faith in Christ, the snake's venom is no longer fatal—and when we situate ourselves against the prevailing winds of culture, we can easily hear him, smell him, and pinpoint his location. Even so, Christians are still bitten by the snake. How? We turn our backs—not our faces—to the wind and move with it, dulling our senses to sin and allowing the snake to surprise us when it strikes.

The question for us is, do we want to be snake-proof? Do we want to escape the bite of sin and avoid its unpleasant shock? The answer may seem obvious, but unless there is a readiness in us to be free from sin's bite, we will stumble upon the same old snake over and over again.

Read: John 5: 2-9

Is your back against the wind, or is your face toward it? Do you want to be snake-proof?

Intelligent Living

*"They have forsaken Me, the fountain of living waters, to hew for themselves cisterns,
broken cisterns, that can hold no water."*

JEREMIAH 2:13

Intelligent living. Intelligent life. "Any intelligent life out there?" we hear folks ask. Usually they're making reference to other galaxies or planets, but I wonder if we shouldn't be asking the question of this planet...of our own lives. Are we really demonstrating intelligent living?

Chuck Swindoll tells a story taken from Native American folklore about an Indian brave who found an eagle's egg. The brave could not climb up to the eagle's nest, but he wanted to save the baby eagle inside, so he placed the egg in a prairie chicken's nest. The prairie hen sat on the eggs, and eventually, they all hatched: a handful of prairie chicks...and one little eaglet. Not surprisingly, the eaglet grew up like a prairie chicken, grubbing for worms and never flying more than a few feet off the ground. But one day as an old bird, he saw an eagle soaring in the sky, its wings spread wide to catch the wind. This old eagle asked a prairie chicken friend what kind of bird that was, and the friend said, "Well, that's a mighty eagle—the most magnificent bird in all the world. But don't think much about him, because eagles have nothing to do with you and me. We'll never fly that way." So the changeling eagle lived out the rest of his life earth-bound...with wings that were made to fly.

Isn't that tragic? But aren't we like that changeling eagle? We were meant to fly in relationship to the Lord Jesus Christ, but we've traded His power and His strength for hum-drum lives that can offer us little. Is there intelligent life down here?

Read: I Peter 1: 2-9

Considering your riches in Christ, and the power of His Holy Spirit—are you living intelligently?

My Wicked Heart

MEMORIZE

"The heart is more deceitful than all else, and is desperately sick; who can understand it?"

JEREMIAH 17:9

The man peering out from the pages of *U. S. News & World Report* was only twenty-one years old, but he looked worn out and used up. He was dressed entirely in black, and wore a small button on his jacket that read "I Am A Mess." Anyone who knew John Simon Richey would concur with that statement. He was the leader of a punk rock band, and his life was ruled by his addictions. Drugs. Alcohol. Sex. Violence. He murdered the woman he lived with, served time in prison, was released and then killed a man in a drunken barroom brawl. Shortly after being released from prison a second time, he overdosed on heroin. No one was surprised when Richey—known by millions as rocker Sid Vicious—was dead before his twenty-second birthday.

Sid Vicious' life illustrates the natural end of a depraved heart. He was a mess because his heart was a mess. Your heart is a mess, too, and so is mine. That's the doctrine of the depravity of man. Sid Vicious said, "I Am A Mess." The apostle Paul said, "For I know that nothing good dwells in me, that is, in my flesh…". The language is different—but the concept is the same. Your depravity and my depravity is never going to get any better on its own. We might be able to mask or sublimate the manifestations of our sick hearts, but we cannot improve their condition.

Left unchecked, depravity gives way to permissiveness, and permissiveness degenerates into immorality. Immorality eventually leads to guilt, which, when rationalized, leads to rebellion. That is the way of the world. But there is a better way…a way that leads to life. It is called surrender. The only cure for a depraved heart is to receive a new one through the blood of Jesus Christ. In Him, "the law of the Spirit of life…has set you free from the law of sin and death."

QUESTION

Read: *Jeremiah* 17: 1-10

Have you looked at your heart lately? Are you a mess, or is Christ on the throne?

The Sting of A Lie

MEMORIZE

"Let none of you devise evil in your heart against another, and do not love perjury."

ZECHARIAH 8:17

It was a headline sure to catch the eye of a pastor, and it certainly caught mine. It read, "Full of Grace," and the accompanying story told of a gracious man unjustly accused. His name was Cardinal Joseph Bernardin of Chicago—a Catholic prelate accused of sexual abuse by a former parishioner some twenty years after the alleged incident had taken place. I believe the story first broke on CNN when Steven Cook came forward in a special on sexual abuse by the clergy—particularly in the Roman Catholic Church. Cook was diagnosed with AIDS when he made his accusation, and it quickly became the kind of sensational fodder on which the media feed.

A man eligible to become Pope had "fallen from grace," the reports said. Only months later did the real truth emerge. Steven Cook "remembered" the abuse after being hypnotized by a new age guru, and somehow through suggestion Bernardin was implicated. Under the pressure of deadlines and the sensationalism of the story, a thorough investigation was not made before the allegations were aired. (Imagine the ratings an accused Cardinal could deliver!) Eventually, Cook retracted his statement, saying he had been mistaken—that Bernardin had never harmed him. But even before he did, this cardinal had begun to pray for his accuser. He admitted that he felt angry. Frustrated. Even helpless. But this did not stop him from lifting Steven Cook up to the throne of grace.

CNN subsequently offered the Cardinal fifteen minutes of airtime to clear his name, but the damage was already done. Cardinal Bernardin, a man whose life was marked by grace and service, would die himself with a lingering shadow on his life and ministry. Have you been wrongly accused? Could you surrender your anger and frustration as this man did and actually pray for your accuser?

ACTION

Read: *Matthew 5: 38-48*

The next time you experience persecution, make a conscious choice to pray for your accuser.

Have A Goal In Mind

"The Son of Man is going to be delivered into the hands of men;
and they will kill Him, and He will be raised on the third day."

MATTHEW 17:22-23

The mother of four young children was running errands on a Saturday. She had groceries to buy, dry cleaning to pick up, and a long "to-do" list to tackle. After a couple of hours, the troops became restless. Two were fighting. Two were crying. In between traffic lights, she was trying her best to placate everyone. Then it hit her: the kids are hungry. We'll get some lunch, and then we can finish our errands. She drove into Wendy's with one mission in mind: to feed her children. She ordered "fun meals" all around, drove to the window, and picked up the food. Before she was back on the freeway, one of the children began to wail. "I didn't get a burger! There's no burger in here!" Mom quickly retraced her route, wheeled up to the fast food restaurant, and marched inside with her incomplete fun meal in its Wendy's bag.

"My girl didn't get a burger when we came through the drive-through just now. Put a burger in this bag, please." The girl behind the counter just stood there and stared. "Maybe you didn't hear me," the mother said, more firmly this time. "I need one more burger. Put it in the bag and hurry—I've got four hungry kids in the car." No response. The mother's patience was almost gone, and her choleric personality kicked in: "I said, I need another burger. Put it in this bag RIGHT NOW!" Without saying a word, the young lady at the counter reached back, got a hamburger, and dropped it in the bag. "Thank you very much," the mom said sarcastically, and she turned and walked out of...McDonald's.

It is amazing what can be accomplished with a clear-cut sense of purpose! I know of no one who ever rivaled Jesus Christ for a sense of purpose. He came for one reason, and one reason only...and He never lost sight of His mission. Those who hindered Him, even friends, soon understood that His focus was unwavering and strong.

Read: *Matthew 16: 21-23*

Can you articulate your goals in life? Are they worthy? How focused are you on their pursuit?

A Time For Boldness

MEMORIZE

"Cast your bread on the surface of the waters, for you will find it after many days."

ECCLESIASTES 11:1

Alex Haley in *Roots* wrote these words: *"Through his sorrow Kunta was surprised to hear that the old gardener had been called Josephus. He wondered what the gardener's true name had been, the name of his African forefathers, and to what tribe they had belonged. He wondered if the gardener himself had known. Most likely, he had died as he had lived, without ever learning who he really was."*

Can you think of a greater tragedy than that? To die and never really discover who you were, or for what purpose you were created? King Solomon wrestled with that question his whole life long. "Who am I?" he wondered. "Why am I here?" Finally, at the end of life, he gained the perspective he had sought all along. And when he did, he shared his wisdom through a series of life-teachings we call "proverbs."

His teachings can be summed up with one imperative, expressed in several ways. "Be bold," he exhorted his readers. "Live boldly, exuberantly, passionately. Don't just punch in...really live." I read a while back of a guy named S.L. Potter in LeMesa, California, who bungee jumped on his 100th birthday! His four children, ages 68 to 74 were against it—but in spite of their reservations, S.L. climbed a 200-foot tower and flung himself off. Do you know what his first words were when they unstrapped him from his bungee cord? "Give me back my teeth!" No one should live more boldly than the Christian, because no one has more assurance of God's love and leading. Don't live never knowing who (and whose!) you are. Live boldly!

QUESTION

Read: *Ecclesiastes* 11: 1-6

 What would bold living look like in your life?

Have I Stayed Too Long At The Fair?

"The conclusion, when all has been heard, is: fear God and keep His commandments."

ECCLESIASTES 12:13

There is an old song that asks the musical question, "Have I stayed too long at the fair?" The idea is that life is losing its luster, perhaps because we've overstayed our welcome, or expected things it failed to deliver. It is the song of someone older who is looking back at his youth with disappointment. "I wanted to live in a carnival city with laughter and love everywhere. I wanted my friends to be charming and witty, I wanted someone to care. I found my blue ribbons all shiny and new, but now I've discovered them no longer blue. The merry-go-round is beginning to taunt me—have I stayed too long at the fair? There's nothing to win and no one to want me...have I stayed too long at the fair?"

If we buy into this world's system of priorities, eventually everything we've chased will disappoint us. Unless we're living for God in Christ, we will reach old age and say, "It's all meaningless. I've stayed too long at the fair." This happened to Solomon, or "Solo-Man" as I've called him. At the end of his life, he cut to the chase and said, "I've had it all—and none of it amounted to much." He pursued love, riches, knowledge, religion and power. He attained a measure of success in all of them, but none satisfied.

Far too many of us could say with Solomon, "I've stayed too long at the fair." Maybe you've bought into the world's system, and all you have to show for your efforts today are depression, despondency, broken relationships and broken dreams. But for the man or woman who has spent a lifetime pursuing Jesus Christ, every day is sweeter than the day before. My friend Jane Elder, who pursued Him for 90 years, never sang "I've stayed too long at the fair." Jane's favorite song was "The longer I serve Him, the sweeter He grows." What about you? Which song would you rather sing in the twilight of life?

Read: *Ecclesiastes* 12: 1-7

Have you begun with the end in mind? Are you pursuing things that will ultimately fill you, or leave you empty?

Character Counts!

"For he was a good man, and full of the Holy Spirit and of faith."

ACTS· 11:24

His name was Barnabas, and as players go, he was a minor character in the story of the first century church. But in the life of a man named Paul, he was huge. Barnabas didn't get top billing in the book of Acts; Peter and Paul were the main men. Barnabas was a "background" kind of guy: quietly serving and loving and encouraging those on the front lines of battle. Is there a Barnabas in your life?

We need encouragement from others. And we need to be encouragers for others. When Barnabas saw all the good work that was going on in Antioch, "he rejoiced and began to encourage them with resolute heart to remain true to the Lord." In other words, he said "Atta boy!" or "Good job!" as often as he could. Studies have shown that praise for good behavior is twice as productive as correction for bad behavior—but most of us are quicker to point out another's shortcomings than to praise their progress.

Barnabas was a man of character—and character is not something you have, it is something you are. Character will be expressed by a man's choices and his behavior. Barnabas chose to use his gifts for the good of the Body of Christ in Antioch, and he encouraged Paul to do the same. Men of character do not believe that they are diminished by another man's successful contribution. Barnabas wanted the church at Antioch to benefit from Paul's powerful preaching and teaching, so he encouraged his brother in Christ to join him in the work. Who are you encouraging today?

Read: Acts 11: 19-26

 Would those closest to you consider you an encourager? Is your character a blessing to others?

A Place to Stand

MEMORIZE

"All scripture is inspired by God and profitable for teaching, for reproof,
for correction, for training in righteousness."

II TIMOTHY 3:16

We are beginning a new millennium. Can you believe it? I remember as a boy wondering if I might live to see the turn of the century. The post-war fifties seemed to speed by, and then the turbulent sixties…but it was the 1970's that ushered in the beginning of a revolution in America. Was it economic? No. Political? No. Educational? No. It was a moral revolution where authority of every kind was questioned, undermined, and ultimately disregarded. And chaos has been the result.

Some of you may have read a book called *The Lord of the Flies*. It depicts an island of "lost boys," some good and some bad, who set up their own form of rule. Any time they had a problem or dispute, they consulted a conch shell for wisdom. If they listened hard enough, the shell would tell them what was right. But one day in a fight the shell was shattered, and the boys' source of authority was destroyed. Suddenly, anarchy set in. Might made right. There were no longer good boys and bad boys. Every boy on the island became a savage.

The conch shell is broken. There is a cry today in families, churches, and the marketplace for moral authority. The Bible is a source to which we can look and say with confidence, "This is right," or "This is wrong." You and I need authority in our lives. And as we enter the twenty-first century, we need it more than ever. I believe the Bible—the Word of God—is that authority we need. It's precepts give us a place to stand, and a foundation for right living that is unshakable and true.

ACTION

Read: II Timothy 3: 14-17

Are there areas of your life that are not under the authority of God's Word?
Identify them today.

A Rock In A Sea of Amnesia

"God will judge the secrets of men through Christ Jesus."

ROMANS 2:16

Writer Tom Wolfe summed up the amoral climate of the 1970's with a personal story. Wolfe told of visiting a major university with his friend Harris, whose daughter Laura was a student there. They found her dorm, went to the room, knocked on the door, and finding it unlocked, walked inside. The room was dark, and a boy and girl were in bed together. Wolfe said that he and Harris backed out of the room as if they'd been looking down the throat of a snake. His friend, visibly shaken, said "I'm sure that's Laura's room...but that was not my daughter." The two men asked around, and found Harris' daughter in the library. He began to tell her what he'd seen, but before he got far she interrupted him: "Oh, Daddy, don't be such an old fogey. Two days a month everybody's room is a free room. So, we just go to the library or something during that time." Wolfe said Harris didn't accept that explanation, and began to argue with his daughter that such behavior was wrong. But by the time the visit was over, and Harris and Wolfe had driven back to the city, Harris had reconciled himself to this "new morality." Before long, he neither spoke of it, nor remembered his outrage. "It got lost," Wolfe said, "like a rock in a sea of amnesia."

We live in the age of the beer-commercial philosophy: "You only go through life once...live it with all the gusto you can." Some say our culture is immoral, but I do not believe that. For a culture to be considered immoral presumes some widely-accepted standard of morality...and we have none. This is the age of "anything goes," where truth is considered relative, and where "right" is "what's right for me...right now."

Biblical, Judeo-Christian morality has been lost, like a rock in a sea of amnesia. No one blushes any more because no one needs to. Virtually any behavior or "lifestyle" is accepted in the name of tolerance. Our standards have changed, or disappeared altogether. But God's standards have not changed even one iota. They are timeless, immutable and true. And one day, every man, woman and child will be judged by them. Have we ever needed Jesus more than we do today?

Read: *Romans 2: 11-16*

 Examine your life to determine whether there are any areas where tolerance should be replaced by God's standard of righteousness.

Unbendable Rules

"For this is the will of God, your sanctification..."

I THESSALONIANS 4:3

Often I'm asked, "Do you believe AIDS is the result of God's judgment on homosexuality?" or, "Do you believe herpes is His judgment on sexual promiscuity?" My answer is...yes. I do. And I believe God also judges every lie we tell, every act of thievery we commit, and every prideful thought we entertain. When sin is committed—public or private—we can be sure that judgment will follow. How do I know? The Bible tells me so. And if I could not read, the very universe would echo what His holy word teaches. We live in an ordered, moral universe, and when we break God's laws there are inevitable consequences.

Suppose I had a little boat, and I told you I planned to sail it across the ocean. Then suppose I went on to say that I had no charts, no navigational devices, no knowledge of the stars and no clue about sailing. "How are you going to get across the ocean?" you might legitimately ask. "I'm just going to do it any way I choose," I would answer. And very likely you would shake your head and walk away thinking I was a very, very stupid man.

It doesn't take a rocket scientist (or in this case, a maritime scholar) to predict the outcome of my ill-planned voyage. My little boat (and its sailor, yours truly) would no doubt become fish food at the bottom of the sea. Judgment is built into the very fabric of this world, and if I refuse to be led by the stars, I will eventually have to answer to the rocks. When we operate outside the moral parameters set in place by God in His word, we will ultimately be forced to deal with His wrath. It's that simple.

Read: *I Thessalonians 4: 1-8*

Consider the consequences of sin in your life. Can you see a direct correlation between your disobedience and your discomfort?

Home-Made Gods

*"And when all the people saw it, they fell on their faces and they said,
'The Lord, He is God; the Lord, He is God'."*

I KINGS 18:39

When man has had no god to worship, he has often made one for himself. Usually these homemade gods deified a man's own pet vices. Man enjoyed drinking, so he made himself a god named Bacchus, who smiled on wine and revelry. He wanted to make war on his enemies, so he made himself a god named Mars who promised victory in battle. Down through the ages, man has sought to make gods that would aid and abet him in his chosen lifestyle.

But what happens when these "home-made gods" meet the true and living God? The Bible records just such a confrontation in I Kings 18, when God Almighty won a showdown with Baal. It was not a theological debate, but rather a demonstration of power and a call for decision. The word "baal" means "owner," and Baalism was a lifestyle of materialism, possessions and self-rule. (Sound familiar?) Baal-worshippers were "top of the heap" folks who had money, power and autonomy in their day.

Baal worshippers believed they had the world (and their home-made god) by the tail. Worshippers of Jehovah God believed that He had them! All the singing and crying and praying in the world could not bring down Baal to light a fire on his altar. But one man's prayer to the one true God brought fire so hot it consumed an altar that had been soaked three times with water! When the onlookers saw this, they became believers: "The Lord, He is God," they said. "The Lord, He is God."

Read: I Kings 18: 17-39

 Are there any home-made gods in the closet of your heart?

A *Basket* Case

"And I was let down in a basket through a window in the wall..."

II CORINTHIANS 11:33

The apostle Paul was not an instant hit as a Christian apologist. In fact, he spent ten years virtually in exile after his dramatic Damascus Road conversion. For three years, he was in Arabia studying the scriptures—using his scholar's mind to piece together the prophecies of the Messiah contained in the Old Testament with the Messiah who called him by name on the road that fateful day. Then he returned to Damascus, bursting with insight and no doubt ready to set the world on fire. But a funny thing happened. The Jews didn't want to listen...they wanted to kill him. So Paul went out of town in a slightly more humble way than he must have arrived: he was lowered over a wall in a basket!

Through disappointments and setbacks like this, God showed Paul that, although he was immanently qualified to preach to the Jews, he would become the primary evangelist to the Gentiles! He had perfect credentials to win the Jews, and absolutely no common ground with the Gentiles. After he was run out of Jerusalem as well as Damascus, Paul went away to Tarsus—literally "home to mama." Soon ten years had gone by, and Paul had failed in every effort at preaching the Gospel.

Have you ever felt like that? Does it seem that, in spite of all your giftedness and willingness to serve, God has placed you on the shelf? If so, take a lesson from Paul. What he discovered in his "decade of failure" was that, at best, he was a "basket case." The secret of the victorious, Christian life is not found in impeccable credentials or innate abilities. Rather, it is found in this: "Christ in you, the hope of glory." Nothing more. Nothing less.

Read: II *Corinthians* 3: 4-11

Are you relying on your own skill and natural ability to serve God, or have you surrendered your agenda to His perfect will?

Nothing More Than Nothing

MEMORIZE

"And who knows whether you have not attained royalty for such a time as this?"

ESTHER 4:14

A sparrow looked at a dove and asked him this question: "How much does a single snowflake weigh?" The dove answered, "Nothing more than nothing." Then the sparrow told this story. "Last week when the snow was softly falling, I was nestled in a fir tree's branch, as close to the trunk of that tree as I could get. As I watched the flurry from my hiding place, I began to count the snowflakes as they landed on the branch. I counted and counted until I came to three million, four hundred ninety-three thousand, seven hundred and twenty-one. Then one more snowflake fell—nothing more than nothing—and the whole branch broke off and tumbled down below."

With that the sparrow flew away, and the dove thought and thought. Nothing more than nothing—a single snowflake—made a difference in the sparrow's story. I wonder if you might be that one person—nothing more than nothing—that might make a difference in your world, your home, today? Mom—what can you teach your children that no one else can? How many hugs can you give? Dads—how often can you play catch or checkers or Monopoly, or listen to your child's latest victory or struggle with your undivided attention? Husbands—how many acts of kindness can you show your wife? Wives—how many loving touches can you give your husband?

You see, you and I can make a difference. A hundred couples with vibrant, God-honoring marriages could touch and influence a thousand other couples. Ten men who are devoted to their children before job or self could influence a hundred more. A handful of women who pray for one another's faithfulness to honor God could change a generation. How much does a single snowflake weigh? Nothing more than nothing? Or more than enough?

ACTION

Read: Matthew 24: 46-51

Let your actions today show the love of Christ to your family, friends or co-workers.

Changing Coats

"If...My people who are called by My name humble themselves and pray,...and turn from their wicked ways, then I will hear from heaven,...and will heal their land."

II CHRONICLES 7:14

We live in the polling age. Should marijuana be legalized? Take a poll. Is abortion every woman's inalienable right? Take a poll. Is pre-marital sex wrong? Take a poll. But poll-taking is no barometer of right and wrong, only of popular opinion. The standard has been established on right and wrong, and it was set by God Himself. Unfortunately, our culture seems to live and die by the standard reflected in the polls.

Once upon a time there was a man named Ed. (I'll give him my own name in this fictional example.) Ed lived to make other people happy, and he lived in a land where everyone wore coats. These people never removed their coats, and because Ed wanted to fit in, he tried to wear the color of coat that would please people most. His mother liked blue, so Ed wore blue. When he did, she praised him. When he wore another color, she said, "Yuk, Ed. Put on your blue coat." But Ed's boss liked green and all his co-workers wore green. The blue coat was quickly discarded, and replaced by a green one. When Ed wore green, his boss applauded. When he wore another color, his boss said, "Yuk, Ed! What happened to the green coat?" Soon Ed got very adept at changing coats. He carried several colors with him at all times. When he wore the right coat, he was praised: "Yea, Ed!" When he wore the wrong coat, he was booed: "Yuk, Ed!" You can imagine what eventually happened. Ed became a "Yea-Yuk" man. He could please almost everyone, almost all of the time. He was popular and powerful. But he lost the ability to choose right and wrong for himself. He simply became a reflection of the desires of others.

Read: Mark 15: 1-5

Are you a "Yea-Yuk" man or woman? Are there too many coats in your closet?

The Lost Ark

MEMORIZE

"The glory has departed from Israel, for the ark of God was taken."
I SAMUEL 4:22

The popular movie *Raiders of the Lost Ark* familiarized a whole new generation with an ancient biblical relic that has been largely forgotten: the Ark of the Covenant. The ark represented God's presence among his people, and His awesome holiness. Not only is the actual ark lost today, but I believe we have lost what it represented as well. We have lost the sense of God's holy presence among His people. Nothing is viewed as sacred anymore. Cameras intrude into bedrooms, courtrooms, and all areas of our private lives. Networks air suicides to capture ratings. Ordinary people and celebrities mock God openly. We have lost the reverence of God that is critical to our very survival. Listen! Even the seraphim who surrounded the throne of God knew when to cover their eyes. Even the sun knew to hide its face on Good Friday. How we need to bring back the ark to our land, to recover our sense of the sacred.

How do we bring back the ark? The same way Israel did. We repent, confessing our sin to the living God who makes ethical requirements of us. We return to Him with our whole heart, acknowledging His authority over us. Then we remove the foreign gods from among us. Foreign gods? That's right. "Little-g" deities like the god of comfort, the god of beauty, the god of gain and ease and activity—all of these must go if the ark is to return. Then we are to serve God only, and God alone. He is not to be just a part of our agenda, but our entire agenda. He is to be involved in every endeavor, every relationship, every dream and desire.

There's an agricultural truism that fits here, I believe. When a farmer whose crops were choked out by weeds would blame the soil, he would be told "any soil that will grow weeds will grow beans." A life that is sensual can also be a life that is pure. A life that is prideful can be a life that is humble. It *is* possible to live in the presence of God in a wicked world. The ark can still reside among us!

ACTION

Read: I Samuel 7: 3-12

Using a concordance, search for verses that tell of the holiness of God, and meditate on what you read.

Pacesetter, Conductor, Father

"Correct your son, and he will give you comfort; he will also delight your soul."

PROVERBS 29:17

I'm not a big auto-racing fan, but on Memorial Day, I like to watch the Indianapolis 500—and my favorite part of the race is the start. If you have never seen it, you have missed something. A specially-designed pace car goes ahead of the 30 or so other race cars, looping the track several times to set the proper pace. Then when the starter agrees that all cars are in position, he lowers the green flag and the race is on. What happens to the pace car? He gets out of the way as quickly as possible, because the high-powered cars behind him are about to move out at an unbelievable speed!

I'm not a huge fan of the symphony, either, but I appreciate the role of the conductor. I've learned that the price of a symphony ticket is many times determined by the expertise or renown of the conductor. And when a conductor steps into the spotlight and lifts his baton, an orchestra full of highly skilled, first-rate musicians are waiting for him to cue that first note and establish the tempo the music requires.

Every family needs a pacesetter. Every family needs a conductor. His name is "Dad." Fathers are to be the pacesetters for their families—especially in the lives of their children. Dads lead their children around the track, establishing the pace for 18 years or so in the existential classroom of family living—then they get off the track and get out of the way, because their sons and daughters are ready to run the race we call life. As conductor, the father establishes the tempo of the home, and seeks to insure that the music pouring forth from his family matches the Composer's perfect design. How about you, Dad? How are you doing? Would your family recognize you as a pacesetter and conductor, or an absentee landlord?

Read: I Samuel 2: 22-35

If you are a father, ask your children how they see you. You may be surprised at what you hear.

The Idol of Doctrine

MEMORIZE

"Little children, guard yourselves from idols."

I JOHN 5:21

Did you know that even the things of God can become idols? They can. Doctrine is the means by which we approach and know God, but it is of no use on its own. It is a map, or the lens on a telescope, enabling us to grasp the untouchable reality of God. But doctrine is not a thing to be worshipped or revered. Only the God it points to deserves our worship. Everything of God that is real can be counterfeited by Satan. Beware of the idolatry of doctrine, or of ideas.

Certainly we want to know more about the Lord. We are curious, like the little girl riding through the countryside with her father. "Daddy," she asked, "how big is that lake?" He said, "I don't know." They drove on a little farther and she said, "Daddy, how high is that mountain?" Again he said, "I don't know." She gazed out the window in silence for a few miles. "Daddy," she asked, "how long is this road?" Her father shook his head and said, "Sweetie, I just don't know." She said, "Daddy, you don't mind my questions, do you?" He said, "Oh, no, honey. How else are you going to learn?"

We must learn to seek a relationship with God, not merely facts about Him. We can know, teach and apply scripture without knowing God through Jesus Christ. But what a sad, sad waste! Doctrine is of no use without relationship, and unless we know the Living Lord through His Son Jesus Christ, our learning is nothing more than idolatry.

QUESTION

Read: *Daniel 3: 8-18*

Do you know God, or do you only know about Him?

The Idol of Emotionalism

MEMORIZE

"And we have seen and bear witness and proclaim to you the eternal life which was with the Father and was manifested to us."

I JOHN 1:2

Emotions are a vital part of the Christian experience. The remorse for sin leads to repentance. The thrill of praise enhances our worship. The gratitude for salvation spurs us on to obedience. But God-given emotions, like doctrine, can be counterfeited by the great deceiver, Satan. When this happens, when we seek the feelings associated with worship rather than God Himself, our emotions become an idol.

Certainly conversion itself is a dramatic, life-changing experience, but not all conversions have the emotional impact of the apostle Paul's, or Augustine's, or John Calvin's or Martin Luther's. For some who come up in the church, accepting Christ comes as naturally as breathing. They do not have to go through hell before they come to God. And who is to say their experience with Christ is any less valid than that of one whose life was on the brink of destruction before they found the Lord?

Beware of substituting the love of feelings and drama and emotion for the love of God. Some of us come to Him in tears; others in quiet surrender. Some come running, others walk, others are led by another, but the end result is the same. The bottom line is this: God is sovereign, and He will do it His way. It's not about how we feel—it's about who He is. We are not to tell God what to do...we are simply to report to Him for orders.

QUESTION

Read: I John 5: 1-12

Are you looking for an emotional "high" from Christianity, or are you content to let God meet you as He wills?

Forgiven And Forgiving

"But Jesus was saying, 'Father, forgive them; for they do not know what they are doing'."

LUKE 23:34

A fable tells of Ralph and Hilda, a baker and his wife. Ralph was tall and lean, and he was an unusually righteous man. He spoke in moral platitudes, and always did right. Hilda was soft and round—and as fun-loving and joyful as Ralph was cold and aloof. One night Ralph came home late from the bakery and found Hilda in the arms of another man. The whole town expected him to throw her out, but he didn't. He vowed to forgive her "like the Good Book says." But as time went on, it became clear that he had not. Heaven did not smile on Ralph's cheap brand of forgiveness, and soon sent an angel to place a small pebble in Ralph's heart with every look of scorn or belittling jab he gave to Hilda. In time, his heart was so heavy he could hardly stand up straight.

When he cried out in his pain for someone to help, the angel offered to cure his heavy, hurting heart. "How?" Ralph asked. "I will give you the gift of magic eyes," the angel replied. "What is that?" Ralph wanted to know. "With magic eyes," said the angel, "you will see Hilda not as someone who has betrayed you, but as a lonely woman who is trying her best to love you." Ralph wasn't sure he wanted magic eyes, because he had come to enjoy his hatred. But eventually, he said yes, and discovered that every time he looked at Hilda with his new magic eyes, a pebble was removed from his heart. Soon he began to feel good again, and he invited Hilda back into his heart.

All of us have been hurt. We may think the hurt we suffered was too deep to ever forget and forgive, but Jesus can give us His eyes—magic eyes—with which to see our enemies.

Read: *Luke* 23: 33-43

Who do you need to look at with "magic eyes?" Ask God to help you see them as Jesus would.

A Green Leaf In Drought Time

MEMORIZE

"But He knows the way I take; when He has tried me, I shall come forth as gold."

JOB 23:10

In the book *A Green Leaf in Drought Time*, Andrew Murray had some fine advice for those undergoing persecution. He gave them four words of counsel. First, he said, "You are in this straight place by Divine appointment." Second, he said, "You are here in His keeping. He will keep you by His grace and love in this situation." Third, Murray said, "You are here for His training and discipline. God wants to stretch you, to build you up, and He has brought you to this trial to test you by fire." Finally, he said, "You are here in His time. You don't know how long you'll be here, or what your future will hold, but this is where God wants you now."

What if you and I approached every trial we face with these precepts in mind? What if we viewed every hardship as His perfect plan for us? Murray also said, "If there were any circumstance better for you than the one in which you find yourself, Divine Love would have placed you there." That gives our trials a whole new meaning, doesn't it? If you are experiencing a time of difficulty right now, ask God to give you wisdom to see your situation the way He sees it.

His aim is that you and I grow up. Trials are our ticket out of complacency and mediocrity. When we struggle, we grow. Like Job, we can be certain that the outcome of our pain will be a stronger, purer faith.

ACTION

Read: James 1: 1-8

Pray that God will give you wisdom to see your trial as He sees it.

Gone Fishing

MEMORIZE

"Submit therefore to God. Resist the devil and he will flee from you."

JAMES 4:7

S atan is a fisherman. Did you know that? He baits a hook for you or me, and uses a lure that is certain to attract us. He's a good fisherman, too. He's been at it for a long time, fishing for the hearts and lives of men since Adam and Eve lived in the Garden of Eden. He knows the areas in which we are vulnerable, and he is crafty enough to hide the hook from us until it is too late.

I don't know much about fishing, but my oldest son does. He's a good bass fisherman, and he studies fish. He knows their tendencies, their habitat, their favorite lures. But even so, some fish still elude him. Have you ever wondered how a bass gets to weigh six, seven, or eight pounds? They've studied the fisherman like he's studied them. They know his best tricks, and they are not quick to pounce on a lure. They suspect the hook—and they're usually right.

Once we take Satan's bait and the hook is set, we're caught. The trick to evading the fisherman is to steer clear of the lures. We can be sure he knows just how to tempt us, but we also have within us the power to overcome temptation if we will only use it. Jesus Christ gives us strength to resist the devil...and when we do, he will flee.

ACTION

Read: *Luke 22: 1-6*

Identify your favorite "lures," and watch carefully for Satan's next fishing expedition.

The Set of The Sail

MEMORIZE

"Watch over your heart with all diligence, for from it flow the springs of life."

PROVERBS 4:23

An army chaplain of another generation said men would frequently come to him and say, "Sir, I just couldn't resist temptation. I tried, but the pull of sin was too strong, and I'm too weak." The chaplain would respond to his men in this way: "Son, you go down to the port and you'll discover that the wind is blowing in one direction, and one direction alone. Even so, you'll see ships sailing with the wind, and against it. You can stand up to temptation, but it's up to you and your will."

An old poem I've always liked says it this way: *One ship sails east, one ship sails west, with the self-same wind that blows. It's the set of the sail and not the gale that determines which way it goes."* What about the set of the sail in your life? Remember, it is not the wind that rules, it's the set of the sail—or the set of the mind, the heart, the will.

When testing and trials come, resist the urge to make excuses. Don't say, "I was particularly weak at the time," or "I was blinded by prosperity," or "I was frightened by poverty." Ask yourself instead, "What is the set of my sail?" You do not have to be a victim to sin. God has given all of His children the will and the power to resist Satan, and to live lives that are victorious.

ACTION

Read: *Hebrews* 2: 14-18

When you are faced with temptation, imagine your sails filled with the wind of God's Spirit, moving strongly into battle.

You Bet!

"...your faith should not rest on the wisdom of men, but on the power of God."

I CORINTHIANS 2:5

I'm for gambling! If that offends you, please keep reading. I believe that risk-taking is part of the fabric of life, and that God has built into each one of us a desire to venture beyond what we can see. But there is gambling...and there is gambling. There is the kind of high stakes gamble of a God who would wager His only Son for a lost, dying world...and there is what I call "foot of the cross" gambling: the simple, petty gaming of the men who cast lots for the robe of the crucified Christ. Martin Luther, meditating on the mighty grace of God said, "If you are going to sin, sin big." I would say if you are going to gamble, risk it all.

I know that to call faith in Christ a gamble will offend some. The Gospel itself was, is, and always will be scandalous. It offends the self-righteous man the most. It is true that placing our faith in Christ is "gambling" on a sure thing—that is, the power of God to save us...but it is a power we cannot be completely sure of until we have put our full weight down on it. The philosopher Pascal proposed a skeptic's wager that went something like this: If God is the true God, and able to save us, why not place our faith in Him to do so? If we are right, we have gained everything. If we are wrong, we have lost nothing!

What kind of gambler are you? Have you wagered everything on the power of God to save you by placing your faith in His Son Jesus Christ? Or are you holding your cards "close to the vest," carefully watching and speculating and waiting for a more opportune time to risk it all? Don't waste time on the small-time, "foot of the cross" gambling that goes on everywhere, every day. Step into the big time, and say "I believe that Jesus is the Son of God, and I am placing my faith in Him and never looking back." Is it a risk worth taking? You bet!

Read: John 19: 16-24

 If you have placed your faith in Christ already, challenge an unbeliever you love to bet it all.

Stick Out Your Tongue

"But no one can tame the tongue; it is a restless evil and full of deadly poison."

JAMES 3:8

When I was a boy, doctors made house calls, and the doctor who came to our house was our family physician, Dr. Gatlin. I can still picture him in the doorway of my room, with his black case, nodding as my mother ran through my symptoms. But regardless of what she said, I could be sure that Dr. Gatlin would listen to my heart with his stethoscope, and take a flat, wooden tongue depressor and say, "Okay, Edwin, stick out your tongue." If I had fever, he would call Johnson's Drug Store and have them send a sulfur drug. If I were fever-free, he would recommend two teaspoons of milk of magnesia. I'm not sure what he learned about my physical condition from seeing my tongue, but I know today that the tongue can diagnose my spiritual condition in a heartbeat.

To all who desire to be mature Christians, James would say, "stick out your tongue." That is because our words, and how we say them, reflect the degree to which we are sincerely living for God and walking with Jesus Christ.

You see, the tongue is simply a messenger boy of the heart, or a bucket that is lowered into the well of our soul. It can only deliver the message it is given. It can only bring up the water that is already there. Jesus said it is not what enters the mouth of a man that defiles him or makes him unclean, it is what comes out of the man from the heart that defiles him. If hatred and bitterness and jealousy and slander are on your tongue, you can be certain it is because they are in your heart. And once those words are spoken, they can never be reclaimed. There is simply no diagnostician of the heart as accurate as the tongue!

Read: *James 3: 2-12*

What is your tongue saying about the condition of your heart?

Practical Atheism

"Therefore to one who knows the right thing to do, and does not do it, to him it is sin."

JAMES 4:17

Not too many folks will tell you, "I'm an atheist." At least not with their words. But the lifestyles of many say otherwise. I know a lot of people (and you do, too) who are living their lives as if there were no God. They are what I call "practical atheists." Not practicing. Practical. They do not take God into consideration. They leave Him out of their reckoning, their speech, their plans and their deeds.

When German theologian Martin Luther was going through a period of dark depression, his wife Katherine was worried. Day after day, Luther would lock himself in his study and cry and pray and bemoan the state of the world. Finally, Katherine appeared before him dressed in black from head to foot. "What are you doing?" he asked her. "Why are you dressed in mourning clothes?" She replied, "You, good doctor, are acting as if God were dead, so I shall dress as if He were!"

Are you living like a practical atheist—disregarding God's commands and precepts, relying on your own wisdom, and refusing to hope in the goodness of God the Father? Or is your belief in God evident in your speech, your refusal to judge your brothers and sisters, and your surrender to God's leading day by day? Faith without works is dead faith, James would say. Don't let your life deny your belief in God.

Read: *James 4: 7-17*

 Consult God in the decisions you would make today. Ask Him, "Father, is this what You have for me?" Then do what He shows you is right.

A Hospital For Sinners

"Above all, keep fervent in your love for one another, because love covers a multitude of sins."

I PETER 4:8

Dallas businessman Fred Smith tells a modern-day parable about the church that illustrates beautifully what the Body of Christ is to be. A man is hit by a car and left on the side of the road. He is bleeding and seriously injured. Bystanders rush to his side and insist that he be taken to the nearest hospital. "Oh, no," he protests. "Don't send me to the hospital. Please don't call an ambulance." They argue with him: "Look, you're bleeding. You're in bad shape. We've got to get you some help." Again he refuses, explaining that he works on the staff of the hospital, and his co-workers would not understand how he could be so stupid as to be struck by a hit-and-run driver. "Besides," he says, "the people in the admissions office like to get all the details when a new patient is brought in, and I don't even know what kind of car hit me. I didn't get the license number, and I have no idea where my insurance card is. They probably wouldn't even treat me if you took me in."

It's a crazy story, isn't it? Here's a man who is critically injured, but instead of going where he could receive help, he crawls off into the gutter to die alone. He would rather die than suffer the embarrassment of being seen by his friends and associates as a man in desperate need.

But let's be honest. If last night, you were "run over" by some horrible sin, would you be in church today? Would you risk having people know you are hurting and in need of help? Many of us have the idea that church is a place where everyone looks good, smells good and is good. But the truth is, the church is a hospital for sinners, offering grace to one and all.

Read: I Peter 4: 6-19

Where do you go when you are hit hard by sin? Is church—the Body of Christ—the last place on your list?

Patience

MEMORIZE

"You too be patient; strengthen your hearts, for the coming of the Lord is at hand."

JAMES 5:8

The best illustration of impatience in all of Scripture has to be recorded in Exodus. Two brothers were engaged in the same activity at virtually the same time—but with vastly different results. Moses was on Mount Sinai in the presence of God, holding the tablets as God sculpted on them His rules for living. Aaron was at the foot of the mountain, sculpting an idol for himself and the children of Israel. Moses had been on the mountain for forty days, and the natives, as they say, were restless. They asked Aaron to make a god they could worship, and he complied. They could not wait for Moses to come down from the mountain. They were impatient, and Aaron gave them what they asked for.

What was the difference in these two endeavors? Moses was responding to the divine decree of God. Aaron was responding to the pleas of the people. Moses gave the people what God thought they needed. Aaron gave the people what they thought they needed. The words that would be life and peace and promise to them were being carved by the very hand of God, but the Israelites could not wait to read them.

You and I must learn to be patient. Patience does not mean sitting back and doing nothing. It means waiting on God, but doing His will in the meantime. It means using our spiritual gifts, working to bring in the harvest, and speaking out in spite of suffering and persecution.

ACTION

Read: Exodus 32: 1-10

If you are waiting on God and losing patience, ask Him what He would have you do in the meantime…then do it!

No Bad Time To Pray

"Pray without ceasing."

I THESSALONIANS 5:17

There is simply no inappropriate time for prayer. James tells us we are to pray when we are suffering, sick, cheerful, or hurting. We are to pray for ourselves, and for each other.

I read of a missionary who arranged for a promising man from Nigeria to come to America to pursue a university education. The young man observed some athletes running and remarked to one of his professors, "I think I could do that. I'd like to try." The professor made the proper introductions, and soon this young Nigerian was running with the university track team. It became evident that he was very gifted at distance, and the first time he was clocked running a mile his time shattered the national record! The coach was thrilled to discover he had a contender for the national title, and at the big meet, he told his young runner: "Just get on the outside, and run like you do in practice. Don't let anyone bump you or crowd you. Get out in front and stay there!"

The gun sounded and the young man took off. But instead of leading the pack, he was running dead last. His feet felt like lead until the end of the first lap, and then he began to fly. When the coach saw him cross the line in first place, there were tears on his face. The coach embraced his runner, then said, "Son, what happened to you out there? I've never seen a slower first quarter!" The boy said, "My feet felt so heavy I could not pick them up, but then I prayed, 'Lord, if you'll pick them up, I'll put them down.' And the Lord Jesus picked them up so fast I felt like my feet never touched the ground."

In times of trouble, pray. In times of happiness, pray. In times of sin and sickness, pray. It's the very best that we can do.

Read: *James* 5: 13-16

Are you guilty of praying only as a "last resort," or is prayer your first line of defense?

You Can't Face Both Ways!

"He who is not with Me is against Me; and he who does not gather with Me, scatters."

LUKE 11:23

Neutrality, bi-partisanship, and tolerance are admired postures in our post-modern culture. But God does not admire neutrality. In fact, He does not recognize it at all. He clearly states that all those who are not for Him are by default, against Him. Jesus said, "He who does not gather with Me, scatters." Could it be more clear?

Satan is a strongman whose "house" is this world, and he counts as his possessions many who live here. When you and I try to stand alone against this rebel-king, we are sorely mismatched. We cannot do it. If we think that we can ("Oh, I would never be tempted by *that*...") we are displaying what God calls "the pride of life." But there is a stronger One who has come and overthrown the rebel-king. If Satan rules now, it is only by theft, not by right. Jesus Christ is the stronger man who "breaks the power of canceled sin and sets the prisoner free." He has overthrown Satan.

Even so, there are some who wish to remain neutral. They tip their hats to God by attending church occasionally or adopting certain religious rituals. But in truth, their agenda is still their own, and they are not God's. You can't be 90% faithful. Your mate would not tolerate that, and your Lord won't either. You are either for Him 100%, or you are against Him. You can't face both ways.

Read: *Luke 11: 21-23*

Are you trying to have it both ways? Have you gone against God by refusing to be for Him?

The Natural End of Neutrality

"and again he denied it with an oath, 'I do not know the man'."

MATTHEW 26:72

Peter purposed (and promised) to follow Jesus to death and beyond, but when Peter refused to acknowledge Jesus, he eventually denied him. It is impossible to remain neutral...and Peter tried. He moved in a matter of minutes from "I do not know what you are talking about" to "I do not know *the man.*"

The natural end of neutrality is denial. Trapped in a dark courtyard and confronted by servants with the charge of being a Jesus-follower, the man who had sliced off the ear of a soldier turned to jello. He did not flee with the rest of the apostles, but he did not claim his Lord, either. Instead, he tried to dodge the questions, hide his accent, and keep his face away from the light. But when push came to shove, Peter denied Jesus three times. His neutrality quickly turned to denial.

Later in that same courtyard, Peter and Jesus came face to face with one another. When Jesus looked at him, Peter remembered his brash promises in the light of his pitiful failure. I have a question for you. If you came face to face with Jesus this day, and He looked directly at you, what kind of look would be in His eyes? What kind of look would be in yours?

QUESTION

Read: Matthew 26: 31-35; 69-75

How have you denied the lordship of Christ by attempting neutrality?

Thankful Living

MEMORIZE

"Be anxious for nothing, but in everything by prayer and supplication with thanksgiving, let your requests be made known to God."

PHILIPPIANS 4:6

Did you know that the words "think" and "thank" come from the same root? They do. So when you and I think, we should immediately expel words of thanksgiving. Simply put, we are to be thankful people. Far too many of us have a hard time seeing what we have to be thankful for. We are like the little girl who was told by her mother to eat all her spinach, which she hated. She ate it, pushed around the rest of her food, and then asked to be excused from the table. Her mother told her, "You may, but not until you think of something you're thankful for." The little girl thought for a minute, then said, "I'm thankful, Mom, that the spinach has not made me sick yet. Now may I be excused?"

Not too many of us are detained at the table anymore, but I wish that all of us could be made to sit still and quiet until we came up with at least a dozen things for which we can be thankful. Could you do it? Would it take you long?

To be a Christian steeped in negativism is to deny the goodness of the Lord God Almighty. I have seen Christians in other cultures thankful for conditions we would consider desperate. Do you have clothes to wear? Food to eat? Could you get medical care if you needed it? Are your sins forgiven? Are you a son or daughter of God and a joint heir with Jesus Christ? Think about it...and give thanks.

ACTION

Read: *Philippians* 4: 6-13

Sit quietly today and think, until you have a list of at least twelve things for which you are thankful.

Blessings That Last

*"I thank my God in all my remembrance of you,
always offering prayer with joy in my every prayer for you all."*

PHILIPPIANS 1:3-4

"Count your many blessings," the old song says, "name them one by one." It seems the "common blessings" of life—family, friends, home, health—are the most frequently overlooked. It helps to realize that no blessing is just for the moment...it's forever. Blessings "keep," and when difficult times come, we can remember the ways God has blessed us in the past, being confident He will do the same in the future.

One man who understood this truth wrote a letter to a teacher who had taken special interest in him years before. This was her reply: "Dear Willie: I cannot tell you how much your note meant to me. I'm in my 80's and live alone in a small room, lonely like the last leaf of summer, lingering behind. You'll be interested to know that I taught school for 50 years, and yours is the first note of appreciation I have ever received. It came on a cold, blue morning, and it cheered me as nothing has in many years." He got so excited by her reply that he wrote another letter of thanks, this one to a friend some distance away who had lost his wife. He received this letter in return: "Dear Will: Your letter was so beautiful, so real, that as I sat reading it in my den, tears fell from my eyes—tears of gratitude. Then, before I realized what I was doing I rose from my chair and called her name to show it to her, forgetting for a moment that she was gone. You will never know how much your letter has warmed my spirit; I have been walking about in the glow of it all day long."

How long has it been since you have shown appreciation for the common blessings in your life? You have carried them in your heart for years. Isn't it time thanksgiving for them spilled out and blessed someone else?

Read: II *Corinthians* 9: 8-15

Write a note of thanks to someone who has been, and is still, a blessing to you.

Fighting From Victory

MEMORIZE

*"Every place on which the sole of your foot treads, I have given it to you,
just as I spoke to Moses."*

JOSHUA 1:3

We are at war. But the outcome is certain. We are not fighting *for* victory…we're fighting *from* victory. When He died on the cross and was raised from the dead, Jesus Christ defeated sin and de-fanged death, crushing our enemy, Satan. We still battle, but victory is an accomplished act. Jesus did that.

This war *from* victory is a different kind of war, is it not? It's like the war Joshua was asked to fight, claiming the occupied Promised Land that God had already given. "The land is yours," God told him. "You own it, and My word is the title deed. I promised it to Abraham; I will give it to you. But you must fight." He led the nation of Israel in some fierce battles, but Joshua owned the dirt everywhere he put his foot down. He had the deed. He was fighting not for victory against the Amalekites, the Amorites and others—he was fighting *from* victory already made certain by God Himself.

That's how we are. Our battles are not against flesh and blood, but they are very real just the same. We go head to head against the wiles of Satan, but we are fighting from victory, because God has already accomplished it. When Jesus endured the cross and conquered the grave, we became soldiers whose ultimate conquest is assured.

REFLECTION

Read: Joshua 1: 1-7

Re-assess any battles you may be facing now. How does Jesus' victory over sin and death change your outlook?

We're Satan's Target

MEMORIZE

"For all that is in the world, the lust of the flesh, the lust of the eyes and the boastful pride of life, is not from the Father..."

I JOHN 2:16

D o you ever feel like you've got a big bull's-eye painted on your chest? That's because you do! If you are in Christ, you are Satan's target—and he will never stop shooting at you in this life. Where does he most often take aim? John said it well: the lust of the flesh, the lust of the eyes and the boastful pride of life. Most of us know too well what lust is. But what is "the boastful pride of life?" Perhaps a story will help illustrate it.

A young man finished seminary as a brilliant student. He went to deliver his first sermon to his home church looking every bit the erudite pastor. He ascended the Anglican-style pulpit in that church with utter confidence, wearing a new suit, sporting a new haircut, and carrying a new Bible under his arm. As he began to speak, those in the congregation who knew him said, "This young man is our best and brightest. He has multiple degrees and a great education. Just look at him." You could almost see ego oozing from every pore as he spoke with beautiful eloquence. But suddenly, he mispronounced a word. And then another. Then his concentration was shattered. He lost his place. He repeated himself. Frustrated and embarrassed, he finished his sermon as quickly as possible, walked down the center aisle and toward the back of the church. He could not hold his head up, nor could he stop his tears. Someone turned to an old saint in the back pew as the preacher passed, and asked, "What happened to William? So much promise." The old saint said, "If he had gone up like he came down, he would have come down like he went up." That is the pride of life...and we are all susceptible to it.

Beware of placing confidence in yourself, your natural abilities, or even the gifts with which God has blessed you. Pride is at the root of every sin, and only utter dependence on the Lord Jesus Christ can kill it. Until pride is killed out in you and me, we can be sure that we are easy targets for Satan.

QUESTION

Read: I Chronicles 21: 1-8; 14-19

 On what things do you pride yourself? They are nothing apart from Christ in you, who is the hope of glory.

Pursuing Love

MEMORIZE

"Therefore, behold, I will allure her, bring her into the wilderness and speak kindly to her."

HOSEA 2:14

Do you know how God pursues those who run from Him? He pursues them with purpose, and with provision, and with unbending love. The tiny book of Hosea is a mini-pageant of God's pursuing love played on the stage of human life. In it, Gomer leaves her good husband Hosea and goes her own way, taking other lovers and shaming the faithful man she married. But he doesn't write her off or cut her loose. In fact, even when she is with other men, he is concerned for her welfare, and reckoning for her good.

When Gomer sets up housekeeping with another man, Hosea seeks him out and gives him wool and flax and bread, saying, "Give her these, she'll need them." So the man does, and takes credit for them himself, receiving the gratitude and affection that should have been Hosea's.

God's love is like that, isn't it? He keeps on loving you and keeps on loving me, even when we say "God, I've had enough," and run from Him! We flee as far and as fast as we can, then stop to catch our breath and think we've out-distanced Him. But then there's a quiet word or a gentle touch, and God is near again. We say, "Lord, how did you find me here?" and He replies, "My child, I knew a short-cut." Pursuing love is not deterred by our weak protests. Love always knows a short cut.

ACTION

Read: *Hosea* 2: 1-23

If you are running from the love of God, stop where you are. He is much closer than you think.

Love Pays The Price

"...and they will come trembling to the Lord and to His goodness in the last days."

HOSEA 3:5

When Hosea purchased back his wife Gomer in a slave auction, he paid the price for love. She had betrayed him for other lovers, and abandoned their home and family. Hosea, remember, is a pageant played out in human life. It is the story of a husband and a wife, Hosea and Gomer, the story of God and His people, Israel, and the story of you and me and countless other sinners who have run from the God who loves them. But love pursues, and love pays the price. Hosea bought back his wife for fifteen shekels of silver and a homer and a half of barley. God bought you and me with the precious blood of His only Son Jesus Christ.

Can you imagine the scene of Gomer's redemption? She is naked, and men are bidding on her like she is an animal. The auctioneer's voice rings out "Sold!" and she is led to the man who paid the highest price. She lifts her head to see who her new master is, and she looks into the eyes of the husband she once loved, and betrayed. And all she sees in his eyes is...love.

That's the way it is with you and me. The world is bidding for us—pleasure, a good time, success, prosperity—the world is bidding for some right now. But the Father has bid Jesus' shed blood in response, and there is no higher bid than that. Paul said it like this: "But God demonstrates His own love toward us, in that while we were yet sinners, Christ died for us." Love pays the price.

Read: Hosea 3:1-5

Consider the price God paid for you at your worst. What does His love inspire in you?

Precious Dependence

MEMORIZE

"And He said to them, 'Why are you so timid? How is it that you have no faith?'"

MARK 4:40

In times of difficulty, we learn dependence. When the seas of life are smooth, we are able to believe that we rule the waves, but when a storm comes, we see how little power we have over our circumstances. Then, if we are wise, we lay aside all pride and pretense and say, "Lord, I'm helpless. I'm going to cling to You."

If we could interview all the biblical superstars "Barbara Walters-style" and say, "Take me back to the spot where you learned to be totally dependent upon God," what do you think they would say? I believe Abraham would say, "Climb up. I can take you to the very spot on Mount Moriah where my life turned around." Moses would say, "We can't go there anymore...it's under water. But we can stand on the shore of the Red Sea and I'll point it out to you. It's right about...there. That's where I learned Who is really in control." Perhaps Ruth would say, "Come on out to the field of Boaz. I'll show you where I was working when it happened." Jacob might say, "It was there by the river in the middle of the night. That's the place we wrestled, and since then nothing has been the same." John would say, "You'll have to go with me to the isle of Patmos," and Peter would point to a spot by the Sea of Galilee where the risen Savior cooked him breakfast and asked him three questions that were burned upon his heart forever.

I've never known a person—superstar or ordinary Joe—who would identify the transforming moment of his life as a promotion or a windfall or a breathtaking, come-from-behind victory. The hinge points of life are those where we learn precious dependence on God...and we say to ourselves in whispered awe, "Who then is this, that even the wind and the sea obey Him?"

ACTION

Read: *Mark 4: 35-41*

Identify the "hinge" moments of your life...times where you discovered that you are helpless, and that God is your helper.

The Divine Yes

"For as many as may be the promises of God, in Him they are yes..."

II CORINTHIANS 1:20

There's a negative connotation to being a "yes man" today. It's an accusation of weakness or spinelessness. But Paul calls himself a "yes man" in terms of obedience to Christ. In fact, he claims Christ as his example of a "yes man", because all of God's promises were "yes" in Him. In other words, those promises find their perfect affirmation in Jesus.

One of my heroes of the faith was a man named E. Stanley Jones. Jones served most of his life as a missionary in India, but at 87, he suffered a massive stroke. This mighty man of God could not walk, could not speak, could not see and could barely hear. But as he fought to recover, he told his daughter he had one last book to write, and thinking it might give him something to press toward, she agreed to help him. Jones dictated that last book into a microphone. It was called "The Divine Yes." In it he said that he had served the Lord with a measure of health and success all of his life, but that in the darkness and depression following his stroke, he wondered if everything he had preached and taught was in fact, true. His conclusion, in pain and weakness and heartbreak was "Yes! It is true! All the promises of God are 'yes' now that I have experienced them in joy and in sorrow."

E. Stanley Jones' life was one exuberant "yes" to the Lord God Almighty. Paul's life was a resounding "yes" to the leading and lordship of Jesus Christ. There is no shame in being a "yes man" or a "yes woman", when the One we are saying "yes" to is Him.

Read: II *Corinthians* 1: 13-24

Are you a "yes man" or a "yes woman" to Jesus Christ?

Adequate!

MEMORIZE

*"Not that we are adequate in ourselves to consider anything as coming from ourselves,
but our adequacy is from God."*

II CORINTHIANS 3:5

Years ago a fellow went into a Rolls Royce dealership in New York City and began to shop for one of those premier automobiles. He had a lot of questions, and his very enthusiastic and well-informed salesperson answered them all with ease. He had almost exhausted his query and decided to purchase the car when he had a final thought: "What is the horsepower of this engine?" he asked. The salesman said, "You know, I've never been asked that. Let's check with the manager." But the manager had never been asked, either. So they consulted the literature, but were unable to find a precise answer. Not wanting to lose a lucrative sale, the sales manager placed a call to the manufacturing plant, where he was connected to one of the key engineers on the assembly line. "I've got a customer here ready to buy," he said breathlessly, "but first he wants to know the horsepower on this particular model number. Can you help me?" There was a slight pause before the engineer answered the dealership manager's question with a single word: "Adequate."

The apostle Paul was definitely a high-powered, top-of-the-line evangelist. Even so, the Corinthians were hesitant to "buy" his preaching and teaching without a healthy dose of skepticism. They questioned his motives. His abilities. His credentials. Paul finally told them that they themselves were his letter of commendation, and that his adequacy came from an impeccable source: God Himself.

When your abilities, motives and credentials as a believer are called into question, don't panic. Your life will defend you, and the Savior Himself has already made you more than adequate for whatever task He assigns.

REFLECTION

Read: II *Corinthians* 3: 1-6

 Is your sense of adequacy based on anything but Jesus Christ?

Tear Down The Wall

MEMORIZE

"Now the Lord is the Spirit, and where the Spirit of the Lord is, there is liberty."

II CORINTHIANS 3:17

Something happened in 1990 that I wasn't sure I would see in my lifetime. The Berlin Wall, the division between communist East Berlin and free West Berlin, came down. Thousands of people streamed through Checkpoint Charlie, and civilians with hammers and pick axes took the old symbol of bondage down piece by piece. In fact, I have a small piece of that wall, given to me by a friend who was visiting Germany when it came down.

It's an amazing thing to see walls come down in such a dramatic way, and to see freedom take root and grow where oppression once thrived. But some could testify that although walls seem to be coming down around the world today, they are still captured. Still in bondage. Not to a political system or to an oppressive government, but held captive by sin and the pull of the old, unredeemed nature.

To those who are struggling to live the Christian life, to be obedient, to "do better" than before, I have one word: quit! That's right...quit trying. You see, this new covenant we are under is not about law-keeping and striving, it is about grace. The fading glory of the old covenant could only diagnose our sin problem, not solve it permanently. But through the blood of Christ, we have been set free from the bondage of trying harder, and "doing enough." God has already done enough: He sent His Son to die on our behalf, and attributes His righteousness to us when we place our faith in Jesus. *That* will set you free!

REFLECTION

Read: II *Corinthians* 3:12-18

If trying harder to do good could win God's approval, what happens when we try and fail?

The Face of Jesus Christ

*"For God...is the One who has shone in our hearts to give the light
of the knowledge of the glory of God in the face of Christ."*

II CORINTHIANS 4:6

I have a little book in my study titled *The Face of Jesus*. It is filled with different artists' interpretations of how Jesus might have looked. In it you can see Him as an Asian, an African, a European...Jesus as He might have appeared in different cultures and races. But do you know where you can see the face of Jesus today? In the Word! As you and I study Scripture, the face of Jesus comes sharply into focus.

A musical prodigy was born years ago in a small Italian village. He studied violin with an old master teacher in that region, and the master poured his life into his most promising student. When he was eleven, he played a concert in Rome and his performance caused a sensation. Soon he had agents and handlers who booked him into all the major concert halls of Europe. He toured the world as a teenager and a young adult, and by the time he was thirty he was the most renowned violinist in the world. Finally, he was invited to come back to play in his hometown. The village responded with pure adulation. As he played, applause flooded the tiny hall, and cheers of "Bravo" filled the air. Flowers and coins were tossed on to the stage as the star kept playing—and although he acknowledged the crowd's response, his eyes never strayed from a spot in the balcony where his old teacher sat. When the concert was over, he was asked "What were you looking at as you played?" He answered, "I was looking at my old master teacher, who taught me everything I know and poured his life into me. I came here to play for him, and I was watching his face for approval."

"Turn your eyes upon Jesus," the old song says, "look full in His wonderful face...and the things of earth will grow strangely dim in the light of His glory and grace."

Read: II Corinthians 4:1-6

As you work and serve and love today, look in the face of Jesus, playing your life to an audience of one.

Truth Is In Jesus

"...if indeed you have heard Him and have been taught in Him, just as truth is in Jesus."

EPHESIANS 4:21

The Christian has a simple calling, and that is to manifest, or show forth, the truth—and the truth is in Jesus. Some people come to church desiring to be religious, but not desiring the truth. They look upon religion as a low-calorie dessert. It's nice, a little sweet, and not too calorie-laden or addicting. They'll have a bite of it. Religion to them is an add-on to the main course of life, nothing more.

The only problem with this approach comes when a seeker who only wants a bite of religion comes into contact with God's Word and is confronted head-on by truth. Suddenly "religion" is applied to and intrudes upon life. The truth affects how a man runs his business. It affects how he treats his wife. It affects the places he goes and the things he says and does. It even begins to impact his goals and dreams. Suddenly "religion" gives way to relationship—and it becomes far too big for a dessert plate!

C. S. Lewis was an intellectual agnostic when he met Jesus Christ. This brilliant British writer and teacher came face-to-face with the claims of Christ, and even as he wrestled intellectually, his conscience confirmed that he had indeed found the truth in Jesus. Our Savior said it Himself: *"I am the way, the truth and the life."* And so He is.

Read: *I Timothy 2: 1-7*

If you have come to know the truth in Jesus, is that truth manifest in your life?

Almost Persuaded

"But whenever a man turns to the Lord, the veil is taken away."

II CORINTHIANS 3:16

If the gospel is veiled, Paul said, it is veiled to those who are perishing. They cannot see the truth because the god of this world—Satan—has blinded them.

Many years ago, I visited the home of a young couple who was attending the church I pastored. They were a beautiful family: a strong husband, an attractive wife, and polite, well-mannered children. They were lovely people, but they did not have a clue about what it meant to be a Christian. As I talked, the wife indicated that she would like to receive Christ, and one of their teenaged children did likewise. The husband was warm, engaging, and appeared very interested, but he did not follow the example of his wife and child. "Is there any reason why you cannot ask Jesus Christ into your life?" I asked him. "No," he replied. "Well, would you like to?" I said. "I want to someday," he said.

I believed he was so close. Almost persuaded to surrender to Christ. But although we spoke until the wee hours, he never budged. I could not understand it. I was certain he comprehended. There was an openness in him to hear the truth, but not to receive it. It was as if there were a veil over his heart that would not be parted. Later, I learned that he had been having an affair, and shortly after the night we talked, he left his wife and children to be with the other woman. He belonged to the god of this world, and he could not let go—even when he heard the truth.

Read: Acts 26: 24-29

Ask God to make you both bold and sensitive in sharing the truth with those who belong to this world.

Treasure In Earthen Vessels

"But we have this treasure in earthen vessels, that the surpassing greatness of the power may be of God and not from ourselves."

II CORINTHIANS 4:7

Years ago, while visiting Cairo, Egypt, I was privileged to go into the British Museum. I was especially intrigued by the artifacts uncovered by archeologists in the tombs of the pharaohs. One room of such artifacts contained an amazing display of things believed by the Egyptians to be carried into the afterlife: golden bowls, pitchers and goblets, sculptures and all sorts of forged implements. In the midst of this "spread" of wealth sat a few clay pots that looked strangely out of place. Why would the pharaohs leave clay pots along with their most beautiful possessions?

One day the manager of the museum noticed a strange crack in one of the pots that let a bit of light through. He examined it and all the other pots further. What he discovered to his amazement was that the bottoms of these vessels were hollow, and contained exquisite, costly jewels. The treasures of the kings of Egypt were held in earthen vessels.

Paul tells us that God places His treasure—the knowledge of God in Jesus Christ—into men and women like us. We are the "earthen vessels" that contain more wealth than all the tombs of all the kings of Egypt. We may not look like much on the outside, but in our ordinary weakness, the power and wealth of God are magnificently displayed.

Read: II Corinthians 4: 1-10

 How has God displayed His glory through the earthen vessel of your life?

Moving Day

MEMORIZE

"Therefore also we have as our ambition, whether at home or absent,
to be pleasing to Him."

II CORINTHIANS 5:9

George Bernard Shaw said, "There are indeed some fascinating statistics about death. For example, one out of one dies."

What happens when you die? Some people believe that death is simply the end of existence. That a human being, like a dog or a flower or a plant, just ceases to exist when its allotted days are done. Others believe that death begins a kind of new age recycling project in which human beings return to existence in another form. You might return as an elephant or a chrysanthemum…or anything in-between—and the recycling process could recur a half a million times or more. Still others think that a limbo-like state follows death, and that a person remains in this in-between state until all his earthly affairs are rectified; or that the body dies, but the soul "floats" around without a package to contain it.

These earthly tents in which we live sag and wear, and Paul says that in them, we groan. But when the stakes are pulled up and we leave this life, the Bible teaches that Christians go immediately to be in the presence of the Lord, and receive their resurrection bodies. Jesus' own resurrection is our pledge or promise that this is true. So the day of death is not the last day…it is only moving day.

ACTION

Read: II *Corinthians* 5: 1-9

Let Paul's teaching about death and resurrection comfort you when someone close to you dies in Christ.

In "That Great, Gittin' Up Morning"

"For we must all appear before the judgment seat of Christ."

II CORINTHIANS 5:10

S teven Covey wrote a bestseller of the '90's entitled *The Seven Habits of Highly Effective People*. The book had many interesting and very applicable principles of effectiveness in it, not the least of which was this: *Begin with the end in mind.* In other words, know where you want to end up, and adjust your starting point—and every point along the way—accordingly.

I don't know about you, but the "end" I have in mind is to stand before my Heavenly Father and hear Him say these words: "Well done, my good and faithful servant." For every believer, there will be "that great, gittin' up morning" that is judgment day, and on that day, I want to be deemed a good steward in His eyes.

While we are saved by grace, and grace alone, every believer in Christ will be judged. We'll be judged not for salvation—that is ours in Christ, paid in full—but for stewardship. What did you do with your time? What did you do with the gifts you were given? What did you do with your resources and the precious relationships God entrusted to you? Our motive in all these areas should be to picture the end clearly, and desire to hear our Master say, "Well done."

Read: II *Corinthians* 5: 10-11

Could you stand today before the judgment seat of God and truthfully say, "I lived, loved, gave, served, with the end in mind?"

Unequally Yoked

MEMORIZE

*"Do not be bound together with unbelievers; for what partnership have righteousness
and lawlessness, or what fellowship has light with darkness?"*

II CORINTHIANS 6:14

If you are a Christian, and you have a relationship with an unbeliever,
understand one thing: there is nothing you have in common with that
friend that will last forever. Now, Jesus was a friend of sinners, and we
should be, too. But to marry an unbeliever—to be joined together with him
or her as one flesh—is to go against the command of God.

I am the product of a home where my mother was a Christian, and my
dad was not. When a Christian does disobey God's command and marries
a non-Christian, the believing spouse is not to leave. He or she is to stay
and love that mate, praying for them and seeking to win them to the Lord
with their own lifestyle. My mom did that. My dad became a Christian later
in life, but when they married, they were unequally yoked.

If you are single, guard your heart. I do not believe it is wise for a single person who is a Christian to begin a dating relationship with a person
who is not. Why? Because the odds are excellent that you will eventually
marry someone that you date. Why begin a romance that can go nowhere?
It's a prescription for a broken heart. I wish you could sit in my study or read
my mail and hear first-hand from men and women who have fallen in love
with their heart but not their head, and married unbelieving mates. All of
them would tell you to wait for God's best, to guard your heart, and to refuse
to be unequally yoked.

ACTION

Read: II *Corinthians* 6: 14-18

*If you are a single Christian, resolve today to marry only another believer
in Christ.*

"*Dear God...*"

"What harmony has Christ with Belial,
or what has a believer in common with an unbeliever?"

II CORINTHIANS 6:15

Why do Christian men and women fall in love with and marry those who do not share their faith in Christ? Let these two letters from Ray Stedman's excellent book on II Corinthians shed some light on that question. (The first is written by a bride on her wedding day; the second is a hypothetical letter composed by Stedman.)

"Dear God: I know I have not been able to spend much time with you lately, with all the rush of getting ready for today, and I'm sorry. I guess, too, I feel a little guilty when I pray about all this, since Larry still isn't a Christian. But oh, Father, I love him so much. What else can I do? I just couldn't give him up. Oh, you must save him somehow, some way. You know how much I've prayed for him and the way we've discussed the gospel together. I've tried not to appear too religious, I know, but that's because I didn't want to scare him off. Dear Father, please bless our marriage. I don't want to disobey you, but I do love him and I want to be his wife, so please be with us and don't spoil my wedding day."

Stedman says what this bride really meant was this: "Dear God: I don't want to disobey you, but I must have my own way at all cost. For I love what you do not love, and I want to do what you do not want, so please be a good God and deny yourself, move off your throne and let me take over. If you don't like this, all I ask is that you bite your lip and say nothing and don't spoil my wedding day. *Let me have my evil.*"

Don't let your feelings and affections run away with you in the area of choosing a mate. When you marry an unbeliever, the devil is your father-in-law, and you are compromising your life as far as God's best is concerned.

Read: Judges 14: 1-7

Does God's prohibition against marriage with unbelievers seem out of date?
Why does it matter?

The Black Dog of Depression

MEMORIZE

"...we were afflicted on every side: conflicts without, fears within."

II CORINTHIANS 7:5

I have read that at any given time in America, there are over seven million people suffering from untreated depression. It is estimated that over nine million people do seek help each year to deal with various degrees of depression. This much is certain: when you are depressed, you are in good company. The prophet Elijah experienced depression from time to time; so did Job. Writers like Edgar Allen Poe, Fyodor Dostoyevsky and Eugene O'Neill all battled with depression. Abraham Lincoln suffered periods of depression, and Winston Churchill called it "the black dog" that kept him company many days. Charles Wesley, Martin Luther and John Calvin all experienced depression, and Charles Haddon Spurgeon, perhaps the greatest pastor who ever lived, wrote that every genuine man or woman of God will be subject to depression.

Depression does not necessarily stem from sin, or from a lack of faith in God. It is not a sign that God has turned His back on you. Depression can be physiological, circumstantial or spiritual. There are many sources. The apostle Paul's bout of depression recorded in II Corinthians stemmed from his worry over the Christians at Corinth. They were like his wayward children, and concern for their welfare dogged his thoughts constantly. He had poured his life into them, and they seemed to have rejected both his teaching and his love.

His depression was eased by their favorable response to his letter of rebuke, and by their acceptance of his messenger Titus. In other words, the people he was depressed over got right with God. He was also comforted by God through Titus himself, and the good report he brought back from Corinth. When the black dog of depression seems to follow you, examine your heart and be confident of the love of God. He wants to lead you from sorrow to comfort

ACTION

Read: II Corinthians 7: 1-10

 If you are suffering from depression, seek to trace it to its source, and if need be, seek the help of a trusted friend, pastor or counselor.

I Want To Be Rich

MEMORIZE

*"...though He was rich, yet for your sake He became poor,
that you through His poverty might be rich."*

II CORINTHIANS 8:9

A popular song of a few years back said it: "I want to be rich...I want a little bit of love, peace and happiness...I want to be rich." Do you want to be rich? Lots of folks aspire to that. Bill Gates, Microsoft co-founder and the world's richest man, said in an interview that he never aspired to riches. He just found something he loved and did it. He wanted a company that would support him and a few Harvard buddies who were as computer-crazy as he was...and it grew from there. Gates' incredible success was an outgrowth of his passion. Jesus said that where a man's treasure is, his heart is also.

I've said time and again that you can tell more about a person by looking at his canceled checks than you can by any other way. Where you place your treasure is an indicator of where you heart will be. I read of a couple seeking a divorce after twenty years of marriage. The husband anticipated a large financial settlement because he had been quite successful. As he was going through his financial records he discovered a file of old checks, including one to the hotel where he and his wife had spent the first night of their honeymoon. Another check was written to the physician who delivered their daughter. Still another was the down payment to the first house the couple purchased. He became so emotional going through the paper trail of his marriage that he called his wife and said, "I've discovered that I have too much invested in you and you have too much invested in me for us to start all over again with someone else. I wonder if we couldn't get together tomorrow and plan how we'll spend the next twenty years."

This man discovered a great spiritual truth: the way you really get rich is to give.

ACTION

Read: *Luke 12: 27-34*

Look at your checkbook register. Where is your treasure? Where would you like for it to be?

Send In The Clowns

MEMORIZE

"We are fools for Christ's sake."

I CORINTHIANS 4:10

I don't know what you think, but I believe Judy Collins was right. When things get so confused, so complex, so baffling that all we know of life and love begins to resemble a circus—it's time to send in the clowns. We desperately need in this world funny people, foolish people, fun-offering people. We need clowns.

One of my favorite people in all the world was born on April Fool's Day. She loved to laugh, and she loved a good joke, even if the joke was on her. But my friend Jane wasn't just a fun-loving, fun-to-be-around person. She was a fool for Christ. There was nothing—absolutely nothing—she would not do for her Lord's sake, no matter how ridiculous it seemed.

We need, in this hour, Christians who are willing to play the fool for Jesus Christ. Spiritual arrogance is a deadly disease. We have nothing for which to be proud because we have nothing that God has not given us. The apostle Paul examined his own heart and said, "I thought I had lots of reasons to be proud, but on second thought—I'm nothing but a fool for Christ. He's the only thing that matters…the only thing that will last." With that in mind, is there anything Jesus Christ could ask that is "beneath you?" Be a fool for Christ.

QUESTION

Read: I *Corinthians* 4: 6-10

Is there anything you would not do for the Lord's sake?

The Battle For The Mind

MEMORIZE

"...and we are taking every thought captive to the obedience of Christ."

II CORINTHIANS 10:5

I n his book *The Magnificent Mind*, Gary Collins tells the story of Phinneas Gage. Gage was working as a mining foreman in September of 1848 when an accident occurred that changed his life forever. As he leaned over to look down into a blasting hole, some dynamite exploded prematurely, and propelled a 13-pound, 3-foot tamping rod into his cheek, through his brain and out the other side of his skull. It went through him like a missile, but he never lost consciousness on the long trip to the village doctor. "Something passed through my head," he told the doctor as he was examined. The doctor could put his fingers in the hole in Gage's skull. For several weeks Gage had headaches, and infection set in to the wound, nearly taking his life. But in two or three months, he was back at work in the mines—except his personality had radically changed. Where once he had been prompt, courteous and patient, he was now rude, discourteous and impatient. "Gage is no longer Gage," the people who knew him would say. Somehow the rod that passed through his brain had changed his personality, and he was a different man. For the rest of his life he made a living as a circus freak, and when he died, his brain and the tamping rod were placed in the museum of the Harvard Medical School.

The mind is a mysterious, mysterious thing. There is a battle going on in this world, not for territory that can be seen or touched, but for your mind and my mind. The way this battle is won is for us to allow every thought to be captive to the obedience of our Savior Jesus Christ. Doing that requires both inclusion and exclusion. Say for example, that someone attacks you in some area of your life, saying slanderous things about you. You could counterattack, which most of us are prone to do, or you could say to yourself, "That particular thing is not true, but there are many things in my life much worse that are." And then you dismiss that person's attack and walk away from it. That's exclusion. But exclusion alone will not work. We must apply the law of inclusion as well. It works like this: instead of focusing your mind on your anger, or your sense of injustice at being wrongly accused, you focus instead on the positive values of God. In other words, when these thoughts come, you say "I'm sorry, I don't have room for you. My mind is full of truth and faith and righteousness and biblical principles, and I am seeking to have the mind of Christ." Our every thought may not be Christian, but Christ can take every thought captive.

QUESTION

Read: *Philippians* 4: 8-9

 What thoughts do you need to take captive to the obedience of Christ?

He's Alive!

MEMORIZE

*"God raised Him up again, putting an end to the agony of death,
since it was impossible for Him to be held in its power."*

ACTS 2:24

Easter is the season when we usually think of the resurrection, but the fact of Jesus' victory over death applies to every day, every season, every moment of our lives. The truth that Jesus Christ died, was raised from the dead, and lives forever is not just destiny-changing—it's life-changing. Because of His resurrection, we too live, and shall live forever. Because of His resurrection, the horror of death loses its sting.

When our oldest granddaughter LeeBeth was three, she watched a Christmas drama that brought her face to face with the death of Jesus for perhaps the first time. As they began to drive the nails in his hands and feet, her little body would jump with every blow of the hammer. "They're hammering Jesus," she would say. "They're hammering Jesus." All through the rest of the day she said it over and over again—she couldn't get it out of her mind. She told her mother, "Momma, they hammered Jesus. Momma, they hammered Jesus. They hammered Jesus." Lisa would say, "I know, LeeBeth. But the good news is—He's still alive." She was still stung by the picture of His death. "Yes, but they hammered Him. They hammered Jesus." Lisa would patiently say, "They did, LeeBeth, but He's alive."

That night when her Daddy came in to hear her bedtime prayers, she said, "Daddy, did you know they hammered Jesus?" He said, "I know, LeeBeth." Then she thought for a moment and said, "But Daddy—the good news is, He's still alive." He is. And it makes all the difference in the world.

ACTION

Read: Acts 2: 22-36

Tell someone today how the resurrection of Jesus Christ has changed your world.

Handling The Critics

MEMORIZE

"For not he who commends himself is approved, but whom the Lord commends."

II CORINTHIANS 10:18

I'll be honest. I don't like it when people criticize me unjustly and unfairly. Actually, I don't like it when people criticize me justly and fairly, either. And neither do you. If someone says they enjoy having people take pot shots at them, I'd say if they'll lie about that, they'll lie about other things, too. Watch out.

Jesus faced criticism. Moses got his share. King David took a shot or two, and certainly the apostle Paul was no stranger to strong criticism. Since we all find ourselves the object of criticism from time to time, how are we to deal with it? How do we handle the critics? First, I think we need to listen to what is being said. Hold your response in check and pay attention. Then, consider the source. If the criticism comes from someone who knows you well, pay special attention. If it comes from someone who is generally negative, or knows you only casually, consider that as you weigh his comments. Third, don't overreact or underreact. Many times when we overreact to criticism, we become either hyper-defensive or hyper-sensitive. Both are mistakes. But there is a danger in underreacting, too. It is arrogant to dismiss every critic out-of-hand. While they seldom hit the bull's-eye head-on, they rarely miss the target altogether.

One of my favorite criticisms comes from an early screen test for Fred Astaire. Some MGM executive penned these words that must have come back to haunt him a thousand times...a week. "Can't act. Can't sing. Can dance a little." The secret to handling the critics is to know yourself, like yourself, and be yourself. If you are confident that you are operating within your gifts and being obedient to God, you'll survive the sting of criticism and become a better, more effective man or woman of God because of it.

ACTION

Read: II *Corinthians* 10: 12-18

Practice saying these words, just in case you run into some valid criticism today: "You are right. I was wrong. Thank you."

Spending And Being Spent

MEMORIZE

"And I will most gladly spend and be expended for your souls.
If I love you the more, am I to be loved the less?"

II CORINTHIANS 12:15

It costs a lot to be a parent. A lot of sleepless nights. A lot of prayer. A lot of time and energy, and even a lot of money. Every once in a while you'll see a dollar amount of what it costs to rear a child from birth to age 18. The last such figure I saw was astronomical, but it didn't cover the half of it! Parents spend and are spent on their children, and they do it out of love.

I read a story a while back that illustrates this. One morning a young boy placed a bill on the breakfast table next to his mother. He listed everything he felt his mother owed him for "services rendered." It read, "Cutting the grass: $10. Raking the leaves: $5. Cleaning out the garage: $3. Drying the dishes: $2. Total amount owed: $20." His mother didn't say anything, but when this little guy got home from school there was a note on his bed that read: "Ironing clothes: $4. Washing clothes: $4. Folding clothes: $2. Cooking meals: $5. Driving carpool: $5. Baking cookies: $5. Feeding your dog: $2. Helping with homework: $3. Total amount owed: *nothing.*"

Love doesn't charge, does it? Jesus loved you and me, and He was willing to spend and be spent to save us. Those who have nurtured us physically and spiritually have counted it a privilege to do so. Paul told his converts at Corinth that he was more than willing to spend and be spent for their souls. When it comes to the kingdom, no one's keeping score.

ACTION

Read: II *Corinthians* 12: 10-15

Thank someone who has spent himself for your spiritual growth. Then follow their example.

Keep It Simple

MEMORIZE

*"But I am afraid, lest...your minds should be led astray
from the simplicity and purity of devotion to Christ."*

II CORINTHIANS 11:3

There's a move toward simplicity afoot. Have you noticed? Books and articles on paring down your lifestyle and streamlining your schedule abound. It's becoming popular again for mothers of young children to stay at home rather than return to work. But is it possible to simplify your beliefs about God? How simple is a relationship with the living God?

A professor of theology and a professor of astronomy were seated next to each other at a university function. They had little respect for one another's respective fields of study, and were often at odds. The astronomy professor turned to the professor of theology and said loudly enough for everyone at the table to hear, "You know, the whole concept of Christianity can be boiled down to the golden rule, can't it? Isn't that all there is to it?" The professor of theology nodded in agreement, and said, "I guess that's right. Just like the precepts of astronomy can be summed up by saying, 'Twinkle, twinkle, little star.'"

While complete knowledge of God is beyond our human comprehension, the Christian life is actually quite simple. When a man makes up his mind that God is sovereign, that Jesus is his Savior, and that the Bible is his authority, life gets very simple indeed. The closer he draws to God, the less confusing life is, while the farther he moves away from Him, the more complex his situation becomes. When it comes to living the Christian life, less is more. Keep it simple.

QUESTION

Read: II Corinthians 11: 1-15

In what ways are you making following Christ more complicated than it is?

Living In "Crisis Mode"

MEMORIZE

*"The end of all things is at hand; therefore, be of sound judgment
and sober spirit for the purpose of prayer."*

I PETER 4:7

This past summer, two blockbuster movies depicted the end of civilization, and the drama that goes with living life "in crisis mode." Every sense is heightened. Relationships are more precious, and more challenging. Every decision is a major one. Peter wrote to his audience that they, too, should be on the alert, living as if Jesus' return were immanent.

Several years ago, I got a sense of this kind of "crisis mode" focus. Our youngest son Cliff had been away to a North Carolina summer camp for several weeks, so Jo Beth and I decided to fly up for his final week, then fly back home with him. When camp was over, the three of us boarded an airplane in Asheville, North Carolina for a short flight to Atlanta. As we were getting settled in our seats, the flight attendant began to give the standard emergency instructions that no one seems to listen to anymore. Shortly after takeoff, Jo Beth turned to me and said, "I smell smoke." We looked around and thick, white smoke seemed to be coming from the back of the plane. In a minute or two, it got even thicker. The flight attendant stood again and said, "Ladies and gentlemen, we are having some difficulty of an unknown nature, so I want to review the emergency information you received at takeoff. She had a rapt audience, including yours truly. I was concerned that Jo Beth and Cliff might not be paying attention, but I need not have been. They were as focused as I was. They turned the plane around, landed again in Asheville, and all was well. But for those last few minutes of the flight, that attendant had my undivided, complete attention.

We need to learn to live as if tomorrow might be the last day of our lives. In fact, we need to learn to live as if the next hour would be our last. Can you imagine the sharp focus our lives would take if we believed that at any moment the curtain of history could be drawn and the Son of God would return?

QUESTION

Read: I Peter 4: 1-7

How would hearing "the end is near" sharpen your focus? What would immediately change in your life?

Love Makes A Difference

"We love, because He first loved us."

I JOHN 4:19

Christians should be world-class lovers. No one should be better at demonstrating love in action than a follower of Jesus Christ, because we have the best example of love there is. We are to be fervent—stretched out—in our love for others.

Dr. John McGuire was a professor of English at Howard Payne University for many years. One day the president of the university called Dr. McGuire with a special request. "I've admitted a young man with a very poor academic record. He doesn't look like college material, but he is so determined and motivated to succeed that I'm taking a chance on him. I want you to take him under your wing and give him all the help you can." It was a struggle, but the young man's writing and study skills gradually improved. At the bottom of every paper he submitted to Dr. McGuire for review, he would write these words: "Prof, when I'm a great doctor, you'll have a part in it." A few years after he graduated from Howard Payne, the student sent his former professor an engraved graduation announcement from Baylor College of Medicine. On the bottom he wrote, "Prof, when I'm a great doctor, you'll have a part in it." A few years later, another announcement came, saying that the young man had completed his studies in surgery at an eastern university. At the bottom he wrote, "Prof, when I become a great doctor, you'll have a part in it." That man who had once been a struggling undergraduate became the chief of surgery at Walter Reed Army Hospital in Washington, D.C.

Love makes a difference. And nobody is better equipped to love than the man or woman who is in Jesus Christ. We love because He first loved us.

Read: I John 4: 10-21

 Ask God to show you someone who needs to be loved with the love of Jesus.

I SEE JESUS...

The true miracle of life is not that we see Jesus…but that He sees us! The Bible tells us that His eye is on the sparrow, and that His attentiveness to us is even more sharply focused. What a joy to know that we are the apple of His eye, and that His thoughts are toward us all the time.

Jo Beth Young

Don't Quit

MEMORIZE

*"Let those who suffer according to the will of God entrust their souls
to a faithful Creator in doing what is right."*

I PETER 4:19

Many of the blessings we enjoy today are ours because someone did not quit. From religious freedom and educational opportunities to life-saving medical inventions and vaccines, we are helped enormously by the efforts of those who persisted before us. When suffering or hardship comes and we are tempted to quit, that is just the time to keep trusting in our faithful Creator and press on.

Peter gave words of encouragement to the early church when they were tired and afraid. He said in so many words, "Never quit. Don't slow down. Don't stop. Don't get discouraged. Don't let hardship or difficulty or temptation or testing get you off the track. You know you're going to come through if you trust the One who has brought you safe this far." Peter must have remembered a time when many who had begun to follow Jesus fell away, and the Lord asked His disciples if they, too, wanted to leave Him. It was Peter who answered Him, "Lord, to whom shall we go? You have words of eternal life, and we have come to know that You are the Holy One of God."

Once we have begun to follow Jesus, there is nowhere else to go but on with Him. Nothing else makes sense. Nothing else gives life. And no one is worthy of our complete trust but our faithful Creator, who has proved Himself time and again. I like the words of the old hymn, *'Tis So Sweet to Trust in Jesus*: "Jesus, Jesus, how I trust Him! How I've proved Him o'er and o'er. Jesus, Jesus, precious Jesus! Oh, for grace *to trust Him more.*"

REFLECTION

Read: John 6: 66-71

Consider how God's faithfulness has been proved in the past, and look for that same faithfulness in times of suffering and trial.

Where Justice Meets Mercy

"I will sing of lovingkindness and justice, to Thee, O Lord, I will sing praises."

PSALM 101:1

Sometimes the real issues are not readily apparent, but are just below the surface. I believe this was the case when Jesus was called on by the scribes and Pharisees to deal with the woman caught in adultery. At first glance, it would seem the issue was the breaking of the ninth commandment. But it was not. This woman was a pawn in a power game between Jesus and the ecclesiastical elite of His day. She was a chess piece in a high stakes match of wills.

Jesus was in a seemingly lose-lose situation. If he said "stone her," as Jewish law commanded, he was usurping Roman authority—because the Jews were not allowed to deliver the death penalty. But if he said, "let her go," he broke the laws of Moses. He did neither. He wrote in the dust of the ground for a moment, then suggested that any of her accusers who were themselves without sin should go ahead and stone her. The sound of stones dropping to the ground one by one must have followed. The implication was clear: only the sinless could judge the sinner. They wanted Jesus to declare Himself a man of justice or a man of mercy. But he was neither. He was the God of justice *and* mercy.

The real question was, "How do you resolve justice and mercy?" And it is still asked today. "How could a loving God send people to hell?" He does not. He requires justice. And in His mercy, He provides a way for hopeless sinners to be made righteous. On the cross, Jesus caused justice and mercy to kiss one another through His blood.

Read: John 8: 1-11

As you read the account of this woman, put yourself in the roles of the accused, and the accuser. How do you see Jesus from each perspective?

It's Math And Mystery

*"Then the Lord God said, 'It is not good for the man to be alone;
I will make him a helper suitable for him'."*

GENESIS 2:18

The New Testament tells us that marriage is a mystery. I have been married over thirty years, and I agree. It is a mystery. But the word "mystery" in this case does not mean a riddle, or a confusing puzzle. It means a divine secret—one that can only be revealed and unfolded by God Himself. The only way for man to understand the mystery of marriage is to ask the God who established it to interpret it for us.

But if marriage is mystery, it is also mathematics. My freshman year in college, I was a pre-engineering student. I spent most of my time working equations, and I discovered something very early on that was important: if you begin with the wrong premise, you'll end with the wrong answer. If your equation is set up improperly, if you feed in the wrong variables at the beginning, regardless of how conscientiously you work, you will never arrive at the right answer.

According to God, in the mathematics of marriage, one plus one equals…one. Not one-half plus one-half equals one, or one plus one equals two. One plus one equals one. God's mysterious marriage math irritates feminists, puzzles unbelievers and confounds the sociologists who suggest living together or "serial monogamy" as bright solutions to man's alone-ness. But they begin with the wrong premise. It was God's idea that marriage would be a relationship of happiness and joy and fulfillment, part mystery, part mathematics, and all for our good and His glory.

Read: *Song of Solomon* 7: 10-13

If you are married, check your math. Have you begun with the wrong premise or equation?

The Tuning Fork of God

"Bless the Lord, O my soul; and all that is within me, bless His holy name."

PSALM 103:1

Do you know how to worship? I don't mean do you know how to kneel, sing two or three songs, give an offering, jot down a few sermon notes and shake hands at the door on the way out—I mean, do you really know how to worship the Living God? In Psalms 103, David calls *himself* to worship, and in so doing, he shows us how to worship God with all that we are.

First, worship is personal. Although we may be in a crowd of other folks, God does not see us as one big mass of people, but as individuals. "Bless the Lord, O *my* soul," David writes. We are to adore or "bless" God individually, so there is a private aspect to our public worship. Our "soul," or the sum total of our entire personality, is to be involved. Also, we are to worship him internally, with all that is within us. That means my conscience, my will, my purpose, my emotions, my spirit, my energy…all that is within me is to worship God. My inward presence, not my outward posture, is the key. Finally, we are to worship God intelligently, remembering His benefits—that is, all that He has done for us. True worship engages not just our emotions, but our mind.

All of the strings of our lives are being tuned by God. He didn't just tune us when we were born and let us go through life becoming more and more off-key. He continuously tunes the lives of His children, touching one string, then another, and bringing it back to perfect pitch. The last time you were sick, could God have been plucking a string to slow you down and re-focus your attention on Him? What about that promotion you received at work? Was God touching another string to see how you handle success? In all the in's and out's of life, God the Father is running His loving hands over the strings of your life and my life, getting us in tune with Him—and worship is the tuning fork that establishes the pitch: *"Bless the Lord, O my soul; and all that is within me, bless His holy name."*

Read: Psalm 103: 1-22

Plan a time of private worship today, and bless God with all that is within you.

Satisfaction

*"For He has satisfied the thirsty soul, and the hungry soul
He has filled with what is good."*

PSALM 107:9

Mick Jagger and the Rolling Stones spoke for a generation when they sang, "I can't get no satisfaction." Every one on the planet desires it. Some have it, but most do not. Three decades after the Stones' driving anthem, many who sang along are still vainly seeking satisfaction. Like cows seek the greener grass in the next pasture, they crane their necks through barbed wire for a scant taste of something different, something more.

Let me tell you something. You can poke through that fence. You can change jobs. Leave your mate. Hide from your children. Book a flight on the Concorde. Make more money and spend it all and then some. But apart from God in Jesus Christ, *there is no satisfaction*! It's that simple. Every field that looks green from a distance is filled with beggar-lice, brown spots and cockleburs up close. Nothing but Jesus satisfies the deepest desires of a person's heart.

The man who has everything but Christ has nothing. And the man who has Christ plus nothing, has everything. The heart is restless—forever seeking satisfaction—until it finds its rest in Him.

Read: *Psalm* 107:1-9

Make a list of the things you secretly think would bring satisfaction. Then find someone who has those things, and ask them if they are truly satisfied, or if they are still looking for something more.

Far Removed

"As far as the east is from the west, so far has He removed our transgressions from us."

PSALM 103:12

It's easy to adore One who can remove our sins so lovingly and thoroughly. Through the blood of Jesus Christ, our sins are taken away. The Bible says God's lovingkindness to us is as high as the heavens. How high is that? Well, the farthest object the human eye can see is estimated to be ten billion light years away—and a light year is the speed of light traveling at 186,000 miles per second! Multiply that by 60 seconds in a minute, and then by 60 minutes in an hour, and then by 24 hours in a day, and 365 days a year...you get the picture.

His lovingkindness goes that distance for us. And our sins, we are told, are put away as far from us as the east is from the west. Not north to south, but east to west. You see, north to south is a measurable distance, because the North and South Poles are stationary points on the globe. But east and west are different. You can start going east, and you can go east until you die, and you'll never be going west. You'll still be going east. If you go west (and keep going) you'll be going west until you die. Do you see what the psalmist was saying? God's love and mercy are immeasurable, and our sins, when they are in Christ, are never going to find us again.

There is only one point in the world where an infinite vertical line and an infinite horizontal line meet, and that one point is Calvary. At the cross, God's mercy intersected our sin, and through the blood of Jesus Christ, cleansed us once and forever. Is it any wonder we adore Him?

Read: *Luke 5: 15-26*

 Praise God for how perfectly and thoroughly your sins have been removed through the blood of Jesus.

Intimacy Starts With Listening

MEMORIZE

*"Let me see your form, let me hear your voice;
for your voice is sweet and your form is lovely."*

SONG OF SOLOMON 2:14

Some say finding true relational intimacy is as difficult as finding gold. Many husbands and wives are tired of feeling estranged, lonely and uninvolved. They long to exchange their emptiness for a loving, intimate relationship with their mate. And I can tell you something: real intimacy with the one you love is possible. Some prospectors do find gold—and the one who finds relational intimacy with his or her mate finds something a lot more valuable than gold.

How is this intimacy achieved? I believe it begins with the ears. That's right. When a husband or wife decides to plumb the depths of their mate's heart, mind and emotions, they must begin by listening—really listening. I hope it is no surprise to anyone that being in the same room while another person is talking does not constitute listening! My middle son Ben taught me this lesson in a graphic way many years ago. He would talk to me as I was reading the paper or just sitting quietly. Realizing he did not have my full attention, he'd crawl up into my lap, take my face in both of his hands and say, "Daddy, I'm telling you something. Are you listening?"

Don't just hear with your ears. Listen with your mind and heart for the emotions behind the words. Is your mate worried? Glad? Frightened? Hopeful? Do they want your advice, or just your agreement that what they are saying is indeed significant? You won't know unless you listen. Listen with your body, too. Lean in when your mate is speaking. Touch them gently as they talk. Make eye contact. Nod. Put anything you might be working on down. There is nothing more precious than a moment in which your mate opens the door to his or her heart. Don't miss the opportunity for deepening intimacy because you were too lazy or distracted to listen.

ACTION

Read: *Song of Solomon 2: 8-14*

For five minutes today, shut everything down, and ask someone important in your life, "What's really going on with you?"

Do The Right Thing

"But prove yourselves doers of the word, and not merely hearers who delude themselves."
JAMES 1:22

James said, "to one who knows the right thing to do, and does not do it, to him it is sin." Some folks have the mistaken idea that sin is something you do that you shouldn't. It could also be something you don't do that you should. Theologians call these undone acts of obedience "sins of omission."

There is a Japanese legend about a very godly man who died and went to Heaven. A heavenly guide was taking him around the Holy City, and he was astounded at all that he saw. It was more beautiful than he had heard or read; more perfect than he could ever have imagined. The streets were gold, jewels glimmered in the light that never subsided. There was music and praise and celebration and joy everywhere he looked. As he walked farther, he came to what appeared to be a little shop. Inside, there was row upon row upon row of what looked to be dried mushrooms! As he looked closer, he saw they were not mushrooms at all...but human ears. "What does this mean?" he asked his guide. "Why are these here?" The guide said, "these ears belonged to people on earth who worshipped God and listened to His precepts, but never did anything about what they heard. Their bodies went to Hell, and only their ears got to Heaven."

Certainly we do not go to heaven "in pieces." But the point is well illustrated. We are to be doers of the Word—not merely hearers only.

Read: James 1: 22-27

Is there an area of your life where you have not made the leap from hearing to doing?

One "I Do,"
Many "I Don'ts"

"Then they called Rebekah and said to her, 'Will you go with this man?' and she said, 'I will go'."

GENESIS 24:58

Those who are single are always interested in knowing how married couples chose their mates. "How do you know the one who's right for you?" they ask. With the divorce rate nearing 50%, and with Christian couples divorcing at a rate nearly equal to the general population—it's a good question. As someone said, it's better for your plane to have mechanical problems on the ground, trying to take off, than in the air, trying to land. In other words: do your serious checking up front! Your aim is to say one "I do," and in the process, you'll say many "I don'ts."

The story of Isaac's selection of Rebekah as his wife is recorded in Genesis 24. It seems archaic, but it contains some excellent principles. Isaac sought a wife with enough similarities to his background to be compatible, and enough differences to be interesting. He sought a God-fearing, kind, chaste woman...and one to whom he was attracted. And prayer was an integral part of the process. All these are excellent guidelines, I believe.

A columnist in my hometown has another suggestion that I think is a good one. He called it "The Window Washing Test." Leon Hale recommends that every couple seriously contemplating marriage should wash the windows on a house with at least seven rooms. Let one person work the inside, and the other the outside. The first part of the day will probably go fine. "You missed a spot, sweetie. It's on your side." "Oh, you're right. It is." But by late afternoon, Hale said, you're hot, tired, and thirsty. Your patience is running low. "It's on your side," one might say. "No, it's on yours. You're just not rubbing hard enough," the other would respond. Soon you're shouting through the window. Hale concluded that if you can wash windows for a day with someone, and at the end of that day you can still laugh and smile and embrace—you just may be on to something.

ACTION

Read: *Genesis* 24: 15-60

 If you are trusting God for a mate, keep praying, keep trusting, and go about whatever tasks He has placed before you, confident in His providence.

Qualified To Judge?

"He summons the heavens above, and the earth, to judge His people."

PSALM 50:4

Have you ever asked the question, "Why does God allow tragedy to happen?" Or, "Why do good people suffer?" "Why cancer?" "Why murder?" "Why deceit and brokenheartedness?" God is the recipient of so many of our "Why?" questions. But the heavens declare the righteousness of God as our judge. He cannot rule wrongly. He is completely just.

There's an old story in which God is accused of living a very sheltered life. All the people of the world are standing before Him awaiting judgment, and they are complaining. "You're not qualified to judge us," they claim. A German Jew pulls up her sleeve and says, "I was in a Nazi concentration camp where we were beaten and tortured and killed. What could you know about that?" Another man, an African, spoke up. "Do you see these rope burns? I was hanged for my black skin, and my brothers suffocated on slave traders' ships. What could you know about that?" Soon all the suffering people of the world began to murmur against the judgment of God. "You don't know what it's like," they cried. "You've never been where we've been. You live in Heaven, where you sit upon your throne. You're not qualified to judge those of us who have suffered, because you have lived a sheltered life." Then they described the kind of God who would be qualified to judge them: "He would be an ordinary man with no special power to help himself; the legitimacy of his birth would be questioned. He would advocate an unpopular cause, one so radical that he would be hated and condemned by worldly authorities. He would be asked to communicate something that no man had seen, heard, tasted or touched. He would be betrayed by his friends, indicted by a crooked jury, tortured and put to death, feeling absolutely forsaken by all."

When all the requirements for a God who might judge were read and agreed upon, the masses grew silent. No one moved. No one spoke. They realized that God had already served the sentence they had prescribed. God's credentials to be our judge are impeccable. His ways are perfect. His justice is pure. And when we can see Him face to face and ask Him every "why?" we've ever wondered, the answers won't matter anymore.

Read: *Psalm 50: 1-6*

Have you ever questioned the judgments of God? Consider His credentials for ultimate righteousness.

A King's Confession: "My Bad."

"Against Thee, Thee only, I have sinned, and done what is evil in Thy sight."

PSALM 51:4

I've stood at the door of the church on many Sundays and heard this comment over and over again: "Preacher, that sermon was just for me. You were talking about me, and I know it." The truth is, I'm not preaching "at" anybody. If someone is convicted, it is the Holy Spirit touching a heart, not me aiming for it.

This kind of conviction happened to King David after his affair with Bathsheba, and his murder of her husband, Uriah. David heard these words of Asaph in worship: "you hate discipline, and you cast My words behind you. You let your mouth loose in evil, and your tongue frames deceit." When he heard them, the Holy Spirit whispered, "David, it's you." And King David said, "I have sinned," or, in today's cultural slang, "My bad." David owned his sin. And he confessed it publicly in a song of his own—Psalm 51.

Before he was ever confronted by the prophet Nathan, David was stung by the words of a song sung in worship. That the king would eventually (although he was confronted in private by Nathan) confess his sin in public was nothing short of a miracle! David was at the pinnacle of his career. He was powerful. He was popular. And he could have denied Nathan's charge, but he could not deny God's conviction.

King David confessed to God and to the people. And he pled for the mercy of God based on His lovingkindness, and nothing more.

Read: *Psalm* 50: 16-23

Has the Holy Spirit convicted you of a specific sin? Have you confessed it and asked for forgiveness?

Heart Surgery

MEMORIZE

"Create in me a clean heart, O God, and renew a steadfast spirit within me."

PSALM 51:10

What medicine and technology can do for the human heart is nothing short of amazing. I know. I've experienced it first hand, through a nifty little procedure called angioplasty. Angioplasty opens a blocked vessel using a "balloon" catheter to press the blockage against the vessel wall, allowing blood to flow more freely. In my case, it took just a few minutes to alleviate the problem caused by fifty years of southern fried chicken, hot dogs, biscuits and gravy and pecan pie. But I didn't get any new hardware. The doctors just fixed up what I had before.

Sin has done more damage—permanent, irreparable damage—to our hearts than fat, cholesterol or a lack of exercise ever could. The heart that is sick with sin cannot be fixed up…it must be replaced. We need a new heart, not a better old one. No amount of patching, bypassing or medicating can help us. Only a new heart will do.

David prayed to God to create in him a clean, new heart. The Hebrew word he used for create was "bara," and it means to make something out of nothing! When you and I see the damage sin has done to our hearts, we begin to understand that, apart from God's amazing grace, we are beyond repair. We need a new heart, and the kind of new start, that only the blood of Jesus Christ can provide.

ACTION

Read: *Psalm* 51:10-13

Thank God for the new heart that is yours if you belong to Jesus Christ.

The Poison of Envy

"Whom have I in heaven but Thee? And besides Thee, I desire nothing on earth."

PSALM 73:25

The wicked still prosper. Have you noticed? Embezzlers get rich, if they don't get caught. Liars win the race. Scoundrels get the girl. Mean-spirited gossips get voted "most friendly." Go figure. But we do go figure…and that's where the trouble really begins. Because when we start to speculate about why the wicked prosper, we can't help but envy their success, even when it's ill-gained.

The psalmist saw the same thing. He told God, "My wicked neighbor has the world by the tail! He's prosperous, fat, happy and proud. And that's just the outside. I don't even want to begin to speculate about what's in his filthy heart. And here I am, playing by the rules and struggling just to make it through the day. What gives, God? Are you paying attention?"

If we let this kind of thinking run free, we'll certainly be the most miserable among men. The answer to envy is worship. In worship, we see God as He is, and we understand how little we understand! In worship, our focus is removed from our neighbor and ourselves, and riveted on God alone. When that happens, we gain perspective, understanding that the end of wickedness is ruin and loss, and the end of the pursuit of God is joy forever.

Read: Psalm 73: 1-28

What do the words, "God is the strength of my heart and my portion forever" mean to you?

Greed Is Killed By Giving

"...beware, and be on your guard against every form of greed..."

LUKE 12:15

I've been a pastor for thirty-plus years, and I've heard the confession of just about every kind of sin you can imagine, except one. In all my years of pastoring, I've never heard anyone confess to the sin of greed. Not one single time! Yet, in every listing of the seven deadly sins, greed is present, and the evidence of greed in our everyday lives is very real.

What most people don't understand is this: you can be a greedy rich person, or you can be a greedy person who is poor. And greed is a monster that saps your strength, your energy and your emotions. Left unchecked, it will dominate your life.

A Gallup survey done in the late 1970's revealed that 50 percent of college freshmen were just as interested in having a meaningful life as they were in achieving financial security. In a similar survey conducted in 1987, 81 percent of college freshmen were more interested in financial security than they were in building a meaningful life! So the sin of greed has made inroads through the years. But for a culture that is bent on getting, and choked with greed, there is a way out. It's called giving. Greed is killed by giving. Do you own something that you cannot give away? Then you do not own it...it owns you. Are you satisfied with what you have, or are you driven by the desire to have "just a little bit more?" If it's more you're after, slay the monster of greed by the virtue of giving. Give until it hurts...then keep giving until it begins to feel better. You'll be surprised at the freedom giving brings.

Read: *Luke 12: 13-21*

   What do you have that seems to own you? Can you kill greed by giving it away?

Where Do You Live?

MEMORIZE

"Lord, Thou hast been our dwelling place in all generations."

PSALM 90:1

One of the first things most parents teach their children as soon as they can is their home address and phone number. Mom and Dad want their little ones to know where they live if they should ever become lost or separated from them. But knowing the answer to the question, "Where do you live?" is helpful for adults, too.

A young Nazi was being initiated into a very elite group of soldiers and was asked by his commanding officer, "Son, where do you live?" "I live in Stuttgart, sir," he replied. "Wrong answer!" barked the officer. "Where do you live?" The soldier thought and answered a second time: "I live in Germany, sir." The officer inched closer to him, and shouted more loudly than before: "Wrong! Where do you live?" Now he had it. "I live in the Third Reich, sir." But he was wrong again. When he was asked the fourth time, the young soldier gave up, saying "Sir, I don't know how to answer." The officer then told him, "From this day forward, when someone asks you 'Where do you live?' you say, 'I live in Hitler'." His residence was not a place...but a person.

Moses, at the end of his life, still did not dwell in Canaan...he lived in the Lord God Almighty. That was his home address. God was his dwelling place. The problem with most of those who are Christians is that they do not dwell or abide in Christ...they just come home for a visit every now and then. They visit on Sundays. On Easter and Christmas. In times of personal crisis, perhaps. But they do not make their home in Him. Jesus said "Abide in me." We do not need to wonder for a moment where we should live.

QUESTION

Read: *Psalm 90: 1-6*

What could you do this week to remind yourself of your home address?

Number Your Days

MEMORIZE

"So teach us to number our days, that we may present to Thee a heart of wisdom."

PSALM 90:12

"Ohne life to live, soon will be past. Only what's done for God will last." Fame, power, popularity, riches and influence will be a memory one day...but the things we do for God and Christ will last forever. With that in mind, we are to number, or measure our days, so that we can present to God a heart of wisdom and a life of meaning.

John was a fellow in a church I pastored years ago. He accepted Christ in his sixties, and when he did, he became a regular at every church service, event and meeting. He was at the church so often that someone suggested I speak to him, so I did. "John," I said, "you know church is church, but you're up here all the time. Don't you think you could miss a meeting or two?" He said, "Pastor, I've been away from the Lord for 64 years, and now that I have found Christ, I want all of Him I can possibly get."

John was making up for lost time—for the years that passed without peace and salvation and fullness. But each one of us needs to measure our days. Do you number yours? If the average life expectancy is 80 years, is it noon in your life? Or 6:00 p.m., or 8:00 p.m.? Take note of the time, and remember that only what's done for *Him* will stand its test.

ACTION

Read: *Psalm 90: 9-12*

Ask someone who knows you well if you are a good steward of your time, and if they believe you are focusing on eternal things.

The Majesty And Glory

MEMORIZE

"O Lord, our Lord, how majestic is Thy name in all the earth."

PSALM 8:1

G od doesn't just have name recognition...He has name respect. David penned these words of praise following his victory in God's name over the Philistine giant Goliath. No doubt God's name was majestic in Israel on that day...but what about today? Is the Lord's name excellent over all the earth? A half billion Buddhists would say no. A quarter billion Hindus would say no. Millions of atheists and agnostics would say no. But there are also millions who would say "O Lord, our Lord, how majestic is Thy name in all the earth." And the day will come when every knee shall bow and every tongue shall confess that Jesus Christ is Lord, to God's great glory!

"How could God's name be majestic today," some might ask, "if there are no more giants to kill?" Is it possible for God to be glorified in our day and age through the lives of ordinary believers like you and me? It is! In fact, our ordinary-ness is His natural avenue for glory. "When we are weak," the apostle Paul said, "He is strong."

This has been God's way throughout history. Moses—the baby in the bullrushes—eventually overthrew Pharaoh and his kingdom. God Himself became a baby in Bethlehem and turned our world "right side up" with His coming. It is almost as if the limitations of His people are a perfect background to display His brilliance. Have you ever bought a diamond? If you have, the jeweler probably showed it to you on a piece of dark velvet. The dark, dull velvet sets off the facets of a diamond beautifully. Can God's majesty and glory shine in our dark world? Yes it can...and does...and will.

REFLECTION

Read: *Psalm 8: 1-9*

Consider the work of His fingers and the depth of His love today.

The Champion

MEMORIZE

"What is man, that Thou dost take thought of him?
And the son of man, that Thou dost care for him?"

PSALM 8:4

Goliath was the Philistine champion who walked the no man's land between the camp of the Israelites and the camp of the Philistines. Goliath ruled that real estate without dispute until a little shepherd guy named David challenged him, saying "I come to you in the name of the Lord of hosts, the God of the armies of Israel, whom you have taunted." And then out-weighed, inexperienced David issued to Goliath what must have seemed like the most ridiculous death threat ever: "I'm going to come down there and take your head off!" And he did!

David took Goliath's title as champion, but his victory was simply a foreshadowing of the one that would be won by the real champion, the Lord Jesus Christ. Jesus is the champion's champion who stepped into the no man's land between holy God and sinful man, and bridged the gap with His own blood. When you are in God's camp, and Jesus is in your heart and life, you too can walk between the lines of God's kingdom and this world with assurance and humility.

Knowing that the champion's champion is on your side should give you the confidence to risk and love and grow here in no man's land. There are giants in the land, it's true, but our Lord is majestic and powerful, and His love for His children is stronger than any foe that challenges us.

QUESTION

Read: I Samuel 17: 20-37

What battles is God calling you to fight in His name and for His glory?

On Borrowed Time

MEMORIZE

*"...when the wicked sprouted up like grass...it was only
that they might be destroyed forevermore."*

PSALM 92:7

There will be a day of reckoning for all...and that includes the wicked who seem to be managing quite well at present. God is just, and men reap what they sow. Mark it down: anyone who is living in defiance of Almighty God is living on borrowed time.

To test this, I did a little experiment. I put together a list of five guys who were real troublemakers back when we were in high school in Laurel, Mississippi. I tried to pick out the worst offenders I could think of: guys who were profane, who were immoral and just out and out rebellious. Then I tried to find out what had happened to them in the years since we were in school together.

One died of complications related to alcoholism. Two others were addicted to drugs and alcohol, and had several marriages between them. Their children and their children's children were having problems similar to their own. The fourth one just disappeared. No one knew what had happened to him, or if he were dead or alive. The fifth guy I checked on was working for the government in Jackson, Mississippi. I called him to say hello, and he told me that God had changed his life. (He even told me he was attending church on Wednesday nights!)

The wicked may seem to prosper for a time, but they do not prosper indefinitely. They are like grass. They have their day in the sun, then they wither and perish.

ACTION

Read: *Psalm* 92: 5-9

Take the high school yearbook test. Look up some folks from your past who disregarded God and see where they are today.

Let's Talk Trees

MEMORIZE

"The righteous man will flourish like the palm tree, he will grow like a cedar in Lebanon."

PSALM 92:12

The righteous man, the Bible says, *will* flourish, while the wicked man will be destroyed. If a wicked man is like grass, the psalmist writes, a righteous man is like a tree. And not just any tree. A palm tree.

What's so special about a palm tree? Well, first of all, it grows upright, in harmony with the pull of gravity. A righteous man is upright, too, and his life is in harmony with the moral universe in which he lives. The palm tree also grows in unlikely environments...places where no other tree will grow. It even grows in the desert, its roots reaching down deep for nourishment. In the same way, a spirit filled Christian can thrive in a spiritual desert. Palm trees grow from the center out, not adding external layers, but being renewed from within. A righteous man may show signs of age or wear externally, but he is constantly being renewed from within by the Holy Spirit who dwells in him. Finally, the palm tree is evergreen. It never loses its leaves or turns brown and brittle. It is always in season. The righteous man is full of life, too. As the years go by he grows in grace, always vibrant, always valuable, always flourishing.

The promise of God for the righteous man or woman is that there will be life and sweetness and produce and growth, not just for a brief season, but for an entire lifetime! The wicked have their day...but it is fleeting. The righteous endure, and their productivity only increases as the years go by.

REFLECTION

Read: Psalm 92: 10-15

 How does your life in Christ resemble the palm tree?

God-Pleasing Worship

"For the Lord takes pleasure in His people;
He will beautify the afflicted ones with salvation."

PSALM 149:4

One of the major problems with our worship is that we evaluate it by asking the wrong question. "Did you enjoy worship?" we might ask someone who's just attended a church service. But the point of worship is not that we enjoy it (although certainly we should), but that God is pleased by it and honored through it. A better question would be, "Did God enjoy your worship?"

I've enjoyed the few Broadway shows I've seen. I once tried to get tickets to *My Fair Lady* and could not—and ended up seeing a new show called *Funny Girl* with an unknown actress named Barbra Streisand. (I guess you could say I fell uphill.) In theater, you have the actors, the audience, and an unseen assistant called the prompter—whose job is to whisper cues to the actors when they forget their lines. Most of us have the idea when we worship in church that the preacher is the actor, God is the prompter telling him what to say, and the congregation is the audience. But this is wrong.

In worship, God is the audience, and the congregation is on stage. The preacher is simply a prompter, helping the people focus their attention on God. If worship is true and God-honoring, He is blessed by every hymn sung, every word proclaimed, every gift given and every testimony spoken. It is all about Him...and all for Him.

Read: Psalm 149: 1-9

 Did God get pleasure in the worship you offered Him today?

Freedom And Responsibility

MEMORIZE

*"So then let us pursue the things which make for peace
and the building up of one another."*

ROMANS 14:19

We are free in Christ. Free from sin and death. Free from legalistic rule-keeping. But we are not free from responsibility—and part of our responsibility is to nurture those who are younger and weaker in the faith, even at the cost of our own personal liberty.

My friend Johnny Baker tells a story that illustrates this beautifully. Johnny was an all-American football player for Mississippi State who went on to play for the Houston Oilers. One Saturday Mississippi State played, and defeated, the University of Houston, which was no small accomplishment. Some alumni at the game passed out cigars to the winning team, and Johnny stuck his in his pocket during the trip home. The next day, back in Meridian, Johnny was sitting on the front porch at his folk's house, by himself. He felt in his pocket, and noticed the cigar, opened it, and put it in his mouth. Johnny didn't smoke, but he said he sort of shifted it around in his mouth, and thought about that big win the day before.

In a little while, a young boy walked up to the porch. "How 'ya doin'?" Johnny said. "Come on up here and sit by me a minute." And the boy climbed up to sit next to his big, football-playing neighbor. Johnny and the boy began to talk, and he said in a few minutes, he noticed the boy had a stick in his mouth. Then he remembered the cigar in his. Johnny talked a little more, then reached up, took the cigar out of his mouth, broke it in half, threw it down, and said, "You know, I think I'll quit smoking." The boy took the stick out of his mouth, broke it, threw it down and said, "Yeah. Me, too."

Our liberty in Christ extends only as far as it does not cause a brother or sister in Christ to stumble. When it does, responsibility supercedes freedom.

REFLECTION

Read: *Romans 14: 13-22*

 Could the exercise of your freedom in Christ in a gray area of liberty be keeping someone else in bondage?

Good Job!

"For the report of your obedience has reached to all; therefore I am rejoicing over you..."

ROMANS 16:19

Words of encouragement are among the world's best bargains. They cost so little and can accomplish so much. To hear one's name along with an affirming, "Good job!" quite literally can change a life.

Growing up, I was the textbook definition of "average." Average is the best of the worst, and the worst of the best, and that was me. But in the tenth grade, we had a new history teacher who did not know that I was only average. We were assigned to write a half-page paper on some patriotic subject, and I went home that night and really worked at that little paper. The next day in class, Mr. West said he had graded our papers, and that they were the worst he'd ever seen…except for one. "One paper, " he said, "was just outstanding. Edwin Young, would you lift your hand?" And from the back row, timidly, I raised my hand, and turned a corner as a student. I began to use what giftedness I had. I developed a love for history, and majored in it in college. I became a fellow in the history department, and graded papers for a professor in that department. All because someone rejoiced in me and said, "Good job."

Has anyone rejoiced over you? Paul rejoiced over his Christian brothers and sisters in Rome, calling many of them by name at the end of his letter. He said, "I rejoice in your obedience, and I have big plans, big dreams for you. I want you to be strong in the faith, and effective in your witness. And by the way—you're doing a great job!"

Read: Romans 16: 19-27

Plan to rejoice over the good work of another today, and tell them they're doing a good job.

Trust, Obey And Follow

"And she named him Moses, and said, 'because I drew him out of the water.'"

EXODUS 2:10

The Dreamworks team in Hollywood has discovered a new star. They've packaged him as the *Prince of Egypt*...but we've known him for a long time now as simply Moses. His story is full of drama and action and conflict, and has been the subject of more than one movie. But at its core, it is a very basic story of one man learning to follow, trust and obey God.

Moses had a rocky start. He was nearly lost at birth, but was adopted into Pharaoh's household instead. He grew up an Egyptian prince, but he was really the son of a Hebrew slave. He lived in two worlds until he was forty, then decided to cast his lot with his own people...but that quickly backfired. His intentions were good—but Moses tried to do what he believed was God's work his own way. Sound familiar to anyone? He killed an Egyptian who was beating a Hebrew, then buried his body in the sand. He thought no one saw, but he was found out. Maybe he didn't dig deep enough, and as those desert winds blew, his victim's toes were soon sticking up out of the sand!

When we take our evil and sin and try to bury it, we're never successful. It keeps coming back up. We're forced to lie more, deceive more, if we want to cover our original sin. Then fear comes in. Let sin come into your life and fear will quickly follow. A man told me once, "I never knew gut-wrenching, paralyzing fear until I began to cheat on my wife. Then I lived every day in sheer terror of being found out." When Moses struck and killed the Egyptian, he looked east and west...but he didn't look up. He was concerned about what men might see, but hadn't considered the eyes of God. Confronted with his sin and rejected by his people, he did the only thing he knew to do: he ran. Until we are ready to trust, obey and follow God, we are not ready to be used by God, no matter how good our credentials or our intentions!

Read: Exodus 2: 11-15

 Is there a secret sin you are hiding that is keeping you out of the game for God?

Timing

MEMORIZE

"Therefore, come now, and I will send you to Pharaoh, so that you may bring My people, the sons of Israel, out of Egypt."

EXODUS 3:10

Timing is so important. It is the common denominator of every great comedian from Red Skelton and Jack Benny to Bill Cosby and Jerry Seinfeld. It is the secret of so many things, from cooking to commodities trading, and it can be the difference between success and failure in any endeavor. Did you know that you can do the right thing at the wrong time and it will end up being the wrong thing? Ask Moses. Timing is critical.

The number one enemy of God's timing is impatience. His plan is best, and His timing is perfect, but we often get impatient. My friend Jeannette Clift George likes to say with a chuckle that God has never been late, although He has missed many good opportunities to come early! I can identify with that sentiment. We have the mistaken idea that to be impatient is a show of strength—but just the opposite is true. When you see someone walking a dog that is straining on the leash, bucking and snorting and choking—do you think the problem is that his master is moving too slowly, or that the dog has not learned to heel?

It is a great day when a man or woman decides to put their talents and abilities and passions to work for God's cause. It is a greater day when that same person waits for God to say how and where and when.

REFLECTION

Read: Exodus 3: 1-10

 Determine to wait for God's perfect timing in some specific area, and quit pulling against His loving lead.

The Baton of Disobedience

*"Now the Lord said to Moses in Midian, 'Go back to Egypt,
for all the men who were seeking your life are dead'."*

EXODUS 4:19

Have you ever been faced with a serious setback along the road of obedience? You are following God and seeking His will, then bang!—disaster strikes. It happened to Moses. He was on his way back to Egypt with his wife and family, and all set to confront Pharaoh, when he became so ill he thought he would die. In Moses' case (and sometimes in ours, too) the problem was an old sin that hadn't been addressed. He had been so busy gearing up for God's program that he had neglected a matter of obedience in his own family. He had failed to circumcise his son. Does that seem petty? Does it seem like a little thing? It was not little in the sight of God.

If you make up your mind that you want God's best for your life, if you commit to seek and follow His will, if God's blessing matters more to you than anything, God will hold you to it. And He'll take you back every time to the place you got off track and give you the chance to begin again. Moses dropped the baton of obedience by failing to circumcise his son. He thought he was ready to do God's bidding, and to face the leaders of the most powerful nation on earth, but first there was a small matter of obedience to rectify at home.

Have you ever watched a relay race in a track meet? A baton is passed from runner to runner, and the exchange can add or subtract vital seconds to the runners' score. If the baton is dropped, it must be picked up. The runner who finishes the race without it—even if he finishes first—is disqualified. When a sin of omission or commission blocks your progress, if you have the human power to do so, you must go back and get it right. Only when you have done so are you ready to move on and be blessed by God in the race of life.

Read: *Exodus 4: 18-31*

 Can you think of an instance of disobedience in which you dropped the baton? If possible, return to that spot and get it right.

Returning To God

"Then Moses returned to the Lord..."

EXODUS 5:22

D o you know the secret of Christians whose lives are full and vital and productive for the kingdom of God? It's not that they never face opposition or failure. Their secret of success is that when they do, they return to God. They just keep going back to Him for guidance, encouragement, wisdom and strength.

Moses was following God's precise instructions when he went to Pharaoh and asked for the release of the Hebrews so that they could worship God in the wilderness. But Pharaoh's response wasn't what Moses anticipated. "If you have enough time to worship," he said, "you've got more time than I thought. From now on, I'm holding you to your production quota of bricks, but you've got to gather all your own materials, too."

Moses was in a jam. He had done God's will, yet he was boxed in by Pharaoh's edict and his own people's anger. Forty years before, he would have run away. This time, he ran to God. When your life bottoms out, run. But run in the right direction. When we run to God, whether we are crying, questioning or complaining, we've come to the right place. The walk of faith is a constant returning to God and venturing out, over and over again.

Read: *Exodus 5: 1-23*

When you find yourself in confusing or crippling circumstances, do you run away, or run to Him?

"With Every Hoof I Have."

MEMORIZE

*"You shall fear only the Lord your God; and you shall worship Him,
and swear by His name."*

DEUTERONOMY 6:13

I f Satan cannot win an outright victory, he will attempt a compromise. As the showdown between Moses and Pharaoh was drawing to a close, Moses was offered two final compromises. "Go," Pharaoh said, "and worship your God. But leave your women and children here with us." Moses refused. "Then take them, too," Pharaoh countered, "but leave your livestock." Again Moses refused. "Not a hoof will be left behind," he told Pharaoh. Deliverance was to be complete; not partial. Moses refused to compromise.

When he left Egypt to worship God in the wilderness, Moses took every Israelite, man, woman and child, and every goat, cow and sheep that belonged to Israel. He wanted to worship God with every hoof he had! The only way you and I can truly worship God is with everything we have. Every possession. Every blessing. Every dream. Everything. Moses refused to offer God partial obedience and compromised worship. What would our lives be like if we did the same?

Are you giving everything you have to God? Or are you only offering partial devotion, partial obedience, partial worship? What has your devotion to God cost you? David refused to furnish God's temple with gifts that had cost him nothing. Moses refused to worship God with anything less than all he had. David knew, and Moses knew, that God asks for everything. C. S. Lewis said, *"In love, He claims all. There is no bargaining with Him."* Are you succumbing to Satan's temptation to love God with less than every hoof you have?

ACTION

Read: *Exodus* 10: 21-29

Ask God to reveal to you anything that you may be holding back in your worship of Him.

The Passover Lamb

MEMORIZE

*"And the blood shall be a sign for you on the houses where you live;
and when I see the blood I will pass over you..."*

EXODUS 12:13

Can you imagine the media attention that would ensue if every first-born of every household in one nation were mysteriously struck dead at midnight? It would be a bigger story than a jet crash, or an international hostage situation, or even a mass cult suicide. Think of it. Every firstborn. In every house. In a single night. Unless...

Unless you were a foreigner who had followed an equally mysterious prescription for deliverance that involved the blood of a lamb. Unless you had slaughtered this lamb and spread its blood over the doorposts of your home as a signal to the death angel to pass you by. Now this is some story, is it not? Can you see the investigators who would follow such a story today? The Columbo-types in rumpled raincoats trying to make sense of the supernatural using finite wisdom? It would be impossible.

The message of the Passover is the same today as it was on that historical night in Egypt: there is no salvation except by the grace of God. In the Old Testament and the New Testament, people were saved in the same way: by the grace of God. The Hebrews who experienced Passover were saved by a spotless lamb, and so are we: the spotless Lamb of God whose name is Jesus. His blood marks us as righteous, and the judgment of God passes over us, delivering us from the consequences of our sin. God's initiative is grace. Our response is faith. That is the prescription for salvation that was first depicted in Passover.

ACTION

Read: Exodus 12: 1-13

 Thank God for His Passover Lamb, whose blood keeps on cleansing us from all unrighteousness.

Seeing Salvation

"Do not fear! Stand by and see the salvation of the Lord which He will accomplish for you today..."

EXODUS 14:13

What do you do when you have followed God into a situation that seems impossible? Three things. First, you eliminate fear. "Do not fear," Moses told God's people as they were hemmed in by the Red Sea and Pharaoh's army. Second, you must stand by, or stand fast. God is working, even if you cannot see His hand. Finally, you must see the salvation of the Lord.

How do I do that, you may ask? What is the salvation of the Lord? It is a backward look, and a forward look. It is the sum total of all that God has done, is doing and will do on your behalf, for His glory. It is a retrospective look at His past promises and blessings, and a prospective view of His future grace. The Israelites could look back and see God's promise to Abraham, His provision to Isaac, and His blessings on Jacob. They could see the ten plagues, the Passover, and their deliverance from Egypt. They could see the pillar of fire and the cloud that had led them to this place.

But the salvation of the Lord has a future component, too. Based on all that God has done in the past, we can look forward and anticipate with confidence that He will continue to display His manifold faithfulness in the future. Are you in a cul-de-sac like the Israelites? Is a crisis immanent? Fear not! Stand by! See the salvation of the Lord.

Read: *Exodus* 14: 1-31

 How can you apply these principles to your own times of testing? Will you?

The "Who" of Worship

"You shall have no other gods before Me."

EXODUS 20:3

Scientist and humorist P. D. East wrote a novel that depicted the world on the brink of disaster. Leaders of the super-power nations were fingering the controls that would bring civilization to a close. Negotiations had ceased. Lines were drawn. Just as the curtain was about to come down, there was a reprieve, and a forty-eight hour moratorium was announced for some sense to be made of the nonsense of war. All the leaders met together, bringing the sources of wisdom from their particular cultures. The Bible. The Koran. Folk wisdom. Social science. All were amassed and the information fed into a giant computer. Then they asked the question of the computer, "What is the formula for world peace?" The machine blinked and whirred and groaned until it spoke these words: "Thou shalt have no other gods before Me."

This is the first of the Ten Commandments given to Israel through Moses. These commandments are not the final word on ethics and morality. Jesus gave us that when He said, "Thou shalt love the Lord thy God with all thy heart, with all thy soul, with all thy mind and with all thy strength, and thou shalt love thy neighbor as thyself." The commandments are, however, the precepts on which civilized morality rests. They are still valid, and they are still truthful. You do not break them. They break you.

When God instructs Israel to have no other "little-g" gods before Him, He is not seeking to prove His existence. He doesn't have to. He is the great I Am. He is saying that He alone is to be worshipped, honored and obeyed. Is He first in your life?

Read: *Exodus 20:3*

Take an "idol inventory." Judging from your checkbook and your calendar, what do you worship?

The "How" of Worship

MEMORIZE

"You shall not make for yourself an idol, or any likeness..."

EXODUS 20:4

The first commandment tells us *whom* we are to worship. The second commandment tells us *how* we are to worship. We are not to place any object that we can see or touch before our praise and adoration and thanksgiving to God.

We naturally desire to put a "face" on God to help us relate to Him. We long to worship something we can see. The Australian essayist Frank Borem tells the story of an old Scotsman who, as a boy, had trouble concentrating in prayer. He told his pastor, "I can't imagine that God is really there and is listening to my prayers." His pastor suggested that when he pray, he place an empty chair before him and imagine that Jesus Christ was seated in the chair. So at a young age, this Scotsman began a practice that he continued throughout his life. Early one morning he slipped out of bed, and hours later, he was found with his cold hand on the empty chair. He died in the presence of the One to whom he had prayed for so many years.

The man in this story used his chair as a visible "cue" to imagine an unseeable God...but he did not worship the chair. He only used it as a reminder of God's presence. It helped his devotional life, and in this way, he became a strong disciple. But when a created thing becomes the object of our worship instead of a vehicle for it, we are guilty of idolatry. Never let anything come between you and your worship of Almighty God.

QUESTION

Read: *Exodus 20: 4-6*

What are some contemporary idols that you might be tempted to worship before God?

The Rock That Is Higher

"And the Lord came down on Mount Sinai,
to the top of the mountain…and Moses went up."
EXODUS 19:20

The top of Sinai was a descent for God, but an ascent for Moses. God came down. Moses went up. God gave the commandments. Moses received them. It is obvious, isn't it, that He is supreme, and that His authority is higher than anything else? The Ten Commandments are not suggestions that have stood the test of time. They are timeless truths, woven into the very fabric of the created universe.

When New Bedford was the center for whaling vessels, one sea captain was known to be superior to all others. His name was Hull, and he was a folk hero in that town. He was asked his secret of successful whaling many times, and this is what he would say: "I go up on deck, and I listen to the sound of the wind in the rigging. I study the tides very carefully, then I take a long look at the stars and chart my course accordingly." Years passed, and times changed. Insurance companies would no longer cover a vessel unless they had someone on board who was trained in modern navigational procedure. Captain Hull had three choices. He could quit his job, hire a younger, trained navigator, or learn the new methods himself. He opted for the latter, and went to school. On his first voyage after completing his study, he was more successful than ever before. The townspeople could not wait to ask him about it. "Did you use all your new instruments and techniques?" they wanted to know. "Oh, yes," he replied. "I went down to the chartroom and read my instruments and worked my equations. Then I went up on the deck, listened to the wind, studied the tides, and took a long, long look at the stars so I could go back down and correct my equations."

We live in a different world than the one Moses knew. But although the times are different, the truth is not. God's commands are still relevant today, and will ever be so.

Read: *Exodus* 19: 18-25

 Ask God to give you a renewed sense of His holiness and authority over your life.

The Price of Anger

MEMORIZE

"For the anger of man does not achieve the righteousness of God."

JAMES 1:20

It was Moses' temper—his anger—that kept him from realizing the central purpose of his life. He was called by God, commissioned to lead, brought out of the fields of Midian and uniquely equipped to bring his own people through the wilderness. But he never stood in the land of Canaan because of his anger.

Psychologists tell us there are five levels or degrees of the emotion we call anger. The first level is irritation. The second is indignancy. Then our indignant spirit turns to wrathful action. Fury follows wrath, and fury fed becomes rage. Anger is a serious thing...and its consequences, as in the case of Moses, can be devastating.

Moses was irritated by nearly 40 years of crying and complaining by the people of Israel. He was indignant that they would still be saying, "If only we had died with our brothers in the wilderness." His wrath began to burn when they cried, "Why did you bring us here?" as if the exodus had been his idea and not God's. And his wrath became fury when he struck the rock at Meribah. God's judgment for Moses' anger was quick. "Because you have not believed Me, to treat Me as holy," He said, "you shall not bring this assembly into the land." Moses' anger reflected the unbelief still in his heart, and his action dishonored God before His people. Our anger, too, can often be traced to disbelief. And when we let it loose in a fit of fury, the God we say is ours is not treated in the holy way that He requires.

REFLECTION

Read: *Numbers* 20: 1-12

Consider the consequences of anger in your life. What did your anger achieve?

Far Enough!

*"...let this land be given to your servants as a possession;
do not take us across the Jordan."*

NUMBERS 32:5

Y ou can have as much of God as you really want. You decide the level
at which you will pursue the things of God. You and I are not saved
just to be safe from Hell—we are saved, or salvaged, to come into
right relationship with God and claim His full blessing and promises. Too
many folks live the Christian life like an old iron bedstead. They are firm at
both ends, but saggy in the middle. They're saved and assured of Heaven,
but their life in between is mediocre, at best. They follow God only so far,
and then say, "Far enough!"

It amazes me that not all of the tribes of Israel wanted to dwell in the
Promised Land. The tribes of Rueben and Gad and the half-tribe of
Manasseh actually opted to live east of the Jordan River! Can you believe it?
They crossed over, saw the land, fought for the land, then re-crossed the
Jordan and settled on the near side!

You say "How foolish they were!" But not any more foolish than some
of us who have experienced the power and blessing of God and retreated to
a "safer" spot to live a "quieter" life! I know of no greater tragedy for the
Christian than to live a life on the basis of that which is second best. These
two and a half tribes were not made up of bad people. They were just disobedient to God in the simplest sense. They decided, "This is as far as I will
go. This is the highest level to God that I am willing to make. I'm not going
to grow. I'm not going to go all the way with Him."

God looks at those who say "far enough" and says, "Come up higher."
But when to do so would mean giving up pleasures, they grow faint and lose
heart, forgoing the full victory and blessing and peace the Father has set
aside for His children.

Read: Joshua 1: 10-18

*Are you living life east of the Jordan? Do you have all that you want
of God?*

What's Your Jericho?

MEMORIZE

"I have given Jericho into your hand, with its king and valiant warriors."

JOSHUA 6:2

There is a Jericho in every life. Your Jericho is the thing that stands between you and all that God wants you to become. It may be a beseting sin that you have tried unsuccessfully to shake. It may be a scar from your past that still hobbles and shames you. Whatever it is, it is blocking you from God's best, and you know it. Perhaps you've tried to handle your Jericho in your own way but have been unable to defeat it. Now what?

God's prescription for the defeat of ancient Jericho was an odd one. March around the city wall thirteen times, he told the Israelites. March in silence. Blow the ram's horn, carry the ark of the covenant before you, and say nothing. Psychological warfare? I don't think so. I think the repetition was for the Israelites' benefit. They had to see that they would be utterly unable to defeat Jericho on their own power. They admitted their powerlessness. And they were patient. They placed their faith in God.

The reason God cannot use so many of us is not the reason we think. It is not because we're too sinful or too hypocritical, or even too weak. It's because we're too strong. We're too boastful and proud and self-confident to tell God that we need help to defeat our Jericho. God specializes in unlikely victories. Depend on Him. Wait on Him patiently, and at His command, shout the shout of faith and watch the walls of your Jericho come down.

ACTION

Read: *Joshua 6: 1-20*

Name the Jericho in your life, and tell God you cannot conquer it without Him.

Regaining Lost Ground

*"...go up to Ai; see, I have given into your hand the king of Ai,
his people, his city and his land."*

JOSHUA 8:1

H ave you noticed it can take thirty minutes (or less!) to get outside the will of God, and thirty years (or more) to get back to the place you were before sin invaded your life? When we lose spiritual ground, when we retreat before the enemy, when we revert to our old ways, it is tough going back. We may confess, make restitution, and start over again with a clean slate, but somehow we don't feel the presence of God like we did before.

Joshua experienced this. He led Israel to a great victory at Jericho. Then God's people suffered a crushing defeat at Ai. When the sin at the root of that defeat was exposed, Joshua dealt with it. Then he humbly received instructions on how to win back the city he had just lost. It was nothing like the way he won Jericho. Joshua learned that following a holy, awesome, powerful God is not a cookie-cutter proposition. One day is not just like the next. One victory does not become the prescription for all victories.

Not only did God have a plan for the re-capture of Israel's lost ground— He had a word of tender encouragement to his defeated leader. "Do not fear or be dismayed," He told Joshua. Defeat is no cause for fear or depression. We will experience defeat in the Christian life, but it is not a permanent condition. It is only a temporary setback. Even when a Christian loses the battle, his God has won the war.

Read: *Joshua* 8: 1-22

*Is God asking you to re-visit an Ai in your life? Listen for His direction,
and do not fear.*

How To Read The Bible

MEMORIZE

"Make me know Thy ways, O Lord; teach me Thy paths."

PSALM 25:4

"The Bible's hard for me to understand," I've heard people say. "I'd like to read it, but I just don't have that much time." There are as many reasons for not studying God's Word as there are people, but there is nothing I know of that is more critical to Christian growth than the Bible. When we read, it is important to look at the passage in context, with an eye toward the history and culture of the time. When there are parallel passages in other books of the Bible, we should read them as well.

We are not to seek Biblical support to validate our own circumstances—we are to seek the truth, and apply that truth to our circumstances. Too many people place themselves above the Bible when they should be placing themselves under its authority.

An old German pastor told his congregation to read the Bible as a shipwrecked person who had lost everything at sea. A shipwrecked person is a *defeated* person. He is needy. We ought to read the Bible with the idea that we have nothing of our own: no righteousness, no merit, no assets. A shipwrecked person is a *desperate* person. If you are out in the ocean and see a piece of debris floating by, you don't wait for a bigger piece. You cling to whatever comes along and hope it will hold you up. We should come to the Bible with a desperate hope to hear from God and to be taught by His Holy Spirit. We need His Word to stay afloat in life. What a shipwrecked person needs most is *deliverance*, and deliverance is the theme of the Bible from beginning to end. It is the scarlet thread of salvation that runs from Eden to Patmos and everywhere in between.

You and I need God's Word like we need air to breathe and water to drink. Don't neglect personal reading and study of the Bible for any reason. It's simply too vital to miss. It will keep you afloat!

ACTION

Read: *Luke 24: 13-27*

If you do not have a good, readable study Bible, look for one today. Ask a Bible study teacher, pastor or Christian friend to recommend their favorite translation.

What's Wrong With The Harvest?

"Do not be deceived, God is not mocked; for whatever a man sows, this he will also reap."

GALATIANS 6:7

Why are so many evangelical churches in America stagnant? Why are more people not coming to know Jesus Christ? If the fruits of our labors in soul-winning are so lean, it is time to ask, "what is wrong with the harvest?"

I'm from a rural background—and I can tell you that when something goes wrong with the harvest, a farmer will do three things. First, he'll take a look at the soil. In the case of soul-harvesting, the soil is the hearts of men. Are Americans no longer interested in God? It would seem so, considering the harvest, but this is simply not true. There is more interest in God, in spiritual things, in this day and age than ever before. People are searching for depth and meaning, asking religious questions and exploring a variety of religions. So the soil looks good to me. The second thing a farmer with a poor crop will do is look at his seed. Was the seed bad? Our seed in evangelism is God's Word. The seed is good—in fact, it is perfect. So perhaps we are sowing sparingly. The Bible says that if you sow sparingly, you will reap sparingly, and if you sow abundantly, you will reap abundantly. Are we sowing mingled seed? The Bible mixed with social ethics or psychology or anything else is rendered less effective by the mingling. If the soil is good and the seed is good, a farmer will look to himself—the sower. You and I are sowers. Not workers. Sowers. And sowers scatter seed. Until you and I want our friends and neighbors and family members to know Christ more than anything—until that becomes our passion and our focus—we cannot expect a rich and bountiful harvest. How are you doing at scattering seed?

Read: *Galatians 6: 7-10*

If you are not comfortable sharing your faith, seek out a friend or leader who "scatters seed" regularly, and ask him to teach you what he knows.

Promises To Keep

MEMORIZE

*"And we desire that each one of you show the same diligence
so as to realize the full assurance of hope until the end."*

HEBREWS 6:11

"**T**he woods are lovely, dark and deep. But I have promises to keep and miles to go before I sleep; and miles to go before I sleep." Robert Frost spoke these words years ago in a university setting. Following his address, a young man asked him, "What did you mean, Mr. Frost, by 'promises to keep'?" Frost said, "I believe we have promises to keep to those who've gone before us, to our ancestors. And we have promises to keep to our contemporaries, to those we are living with right now, today. Finally," he said, " we have promises to keep to those unborn generations who will follow us. And," added the great poet, "I have promises to keep to myself, and to God."

I think Frost compiled a list that applies to every one of us. There is no one on this planet who does not have promises to keep. For the heritage that is ours and for the privileges we possess, we have promises to keep to our ancestors. We have commitments to keep and a sense of responsibility to our immediate families, friends and associates. And we have promises to keep to the future generations, whose lives will be shaped by the actions we take, the words we speak and the deeds we do. We have promises to keep.

How do we make certain we will keep these promises? We determine to live in obedience to God, claiming His promises, following His commands, seeking His will in all that we do. We become promise keepers by placing our lives under His authority, and by becoming imitators of His Son and our Savior, the Lord Jesus Christ.

REFLECTION

Read: *Hebrews* 6: 9-20

 Would your mate call you a promise-keeper? Your children? Your friends and associates?

Getting Lost

MEMORIZE

"For the Son of Man has come to save that which was lost."

MATTHEW 18:11

How do you get lost? How does lost-ness happen? I've been lost in more cities than I can count, and I can tell you—I never intend to become lost. It's not planned. A co-worker of mine tells the story of getting lost in Sears and Roebuck when she was about three years old. She was in the toy department, and going from toy to toy and aisle to aisle. When she looked up, she could no longer see her mom and dad. She didn't intend to get lost, but she did. And when she did, she stood in the middle of the store and cried at the top of her lungs. When an employee asked her what was wrong, she tearfully explained that she was lost. He told her, "Just stand there and keep crying. They'll find you quick."

Sometimes we get lost through carelessness. We just wander away, not considering the consequences. We see something that looks attractive, and we gravitate toward it. Then we wake up, look around, and say, "Where am I? How did I get here?" C. S. Lewis illustrates this in *The Screwtape Letters*, when experienced tempter Wormwood tells his young nephew Screwtape that a gradual approach is best to lure a Christian away from obedience. "No crises," he tells Screwtape. "Keep everything calm and placid. The best and surest way to Hell is a quiet, steady slope."

Are you lost? Are you far from God because of heedlessness or thoughtlessness or drifting? If you are, the Holy Spirit is calling you to come home. And God knows just where you are. Cry out, and He will come to you and bring you home again.

ACTION

Read: *Luke* 15: 1-10

Take a periodic inventory of your spiritual whereabouts. Are you wandering gradually away from the things of God?

In The Far Country

MEMORIZE

*"...the younger son gathered everything together
and went on a journey into a distant country..."*

LUKE 15:13

Lost things—and lost people—don't always know they're lost. But the one who has lost them knows. Sheep don't know they're lost, but the shepherd does. A lost coin doesn't know it's lost, but its owner does. The prodigal son didn't think he was lost. He thought he was living it up and enjoying the adventure of a lifetime, but if you had asked his father, he would have said, "My son is lost."

Where was the father when his son was lost? Some would argue that he never left home, never went after his boy. But I believe the father was in the far country, too. Not a day or night went by that the father was not with his younger son. Loved ones who are left behind know their own special kind of lost-ness. The wife of a man who fights in a foreign country goes to that country in her thoughts a thousand times a day. The loved one of a hostage is held hostage, too. The parent of a sick child fights disease just a surely as their boy or girl does, and feels every pain.

Day after day, hour after hour, the father of the prodigal was in the far country, too. He was suffering the anguish and emptiness that a life of excess brought to his son. There's not a parent alive who has not experienced the hurt of their child if there is real love there. That's a human picture of the supernatural love of God. He goes where we go. He feels every loss, every disappointment, every pain. And He loves us so much that once, for a moment, He turned His back on His own Son so that we could know that love.

ACTION

Read: *Luke 15: 11-14*

If you love someone who is lost, ask God to show you how to pray for them while they are in the far country. And never stop praying that they will come home.

Costly Words

*"...Father, I have sinned against heaven, and in your sight;
I am no longer worthy to be called your son."*

LUKE 15:21

When God forgives, He always gives. God follows His forgiveness with giving every time. We humans do just the opposite, don't we? We forgive, then put the ones forgiven "on probation," letting them linger just outside the warmth of fellowship until we're certain they've suffered enough. The father in the story of the prodigal son forgave like God forgives. When he welcomed his son home, he didn't just say "you're forgiven," he gave gifts symbolic of sonship and restoration. He even threw a party and celebrated.

There's an entry in the *Guiness Book of World Records* that tells of the costliest words ever spoken. Would it surprise anyone to know that they were spoken in a beer commercial? Actor James Coburn simply said two words, the name of a particular brand of beer, and he was paid $500,000. Half a million dollars for two words!

I'd love to sit down and argue with a Guiness Book of Records editor that those two words are not, in fact, the costliest words ever spoken. I believe without a doubt the most expensive words ever spoken were Jesus' words from the cross: "Father, forgive...". The father of the prodigal forgave, and gave. God, too, forgives and gives. We receive His forgiveness on the basis of the cross—the greatest gift ever given—and God keeps on giving: life, joy, peace, fellowship, every day that we are His.

Read: *Luke* 15: 15-24

For a few minutes today, list the gifts God has given you, beginning with salvation.

Older Brother Blues

MEMORIZE

"My child, you have always been with me, and all that is mine is yours."

LUKE 15:31

There's an old adage that says, "Every good party is attended by at least one wet blanket." In the story of the prodigal son, that "blanket" is the older brother. He refused to join the party. He rebuked his father for celebrating the prodigal's return. And he resented the gifts the father bestowed on his younger son. Were it not for the older brother, this story of Jesus' would have ended on a "happily ever after" kind of note. But it would not have the ring of truth to it that it does. There's just no ignoring the "older brother blues."

What was his beef? That while little brother had been partying and disgracing the family name and squandering his half of the fortune, the older brother had been checking in for work every day—being a responsible, respectful son. On the surface, his anger seems legitimate. If sonship were dependent on good behavior, the party should have been for the older son, while the younger son received punishment. But in this story, and in God's kingdom, sonship is entirely dependent on the grace of the father.

Older brothers who believe performance—and nothing else—counts, are sure to miss the celebration. They may be in the Father's house, but they know little of the Father's love and grace. The idea that we can build ourselves up by pushing another down is a tragic misconception. There is enough love in the Father's house for all of His children, and all that He has is ours.

QUESTION

Read: *Luke* 15: 25-32

Do you have the "older brother blues?" Celebrate the return of every prodigal, and the grace which is yours every day.

Asking Big

"Jesus said, 'what do you want Me to do for you?' and the blind man said to Him,
'Rabboni, I want to regain my sight'."

MARK 10:51

I once read a list of the world's worst questions—or at least someone's idea of the world's worst questions. One of them was, "Can I ask you something personal?" (Not a good opener.) Or, "Do you remember me?" (Usually, when someone asks this, I don't.) But of all the wild, crazy questions I've ever heard, few could beat Jesus' asking a man who'd been blind almost all his life, "What do you want me to do for you?"

It seemed obvious. But it wasn't. Jesus was asking blind Bartimaeus—a man who had asked for alms, bread, and handouts for years—if he was ready to ask for the big thing, the thing he really longed for. When a true miracle worker came his way, would he believe enough to ask for the one thing he needed most? Counselors will tell you that they meet few clients who seem ready to address their central problem right off the bat. They sort of circle around it until they are comfortable enough to dive in. It takes courage, and a certain level of trust, to say "Here's what I need more than anything. Can you help?"

Jesus was able and willing to give Bartimaeus that for which he asked. I believe He still walks among His people today and asks, "What do you want me to do for you? What do you really need? What is the deepest longing and desire of your heart?" But because of fear or a lack of faith, we ask Him for alms—the small change, the stuff that doesn't matter much—when what we desperately need is healing. It is almost as if Jesus is asking, "Do you believe enough to ask for the big thing?" Bartimaeus took the plunge. "I want to regain my sight," he said. And immediately, Jesus healed him.

Read: Mark 10: 46-52

Go before your heavenly Father today, and ask big.

Nicknames

MEMORIZE

"You are Simon, the son of John; you shall be called Cephas (which is translated Peter.)"

JOHN 1:42

The apostle Peter was a natural leader. I believe he would have eventually made it to the front of any parade. But he was also volatile, emotional, and quickly swayed by circumstance. When Andrew brought his brother Simon to meet Jesus, there was an immediate affinity between the two of them. Straight away, Jesus looked at Simon the fisherman and said, "We're not going to call you Simon anymore. We're going to call you Peter—the rock." I have a feeling those who knew Simon must have laughed. "Rock? You never know which way Simon's going to go. You're going to call him Rocky? That would be like calling a 300-pound man 'Tiny'."

Peter was a big, strong man—but you couldn't always count on him. And Jesus nicknamed him "Old Gibralter." That sounds like stability—but it didn't sound like Simon Peter. Peter, for the rest of his life, tried to live up to his nickname. Most of us try to live down our nicknames. I had a coach who used to call me "Speed Ball," and I wasn't. I hated it. A friend of mine was nicknamed "Bucket Head" in high school, and it's followed him for years. Most us try to live down our nicknames because they're derogatory. But Jesus gave Peter a nickname that was better than he was!

Peter had weaknesses. He knew them. Certainly Jesus knew them. But Jesus also saw what Peter *could* be. And that's how God looks at you and me. Like the children's song says, we are a mixture of promise and possibility. God has given you and me the most amazing nickname of all. He has called us "my son" and "my daughter." He has stamped His very name on our lives. Let's live up to it!

REFLECTION

Read: *Matthew* 16: 13-19

 Do you have a nickname you're trying to live down? What about living up to the name Jesus has given you instead?

Second Fiddle

*"One of the two who heard John speak, and followed him,
was Andrew, Simon Peter's brother."*

JOHN 1:40

Someone once asked a famous conductor what he thought was the most difficult instrument in the orchestra to play. Without hesitating, he replied "second fiddle." Have you had that role? Maybe you were second-string quarterback, or first runner up to the scholarship winner. Or perhaps you were the second or third child in a family of over-achievers. If so, you know what it means to play second fiddle.

Andrew knew, too. His brother was Simon Peter—the bold, brash, bigger-than-life fisherman-disciple whose highs and lows pepper the pages of the Gospels. Andrew was the brother in Peter's shadow, but he was reliable, consistent and humble. His agenda was simply to do the work of Jesus, and it didn't matter to him who got credit for it. He brought his brother Peter to Christ. He brought others as well. But as far as we know, he never preached a sermon or led a revival meeting. He was strictly a behind-the-scenes guy.

On one occasion, the great Simon Peter stood and preached, and 3,000 people came to Christ. Do you know how many Andrew won that day? Andrew won 3,001—because it was Andrew who first won Peter. He went home and told his big brother, "I've met a man I want to follow. And you should meet him too." And based on Andrew's recommendation, Peter did go to Jesus. So every time Peter stood and wooed great throngs of people to the Lord, Andrew had a part in that work. Second fiddle, you see, is a very, very important instrument in God's orchestra.

Read: John 1: 35-42

Could you be content playing second fiddle if it meant great gain for the kingdom of God?

The Right-Hand Seat

But Jesus answered and said, "you do not know what you are asking for.
Are you able to drink the cup that I am about to drink?..."

MATTHEW 20:22

We all want to move to the top; we want to lead the band. "All of us," said Carl Sandberg, "want to play Hamlet." We long for the lead role in the drama of life, so we can be someone and count for something. From birth, we are little bundles of ego, who learn to say "I" before just about anything else.

James and John, the biblical "sons of thunder," wanted to be seated at Jesus' right and left hands. They asked for places of honor, and they apparently weren't too shy about doing so. But when they did, Jesus asked *them* a question: "Are you able to drink the cup that I drink, or to be baptized with the baptism with which I am baptized?" They said they were. "Then you'll drink my cup," He told them, "and receive my baptism. But the seating arrangement is not mine to determine."

True greatness is not about getting a great seat for the show...it's about following Jesus Christ to the limits of this life and beyond. It's about drinking His cup of suffering, and being baptized into His death. Greatness comes through service. Living comes through surrendering life. James was the first apostle to be martyred for his faith. He followed Jesus all the way, tasting the cup of suffering, carrying the cross, and ultimately dying for his loyalty to Christ. Do you want to be great? Think carefully before you answer....

Read: *Mark* 10: 35-45

 Describe the greatness to which you aspire. Can you drink His cup? Can you endure His baptism?

Come And See

MEMORIZE

"And Nathanael said to him, 'can any good thing come out of Nazareth?'
Philip said to him, 'come and see'."

JOHN 1:46

Nathanael must have been a thinking skeptic. Maybe he was the kind of guy who organized everything—mentally and physically. You know the type. A place for everything, and everything in its place. He wasn't going to be taken in by emotionalism or hype. He was the sort of guy who hung back and studied the situation before making any kind of decision. His friend Philip knew better than to give Nathanael the hard sell. "We've found the One the prophets wrote about," he said. "His name is Jesus, and He's from Nazareth." When Nathanael asked whether any good thing could come out of a place like Nazareth, Philip simply said, "Come and see."

Where Jesus is concerned, "come and see" is an unbeatable invitation. Because He draws men to Himself, and His winsomeness is irresistible. Seeing Jesus—the real Jesus—is the most compelling argument that exists for Christianity. (Or, as one of my sons says, "There's only one good reason for being a Christian…and that's Jesus.")

I once shared Christ with a man who was a Nathanael-type. I offered him books by C. S. Lewis, Francis Schaeffer and other brilliant apologists, but it seemed all he wanted to do was debate. Finally, I took him to see the stained glass windows of our church. We walked around the outside of the building , and looked at all the windows. "What do you think?" I asked him. "They're actually not that impressive," he said. "I couldn't agree with you more," I told him. "Now, let's go inside." When we arrived in the sanctuary, the lights were not on. Instead, the sunlight was pouring through the windows, illuminating their absolute beauty. "That's the way it is trying to know God and Christ from the outside looking in," I told him. "The step of faith that brings you inside is the one that illumines your darkness."

ACTION

Read: Psalm 34: 8-14

Invite a "Nathanael" in your life to "come and see."

Check It Out!

MEMORIZE

"...Unless I shall see in His hands the imprint of the nails...and
put my hand into His side, I will not believe."

JOHN 20:25

Thomas was the only disciple whose name became a synonym for a certain group of people. You don't hear about "walking-on-water Peter's" or "beloved John's." But everybody knows what it means to be a "doubting Thomas." Thomas was the man who said "show me." He needed to see for himself that the resurrected Christ was the real deal.

Thomas saw Jesus die. He saw the blood and the flies. He smelled the stench of dying flesh and heard the Savior utter His last words. He was an eyewitness to it all, and then he disappeared. On that first Easter, the rest of the disciples saw Him, but Thomas did not. They told him, but the picture of the crucifixion was still too fresh and real for him to believe that his Lord was alive again. "I'll have to see it myself," he said. "That's the only way I'll believe." Eight days passed before Thomas saw Jesus for himself. But he didn't have to touch His wounds. He took one look at Jesus, heard His voice, then fell at His feet saying, "My Lord and my God."

I know plenty of folks who are skeptical about the historicity of the resurrection. I'm grateful for doubting Thomas when I talk to them. "There was a guy who felt just like you do," I say, "but he saw for himself, and believed." They, like Thomas, face a choice. When confronted by the person of Jesus Christ, a man can either say "I believe," or "I refuse to believe." Jesus said, "Blessed are they who did not see, and yet believed."

QUESTION

Read: John 20: 24-29

 Do you know someone who needs to "see?" Pray that Christ will show Himself to them in an unmistakable way.

Under New Management

"Even so consider yourselves to be dead to sin, but alive to God in Christ Jesus."

ROMANS 6:11

No one names his child Judas. Have you noticed? The name Judas is associated with betrayal...in fact, it is a pejorative term. But I do not believe Judas was Satan incarnate (as some have suggested), or even that he was a man whose intentions were evil from the start. He had the potential to become a committed follower of Christ, but he allowed his fleshly nature to sway his thinking—and ultimately, his actions.

Imagine that you live in an apartment house owned by a mean, spiteful landlord. You've been late on the rent, and he has charged you exorbitant interest. You are so far into debt to him that you could not move out if you wanted to. This landlord controls your life, and abuses you because you have no recourse. Then one day, a new landlord comes, announcing that he has bought the building. The slate is wiped clean. All debts are canceled. But still, the old landlord calls, saying, "You owe me. You owe me. Pay up." Guilt, fear and habit could keep you in bondage to the old landlord...but you wouldn't have to be. You are under new management. You could ask your old landlord to take up his claims with the new owner.

When pressure and fear and disappointment began to hammer Judas, when he was stumbling and debating about what the future might hold, he could have talked to Jesus. He was with Him every day. But he didn't. He kept listening to the old landlord. When Satan tries to get his hooks in you, you are not doomed to fall. You don't owe him anything. Tell him you're under new management. Tell him to take it up with the new landlord.

Read: John 12: 1-8

 Do you understand that as a Christian, sin has no power over you? When Satan calls, tell him to take his matter up with your Master, Jesus Christ.

One Thing

*"That I may know Him, and the power of His resurrection
and the fellowship of His sufferings."*

PHILIPPIANS 3:10

Philosopher Soren Kirkegaard wrote a book called *Purity of Heart is to Will One Thing*. He contended that a pure heart was a heart with singular focus. The apostle Paul was a man with laser focus on one thing, and one thing only: he wanted to know Christ. From His highest highs to His lowest lows, Paul wanted to experientially know Jesus Christ. He did not claim to have arrived in his quest…but he was focused on it. He was the original, one-dimensional man.

Do the words "one thing" ring a bell with you? When Jesus spoke to the rich young ruler, He said, "One thing you lack…" When He reprimanded Martha for her bitter attitude toward her sister Mary, He said, "One thing is needed…" The blind man who was given sight by Jesus and questioned at length by the Pharisees said, "One thing I know." Paul said, "I do not regard myself as having laid hold of it yet; but one thing I do…" He did not look back—he reached ahead to his "one thing:" knowing Christ, and being all that He had called him to be.

Have you ever watched the runners in a track meet? When a runner nears the finish line, he strains, leans and stretches for that tape. He does not look back to see where the rest of the runners are. He does not look at the score board to check the time. He does not look down to see if he is placing his feet correctly. He runs flat out for the wire, intent on one thing: winning the race.

Jesus Christ is the author and finisher of our faith. He sounds the starting gun. He stands at the tape. He is the One who calls us higher. He is our One Thing.

Read: *Philippians* 3:10-14

 What is your one thing? Describe it in a sentence, like Paul did in Philippians 3:10.

"And Such Were Some of You…"

*"…but you were washed, but you were sanctified,
but you were justified in the name of the Lord Jesus Christ…"*

I C O R I N T H I A N S 6 : 1 1

I always tell folks that if they are looking for a perfect church—and think they've found one—not to join it. They'd only mess it up! When we're dressed up and on our best behavior, it's easy to forget that we are all sinners saved by grace.

The late Ray Stedman was leading his church through a study of I Corinthians. He read them the list of the kinds of sinners that will not inherit the kingdom of God: fornicators, idolaters, adulterers, effeminate, homosexuals, thieves, the covetous, drunkards, revilers, or swindlers. Then he said, quoting Paul, "and such were some of you." With that, he asked those in his congregation who could identify with one or more of these sins to stand to their feet. No one moved until one saintly woman stood. Stedman said that one by one, people began to stand. Before it was over, two-thirds of those present were on their feet.

They had an invitation that night, and a young man came forward and said, "I've been coming to this church for a long time, and everyone looked so holy and good. They sang, they prayed, they listened to the sermon…and they all seemed so perfect that I just didn't think I belonged. But," he said, "when you read that list and I saw all those people stand, I said, 'Hey, I've been there. I've done that. I'm not so different from them after all. Maybe this is my kind of place.'" The Body of Christ is not a museum for saints. It's a hospital for sinners. That's why so many of us feel at home.

Read: *I Corinthians 6: 9-11*

 Thank God that He has washed you clean with the blood of His Son, Jesus Christ.

Redeemed

"But by His doing you are in Christ Jesus, who became to us wisdom from God, and righteousness and sanctification, and redemption."

I CORINTHIANS 1:30

To redeem means to buy back. We are redeemed, bought back, by the blood of Jesus Christ. Isn't that thrilling? When God looks at you and me, He sees not our vanity, our sin, our hypocrisy or our shame, but His own Son's righteousness! God sees me and says, "That's Edwin. He's 100% forgiven. He's right with Me."

Boston pastor A. O. Cronin was walking down the street when he saw a young man with an old, rusty bird cage. In it were a bunch of birds. "Sonny, where'd you get those birds?" Cronin asked. "I trapped them out in the field," the boy said. "If you'd like to get rid of them," Cronin said, "I'll buy them back from you." The boy wasn't sure. "I don't know," he said. "I was going to take them and play with them for a while, then feed them to the cat. Besides, mister," he said, "they're just field larks. They can't even sing." The pastor persisted. "I'll give you two dollars for the birds, and the cage." The little guy said, "I'll take it." The pastor took the cage, opened the door, and set the birds free. The next Sunday morning, Cronin came to the pulpit with the empty bird cage and told the story of the birds he bought back, and the price he paid. "There's only one problem," he said. "The little boy didn't tell me the truth about one thing. He said these birds couldn't sing. But I want to tell you, when I opened the cage and let them go, I heard them singing, 'Redeemed, redeemed, redeemed'!"

That's our song, too. We're redeemed by the word of the cross. Not by worldly wisdom, but by God's word of revelation which is the cross of His Son Jesus Christ.

Read: *I Corinthians* 1: 27-31

Meditate on these verses, asking God to give you a renewed appreciation for the cross of Christ.

Nothing But Christ

MEMORIZE

"For I determined to know nothing among you except Jesus Christ, and Him crucified."

I CORINTHIANS 2:2

The cross of Jesus Christ frightens some. In the cross, they rightly see commitment. A man on a cross is facing in only one direction. He cannot turn back. And he has no future plans of his own. To follow Christ means to deny self, to turn from ego and pride, and to surrender control of your own life.

In England, there is a chapel built over 200 years ago bearing these words over the door: "We Preach Christ Crucified." The chapel's early pastors did preach Christ crucified. People came with testimonies of how lives were changed, and there was vitality in the church. But time passed. Vines grew over the motto "We Preach Christ Crucified," until it read only, "We Preach Christ." The men who stood in the pulpit named the name of Jesus Christ, but preached a social gospel of good works and morality. The vines continued to grow until the motto read "We Preach." And they did. They preached philosophy, ethics, politics and literature. But not Jesus Christ. Not long after that, the little chapel was emptied.

Paul told the Corinthians he had nothing to bring to them except the message of Jesus Christ crucified. It is the message of the cross that divides all of humanity, and saves all who place their faith in Him. When we preach anything less, or anything more, we lose the power of God and the blessing of God.

QUESTION

Read: I Corinthians 2: 1-5

 Is the cross central in the preaching and teaching you listen to?

Higher Ground

MEMORIZE

"I gave you milk to drink, not solid food; for you were not yet able to receive it..."

I CORINTHIANS 3:2

Some Christians spend all their time worrying about falling back into sin. They don't move on and up to higher ground. They don't grow. If you focus all your energy on trying not to fail instead of training to win, you will remain a baby in the faith.

Carl Wallenda was perhaps the most famous aerialist who ever lived. He was one of the "Flying Wallendas"—a family, high-wire act whose feats thrilled audiences worldwide. He wrote, "For me, to live is being on a tight rope. All the rest is waiting." He said in 1968 that the key to tight rope walking was confidence. There was no room to think about failing. But in 1978, Carl Wallenda fell to his death from a high wire strung 75 feet in the air in San Juan, Puerto Rico. His wife said that three months prior to this most dangerous attempt, Carl talked frequently about falling. He checked the installation of the wire. He calculated the wind. He checked the guy wires that kept everything in place. "I believe Carl fell," she said, "because he spent so much time preparing not to fall, instead of preparing to walk the rope."

Do you spend all your time saying, "Boy, I don't want to fall. I'm a Christian now, so I want to live a clean life?" If you do, you are setting yourself up for failure. Don't focus on maintenance. Go for growth. Spend time in God's Word. Seek to understand and apply the truth that you discover. Think about going on to higher ground—not merely protecting the ground you've already covered. In other words, grow up!

ACTION

Read: *I Corinthians 3: 1-3*

Don't be satisfied with the milk of the Christian life. It takes solid food to grow.

Bought And Paid For

MEMORIZE

"For you have been bought with a price: therefore glorify God in your body."
I CORINTHIANS 6:20

I f you belong to Jesus Christ, you are not your own. The Bible says you have been bought and paid for with a price: the precious blood of Jesus Christ.

Let's say you invite me to your home for lunch. You clean up the house, cook a fabulous meal, and put the Bible out on the coffee table, since the pastor is coming. I arrive in a paneled truck with a crew of workers, all of us in blue jeans. We get out with paint cans and brushes, and we paint your house a rainbow of colors. I also decide a wall or two needs knocking down, and your living room furniture needs re-arranging. Then I ask you for the menu, and when you say we're having spaghetti, I suggest pizza instead. Finally you say to me, "What do you think you're doing? I only invited you for lunch. You're acting like this is your house and not mine."

If you have been to Calvary and received Jesus Christ as your savior, the "house" that is your body does not belong to you any more. It is not your house. It is God's house. His Holy Spirit takes up residence in you. And He is well within His rights when He says things like, "That ego has to go," or "Those words don't match what you say you believe. Change them." Jesus Christ has paid the price for you, and you are not your own.

QUESTION

Read: *I Corinthians 6: 12-20*

Are you glorifying God in your body?

Leave The Choice To Him

MEMORIZE

"Who at any time serves as a soldier at his own expense?
Who plants a vineyard, and does not eat the fruit of it?"

I CORINTHIANS 9:7

Has God taught you the principle yet of leaving your rights with Him? Like a hitter in a baseball game who is given the signal to bunt by his coach, we must look to God to see whether we are to "sacrifice," or "swing away."

Twenty-three year old Thomas Edison left Boston for New York in 1873. He was a brilliant inventor, but made his living as a teletype operator. Edison went to the Western Union office to seek employment as an inventor, but was told there was no such job. Instead, he was offered a position servicing and updating the teletype machines, which were quite temperamental. He was told by General Marshall Fawcett, "Just go to work, and I'll settle up with you when we see what you can do." Many months went by. Finally the General came in and said, "Well, son, how much do you think I owe you?" Edison was skilled with his hands but ignorant of finances, although he had given the matter some thought. He determined that a thousand dollars would be adequate, but two thousand would be more fair. He felt three thousand dollars was more than he deserved, but because he desperately needed the money, he decided to ask for five thousand dollars. But before he answered, he remembered the General was noted for his honesty, so at the last moment he asked, "General, what do you think my labor has been worth?" The General said without hesitating, "How does forty thousand dollars sound to you?" Edison said he turned pale, and his lips began to tremble. "F..fi...fine, sir, it sounds just fine." He learned that day the General's generosity exceeded his own greed.

Those who demand their rights in the Christian life rarely grow. Their walk becomes stagnant and cold. But those who put their rights aside and leave the choices to God grow in grace with giant steps.

ACTION

Read: I Corinthians 9: 5-17

 Tell God today that you are ready to surrender your rights, and let Him choose for you.

Behold The Lamb

MEMORIZE

"...worthy is the Lamb that was slain to receive power and riches and wisdom and might and honor and glory and blessing."

REVELATION 5:12

A t the center of the Word of God, Old Testament and New Testament, there is a lamb. He is the sacrifice of Abel's offering. The substitute for Isaac, slain by Abraham on Mount Moriah. The lamb is the centerpiece of the Passover, sparing Israel's firstborn from the death angel. It was a lamb that was killed on the day of atonement, its blood sprinkled by the priests on the mercy seat of the altar, and a lamb who received our punishment in Isaiah's Messianic prophecy. At the baptism of Christ, John the Baptist said, "Behold the Lamb of God who takes away the sins of the world." And in John's vision of the New Jerusalem, the Lamb is on the throne.

Who could guess that beginning in Genesis, the Bible would progressively reveal the Lamb, the Lamb, the Lamb...until all creation would ring with the phrase "Worthy is the Lamb?"

What does the Lamb mean for us today? I'll tell you. The church that is dead and cold and lifeless is practicing the religion of Cain. They are worshipping God with a bouquet of flowers and fruit, but not by the blood of the Lamb of God. The shedding of blood is essential for the forgiveness of sins—and it is the Lamb's blood that atones for us. We don't like the sound of that...it seems messy and foreign and archaic. But there is no other way. *"What can wash away my sin? Nothing but the blood of Jesus! What can make me whole again? Nothing but the blood of Jesus!"* When the church ceases to lift Him up, it ceases to have life. "Behold the Lamb of God, who takes away the sins of the world."

ACTION

Read: *Revelation 5: 6-14*

Focus on the Lamb of God today, thanking Him for His sacrifice, and exalting His Name.

Tire-Kickers

*"...for he who comes to God must believe that He is,
and that He is a rewarder of those who seek Him."*

HEBREWS 11:6

Every church has its share of tire-kickers. I welcome them! The passion of my life is to introduce others to Jesus Christ, so when folks who are just looking come through the doors of the church, I'm thrilled. But not every tire-kicker is a serious seeker. Some who say they are looking for God are actually not looking for Him, but for what they hope He will do for them. And there's a difference. Some are looking for a panacea. They want some area of their life "fixed," and wonder if God can do it. Others are seeking not God, but God's power. They have their own agenda securely in place, and would like just a little of God's "voltage" to power up their plan and put them over the top.

These are the folks who usually pass through the church, then move on. They go away disappointed, believing that God was not interested in them, their pain or their desires. But they are wrong. God is interested in them. But He is not a supernatural errand boy. God Almighty cares deeply for the lost, yet He has established the immutable conditions by which He can be found. They are not easy, but they are simple.

God will be found by every serious tire-kicker, every seeker, who confesses his sin, repents of that sin, and receives Jesus Christ into his life. The words God longs to hear are these: "Lord, have mercy on me, a sinner." They are music to His ears.

Read: *Hebrews* 11: 1-6

How has God rewarded your honest seeking of Him?

Who Is Jesus?

"I and the Father are one."

JOHN 10:30

Christians believe that Jesus Christ is the Son of God. But non-Christians the world over generally agree that—if not divine—Jesus was the very best of human beings. He has been praised as a brilliant teacher, a kind healer, a good man. But, as C. S. Lewis said, these are not options He leaves open for us. He cannot be simply a good man. Peter Kreeft, one of the foremost apologists of this century, says there are only five possible answers to the question, "Who is Jesus?" He is either Lord, a liar, a lunatic, a myth or a guru. These are the only logical options.

There is no escaping this one fact: Jesus claimed to be God. "I and the Father are one," He said. If Jesus were a good man, he would not have lied about who He was. If He claimed to be the Son of God—and was not—He would be a liar. He could not be both a liar and a good man. Claims of divinity might be attributed to lunatics, but there was nothing insane in Jesus' behavior. To say that Jesus was a lunatic would be like saying Mother Teresa was a party animal. Some say Jesus was not a liar or a lunatic, but a myth. He did not make His claims of deity, they argue. They were attributed to Him after his death, along with accounts of all the supernatural things He was said to have done. But manuscript evidence and secular literature deny this premise. Still others argue that Jesus was merely a popular guru or spiritual master whose teachings incorporated pantheism, Hinduism and mysticism. The only problem with this arrangement is that Jesus was a Jew...and Judaism is a monotheistic religion. Christianity is an extension of Judaism, not an incorporation of other religions of the day.

After all the other arguments are refuted, we are left with one premise. Jesus Christ is indeed the Son of God. Probably the strongest argument in favor of His deity is that He claimed it for Himself, and died because of it. If He were not the Son of God, why go all the way to the cross? Why not call off the "hoax?" The claims of Christ stand the test of scrutiny. As G. K Chesterton said, "The only good argument against Christianity is Christians." The only valid, honest reason to reject Christ's claims is because we do not want to be under His moral authority. When Jesus Christ comes into a life, He claims absolute authority over it. That is the true reason most men reject His claims.

Read: *John 6: 41-58*

Who do you say that Jesus is?

Jesus Plus Nothing

MEMORIZE

"He saved us, not on the basis of deeds which we have done in righteousness,
but according to His mercy..."

TITUS 3:5

There are seven hundred million Hindus in the world, and God loves every single one of them. But they do not know the truth. There are three hundred million Buddhists in the world, and God loves every single one of them, but they do not know the truth. There are over nine hundred million Muslims in the world, and God loves every one of them. But they do not know the truth.

We live in a society that believes there are many roads leading to God, and that it doesn't matter which approach you take, as long as you are sincere. But it does matter. In fact, it matters a great deal. A comparative study of world religions will show that nearly all religions have a supreme being, address the afterlife, and offer some kind of moral code of ethics. But they are not interchangeable. Only one is true…because truth is not broad. It is very narrow.

The idea that God is so big that there cannot be one exclusive path to reach Him is not true. The idea that all world religions are essentially the same is intellectually absurd. But the difference between Christianity and every other world religion is that Christianity offers man no way to save himself. Jesus Christ told the thief dying next to Him on the cross, "Today you will be with me in paradise." The thief did nothing for salvation, but believe in the saving power of Christ. He could offer Jesus nothing. He trusted in Jesus plus nothing…and Jesus plus nothing equals salvation.

ACTION

Read: Titus 3: 3-7

Be careful of adding anything to what God requires for salvation.

My Way

MEMORIZE

"...he who does not enter by the door into the fold of the sheep,
but climbs up some other way, he is a thief and a robber."

JOHN 10:1

When young Adolph Hitler was an itinerant artist in Vienna, he became captivated by an artifact in the Hofburg Palace Complex: a spear purported to be the one that pierced the side of Christ on Calvary. Hitler heard museum guides describe the lore surrounding the spear, including the belief that whoever possessed this particular weapon would rule the world. Those words changed Hitler's life. He spent many hours in the Hofburg, studying the occult and Eastern religions, and meditating over that spear. He discovered that Constantine held the same spear when he conquered Rome in 312 AD, and that some 45 other generals, kings and emperors had carried it.

Years later when Adolph Hitler became supreme dictator of Germany, he conquered Vienna without a shot being fired. The night the city fell, Hitler entered the Hofburg Complex, removed the spear from its case and held it to his chest. Historians record that he said, "I knew I held the world in my hands." He believed the spear held some supernatural power, and it is reported that the night he held it for the first time was the very night he decided to exterminate the Jews and Christians in Germany.

There was a unique climate in Germany that gave a megalomaniac the opportunity to take over one of the most powerful nations in the world. There is a unique climate in our country today that encourages ordinary people like you and me to believe that they are gods, and that their subjective opinion of truth is truth. This eclectic atmosphere is called the New Age Movement—and its overriding belief (although it encompasses many) is that we are little gods who can—and should—rule our world. Beware of this subtle, but pervasive, egotistical thinking that ignores the authority of God and the supremacy of Jesus Christ. We cannot do it our way. We must do it His way.

ACTION

Read: John 10: 1-6

 Pick up any major city newspaper or a popular mass market magazine and identify examples of New Age philosophy.

The Word of God

"Thy word is a lamp unto my feet and a light unto my path."
PSALM 119:105

The Bible is the living Word of God, and my life has been built around that fact. My call to the ministry is grounded in its verses, and my marriage is built upon its principles. I have sought to bring up my children on the basis of its truth. The church I serve functions daily by its precepts. We are a Bible-believing, Bible-teaching Body of Christ. So I can truthfully tell you that everything I'm about—every relationship, every role, every assignment—is based upon the authority and truthfulness of God's Word.

When God's people meet for worship and His Word is read, proclaimed, studied and explained, amazing things happen—things that transcend music and words and offerings and emotions—because His Word is alive. It cuts, like a surgeon who would pierce the body in order to heal it. It softens, tenderizing hearts that are hard as steel. It melts icy souls that say, "Nothing can touch me here." It convicts the complacent, leading to repentance. And lives are changed...every time.

Every week I receive letters from people who hear the Word of God and ask, "Did my wife tell you I was going to be at church?" Others say, "You must have known I was coming." It has nothing to do with me. God's Word is living and active, and it has the power to change lives. I know. It changed—and keeps changing—mine.

ACTION

Read: *Hebrews* 4: 12-13

 Ask God to give you a deeper love for His Word, and a passion to study and obey it.

Who Needs Saving?

"For all have sinned and fall short of the glory of God."

ROMANS 3:23

Imagine you are a sales representative with a big presentation to make. You've prepared. You look your best. You have all your ammunition ready. Landing this account could mean the difference between success and failure for your fledgling company. Before you arrive in your potential client's office, you make one last check in the restroom, only to discover an ink stain the size of a Frisbee on your crisp, white shirt. Water won't remove it. You don't have another shirt. You try to hide it with your tie, but to no avail. You are hopelessly, horribly stained, and there is nothing you can do to remove the mark.

Every single man and woman alive is sin-stained. We are not able to remove the blot of sin on our lives, no matter what method we try. But many people resist the idea that they need to be saved from sin. "Saving" is for other people—people whose marks are more obvious than their own. But the Bible says all of us have sinned, and fallen short of the mark of perfection required by a holy God.

There are four realities that sinners like you and me need to know. First, the stain of sin is permanent. It will not improve on its own, nor be removed by human effort. Second, inspection day is coming. You have an appointment with the Lord God Almighty who judges sin, and there is no escaping that appointment. Third, there is only One who can remove the stain of sin. Only Jesus Christ, the Son of God is equipped to cleanse it. Finally—and best of all—Jesus is in the cleaning business! Jesus' clean-up procedure is called salvation, and it takes place when a man by faith receives Jesus Christ into his life. *"Jesus paid it all; all to Him I owe. Sin had left its crimson stain. He washed it white as snow."*

Read: John 3: 1-7

Thank Jesus Christ for His cleansing power over the stain of sin.

Why Should God Let You In?

"I am the way, and the truth, and the life; no one comes to the Father, but through Me."

JOHN 14:6

If God Himself were to ask you, "Why should I let you into My heaven?", how would you answer? I have used that question for many years to determine someone's understanding of salvation. Some people would say, "Well, that's a pointless question, because there is no God." Others would say, "I'm not sure that will ever take place, so your question is irrelevant to me." Still others would say, "I think God will let me into heaven. Although I'm not perfect, I'm better than a lot of people. I've done more good than bad." And a few say, "I've got no chance to get into heaven, except by God's grace and the shed blood of Jesus Christ. I've placed my faith in Him, and I'm counting on Him to get me in."

When folks beg the question, and say "I'm not sure," I press a little further. "Do you think it's an important question?" I might ask. "Oh, without a doubt," they'll usually say. "But I just don't have any idea how to answer it."

It's a big question, isn't it? Where will you spend eternity? Can you think of anything bigger? In comparison with eternity, this life is short. And death, although it is certain, catches all of us by surprise. The Bible clearly teaches that when man dies, he either goes to Heaven to live forever in the presence of God, or he goes to Hell, separated from God forever. With that in mind, shouldn't assurance about our eternal destiny be given a high, high priority? I heard Billy Graham say once, "If you are not ready to die, you are not ready to live." I've never forgotten that; it is absolutely true. If you have placed your faith in Jesus Christ, you are ready. His is the only Name that will gain you admittance to Heaven.

Read: Luke 16: 19-31

Why should God let you into His heaven?

Intellectual Hurdles

"And you will seek Me and find Me, when you search for Me with all your heart."

JEREMIAH 29:13

People believe for all kinds of reasons. Some believe because of the way they were brought up, or because of various experiences they've had. Some believe because of the influence of important people in their lives. But some know the value and depth of believing because they went on a relentless search for truth…and found it.

How should a man conduct a spiritual search? Let me make a few suggestions. First, keep an open mind. The authentic seeker must maintain a healthy balance between solid investigation and a willingness to accept what he finds. Second, pray. A seeker's prayer might go something like this: "God, I'm not even sure I believe You are listening, but if You are, I want to find You. I really do want to know the truth. If you exist, please show Yourself to me." Third, be honest about what you're looking for. Most people who investigate Christianity say, "I'm after spiritual truth." That's fine. But others are looking for instant solutions to life-long problems. Christianity is an eternal solution joined to a life-long process. Finally, be willing to change on the basis of what you discover. Don't view spiritual faith as an accessory item that could complement your lifestyle. It's a relationship that will change your life.

Seekers need to ask questions. Christianity can stand up to even the most careful scrutiny. If you are a seeker, let your quest begin. If you are a believer, encourage seekers. Be an apologist for your faith. That doesn't mean apologizing for believing…it means giving others valid reasons to come to a belief of their own.

Read: Acts 13: 26-42

Encourage the seekers you know to investigate the claims of Christ, or do so yourself.

The One-Way Objection

MEMORIZE

"For the gate is small, and the way is narrow that leads to life,
and few are those who find it."

MATTHEW 7:14

One of the most frequent objections I hear to the claims of Christ is this: "How could God make only one way for people to get to heaven? All religions have some good in them; it doesn't matter what you believe." I call this the "One Way Objection." As America becomes more of a melting pot, I hear it more frequently. Because we have no national religion and our country has become home to so many cultures, tolerance is the watchword of the day. But many have concluded that tolerance of other belief systems means that all belief systems are equally valid. They are not.

Still, the man or woman who says "It's Jesus only," is likely to be called a narrow-minded bigot. Peter Kreeft has only half-jokingly said that "fundamentalist" is "the new four-letter word." To believe in one way to salvation in our day is like attacking baseball, hot dogs, apple pie and motherhood. "What kind of God would have such a narrow requirement?" some ask. And the question itself is a serious charge against God, implying that He has not done enough to provide a way of redemption for mankind.

My answer to the one-way objection is that God Himself, as an ultimate act of redemption, became incarnate in the person of His Son. That Son, Jesus, came into the world not to condemn it, but to save it. He was rejected, slandered, mocked, tortured and murdered. And God accepted that treatment of His Son as punishment for the very people who murdered Him! Instead of punishment, He offered them total pardon, if they would only believe in that Son, and worship and serve Him alone. Could that possibly be unloving and harsh? How could God have done more?

REFLECTION

Read: *Matthew 7: 13-23*

 Reflect for a moment today on the redemption God provided mankind.
Could you call it stingy?

The Hypocrite Objection

MEMORIZE

"Do not judge lest you be judged."

MATTHEW 7:1

"Christians are not perfect," a popular bumper sticker reads, "just for-given." Christians are also the excuse many non-Christians give for not following Christ. The unbeliever's standard of performance for those who profess Christ is often nothing short of perfection. You've heard the charge when a Christian misses the mark: "What a hypocrite! If that's what it means to believe…count me out!"

But that is unfair on two fronts. First, it represents an inaccurate under-standing of what it means to enter into the Christian life. Authentic Christians have made the decision to follow Christ, to turn away from their willful disobedience and rebellion against God, and to accept Jesus' death on the cross as payment for their sins. They have accepted God's leadership in their lives and begun the journey of walking under His management. But they have not arrived at a sinless state—nor will they in this life.

Second, the true hypocrite is not someone who falls short of his or oth-ers' expectations, but one who consciously and knowingly wears a mask. Follow me for a day, and I will disappoint you. Although I love my wife deeply, I fail daily in being the husband I'm supposed to be. I love my chil-dren, too, but I have made mistakes in parenting. I love God and urge oth-ers to do the same, but I remain a sinner who struggles with sin and some-times loses. The good news is that authentic Christianity does not demand perfection—it depends on grace. I am thankful that Jesus is the real issue, not the imperfections of those who love and follow Him.

ACTION

Read: *Matthew 7: 1-7*

If you have any standard of righteousness but Jesus, abandon it.

The Suffering Objection

MEMORIZE

*"And the rain descended, and the floods came, and the winds blew,
and burst against that house; and it fell..."*

MATTHEW 7:27

Storms are a part of life. You needn't live long to discover that life's storms can take many forms. Physical pain is a storm. So is mental or emotional distress. And storms hit the houses of good people.

In the movie *Shadowlands*, Anthony Hopkins portrayed British author C. S. Lewis, whose wife died soon after their mid-life marriage. In one scene from the film, a minister tries to give Lewis a "God-knows-best" kind of pat answer, and Lewis explodes. "No!" he shouts. "This is a mess, that's all anyone can say. It's just a mess." Christians believe in a loving, personal God who cares about His creation, and the Bible teaches that God is all-powerful and able to do anything. Given those two suppositions, it's no surprise that non-believers balk when Christians suffer. It doesn't add up.

Rabbi Harold Kushner concluded in his book *When Bad Things Happen to Good People* that God cares about our suffering, but is powerless to do anything about it. Eli Wiesel said of the God Kushner described, "If that's who God is, why doesn't He resign and let someone more competent take His place?" The answer to this dilemma lies in a thing called free will. God could intervene 100% of the time and rescue us from the fallen-ness of the world and the consequences of our own choices, but to do so would rob us of the free will to love Him. The deeper truth is that He is present in the suffering, and in His sovereignty He is able to make all of it work together for good to those who love Him. No sorrow leaves us where it found us. It drives us from God, or draws us near to Him...but that choice is ours.

ACTION

Read: *Matthew 7: 24-29*

Look for examples in the Bible of how suffering brought men closer to God, and served to demonstrate His glory.

The Verdict

MEMORIZE

"And Simon Peter answered and said, 'Thou art the Christ, the Son of the living God.'"

MATTHEW 16:16

Even today, we have many pictures of Jesus. The six-hour film *Jesus of Nazareth* has been seen by over 100 million television viewers worldwide, and additional millions of film go-ers. The musical *Godspell* was a Broadway hit and later a movie depicting a whimsical, child-like Christ who sang and danced His way into the hearts of His followers. Then Broadway brought us the harder-edged version of the Savior in *Jesus Christ, Superstar*—a sort of cult figure with a rag-tag following and a tragic end. And perhaps the most distorted popular picture of Jesus was seen in *The Last Temptation of Christ*—a disturbed, reluctant Messiah who was a sinner like you and me.

There are "snapshots" of Jesus everywhere...but which one of them (if any) is the real Jesus? Who exactly is He? I have a feeling many in our modern world would like to ask, "Will the real Jesus please stand up?" Not a caricature, an exaggeration or a composite of Him, but the real Jesus. Who is He?

Nearly 2,000 years ago, Jesus asked His small band of disciples this same question. But the real issue then—and now—is not who *others* say Jesus is. We will not be held accountable for their answers. It's who each one of us as *individuals* say He is. Peter rightly answered, "You're the Christ, the Messiah, the Son of the living God." And Jesus said, "That's it! You've got it!" Don't allow others to define for you the identity of Jesus Christ. Search the Bible. Ask questions. Pray for understanding. But find out for yourself. The way you answer this question will matter forever.

ACTION

Read: *Matthew 16: 13-17*

Get alone today in a quiet place and consider the identity of Jesus Christ. If you know who He is, do you know Him?

From Child To Champion

MEMORIZE

*"And they were continually devoting themselves to the apostles' teaching
and to fellowship, the breaking of the bread and to prayer."*

ACTS 2:42

I have never seen a baby being born. When our boys were coming along, dads just didn't do that. My sons, however, have witnessed the births of each of their children. They tell me it is a mysterious, beautiful miracle. My middle son, Ben, described the birth of his first daughter, Nicole, in one word: *awe*. A newborn is a totally dependent, totally vulnerable being. They have nothing. They need everything.

When we are born again, we are not born into spiritual adulthood. We are babies. But we are not meant to stay in the infant stage indefinitely, any more than my six grandchildren are. In the first moments, days, weeks and even years of new life in Christ, the operative word is vulnerable. The babe in Christ is vulnerable to false teachings, to cults, to old habits and relationships, and to addictions. He or she needs a steady, balanced diet of sound teaching, prayer, fellowship and "the breaking of bread." These items are the "staples" of the Christian life, and we must have them to grow strong.

Tom Landry, coach of the Dallas Cowboys for almost three decades, said, "A coach is someone who gets men to do what they do not want to do in order to achieve that which they have always wanted to be." I love that. We may not always want to "do" the spiritual disciplines that are prescribed for our growth, but we do want to grow and become champions for God. With that one goal, every Christian born could live a life that's out of this world!

QUESTION

Read: Acts 2:37-41

Are the disciplines of Bible study, prayer, fellowship and the Lord's Supper priorities in your life?

Hitting Bottom

MEMORIZE

"For Thine arrows have sunk deep into me, and Thy hand has pressed down on me."

PSALM 38:2

The twelve steps of Alcoholics Anonymous are deeply rooted in Biblical authority. These steps that have helped millions were conceived when two recovering alcoholics from Akron, Ohio, hit bottom, and began to seek spiritual solutions for their battle. The first step of the twelve step program is the one that led these men to find a way to stop drinking: you have to hit bottom to wake up and realize you are in real trouble.

Psalm 38 is the sound of a man hitting bottom. The psalm was written by King David after his sin with Bathsheba. It records the suffering of sin, the penalty of sin, the incredible loneliness of sin, and the confession of sin. I wonder how many today would read its words and say, "This is my song. This is my life?"

Healing begins when a man or woman is able to say, "My life is unmanageable. I'm in a flat spin, and I cannot recover on my own power." But because we are so intent on trying to maintain control and present an untarnished image, this is difficult to do. Instead, many of us wind up trying to exercise control over others, too, using money, anger, helplessness or other forms of dysfunction. Amazingly, we even try to control God. Isn't it ironic that the way to victory is not to maintain control, but to acknowledge we have lost it...or never had it at all?

QUESTION

Read: *Psalm 38: 1-22*

Is there an aspect of your life that is out of control? Are you ready to admit it?

Denial

MEMORIZE

"But he denied it, saying, 'I neither know nor understand what you are talking about.'"

MARK 14:68

Have you seen the cartoon of a dead cow on his back, rigor mortis setting in and feet straight up in the air? The caption reads, "Really, I'm fine." We're all experts at denying our problems, aren't we? We deny compulsive behavior. We deny sexual addiction. We deny anorexia and bulimia. We deny overeating and controlling behavior and drug abuse.

In Texas (my adopted home state), we have a saying about denial that's a bit coarse, but gets the point across. "If one person tells you 'you're a horse's tail'," the saying goes, "forget it. If two people tell you 'you're a horse's tail,' you'd better take a look in the mirror. But if three people tell you 'you're a horse's tail,' you'd better buy a saddle." One form of denial is to change external things to alleviate an internal problem. For example, a person who overeats might lose weight, but start smoking. Or an alcoholic might stop drinking only to manifest the symptoms of a workaholic. Such a person moves from addiction to addiction, refusing to address the root problem.

Do you know the way out of denial? It's quite simple. The way out of denial is pain. Pain breaks through the wall of denial every single time. C.S. Lewis said, "God whispers to us in our pleasures. God speaks to us in our conscience. God shouts at us in our pain. Pain is God's megaphone to rouse a deaf world." If there is an area of your life that is out of control, follow the pain and it will lead you to the real root of the problem. Give up denial. Only people who admit problems can find solutions.

QUESTION

Read: *Mark* 14: 66-72

What role has denial played in your life?

God Loves Ragamuffins

MEMORIZE

*"He who was delivered up because of our transgressions,
and was raised because of our justification."*

ROMANS 4:25

Former alcoholic Brennan Manning writes in his book *Ragamuffin Gospel* that the only way anyone can be healed of any addiction or compulsive behavior is to admit—up front—to being a ragamuffin. Manning says we must lose all arrogance and ego, and stop pretending to be better than we really are. To illustrate this, he tells the story of a man named Max.

Max was a first-time attendee at an AA meeting in a small Minnesota town. The other twenty-five or so group members placed Max in the middle of a circle of chairs, and he was introduced to them by group leader Murphy O'Connell. Max was a wealthy, small business owner—very polished, very articulate, very confident. Murphy's first question to Max was, "How long, Max, have you been drinking like a pig?" Max was offended and said so. He shared his drinking habits—seven or eight cocktails a day—and insisted his drinking was not a problem. The group members peppered him with questions, and he maintained his veneer—and his pattern of denial. As the questioning went on, Max admitted to hiding liquor, neglecting his children, and lying to his wife. But he still hung on to his pride and managed to keep dignity about him—until Murphy called his bluff by calling Max's neighborhood bartender to find out what kind of drinker Max really was. Afterwards, Max lost his cool. He screamed. Cursed. Shook his fist at Murphy and the rest of the group. Then he fell to the floor in a fit of rage. Murphy rose, and the rest of the group followed. "Let's get out of here," he said, then he nudged Max's form on the ground. "You are scum," he said. "Get out of here. I don't want to see you again. We don't have room for liars." Later on that day, Max begged to be reinstated. He got honest, and he got humble. He admitted he was nothing but a ragamuffin, and God did a work in his life.

It's not easy to get honest and humble. But if you can, God can begin to heal even the sorriest ragamuffin.

ACTION

Read: II Corinthians 12: 9-11

Confess to God ways that you try to seem better than you are.

Practical Insanity

MEMORIZE

"And Jesus said to him, 'If you can! All things are possible to him who believes'."

MARK 9:23

D o you know what the practical definition of insanity is? A person is practically insane who keeps repeating the same behavior and expecting different results. In whatever area of life we continue to do this, we are what I would call "as crazy as a road lizard." And a road lizard is crazy. It might run at you...or it might run away from you. It might run into the path of a car, in circles, or in a straight line.

We may try to hide our particular brand of insanity, but the first step to healing it is to admit we are out of control in that area, and need help. The second step is to believe that Almighty God can heal and restore us. And the third step is to abandon our will totally to Him. Jim Dethmer has a wonderful illustration of this kind of abandon. Imagine you are on top of one of the World Trade Towers in New York City. There is a terrible fire, and you cannot escape. Then, from out of this towering inferno, you see a wire stretching from the other tower to yours, and a man with a wheelbarrow walking on that wire toward you. He asks you to get in the wheelbarrow, and allow him to take you to safety. What do you do?

You and I are like that man in the burning building. We are trapped in our sin and Jesus Christ has walked the wire of the cross to save us. We know we need to get in. We know we should get in. The question is, will we get in? We cry, along with the father of the young boy possessed, "I do believe; help my unbelief." You need an escape from that area of your life in which you are "road lizard crazy." Will you get in the wheelbarrow?

ACTION

Read: *Mark 9: 14-23*

Identify any area of your life in which your behavior is "practically insane."

The Blame Game

"If I want him to remain until I come, what is that to you? You follow Me."

JOHN 21:22

Our building is on fire. We're perishing. The Son of God comes to save us, offering us a way off the building, if we will only get in His wheelbarrow. If we get in, He will carry us to safety. If we do not, we will surely die. The question is, why don't we get in the wheelbarrow?

One reason we don't abandon ourselves totally to God is that we would rather blame others than address our real issues. We play the blame game. It works like this. I have a very hard day at work, and I want nothing more when I get home than to talk to my wife, and receive some affection from her. But when I get home, I don't say, "Joby, I've had a bad day, and here's what I need." Oh no. Instead, I pick a fight. "Did you not get a new light bulb for the bathroom?" I might ask. "No," she'd say, "I went to the store but I forgot." Then she might give me a telephone message she'd taken earlier in the day. "Did you get his number so I can call him back?" I'd say. "No," she'd say, "I thought you had his number." And we're off! Instead of quiet talk and affection, we've got hostility and harsh tones. All because someone (in this example, me!) could not own his own feelings, and resorted to blaming another instead.

Blame and the ensuing conflict it promotes do not equal intimacy. Some folks make the mistake of equating emotional intensity with emotional intimacy. They are not the same. In fact, they are not even close. But blame keeps us from being real, with others and with God. I don't know what your issues are, but I do know that blame will not solve them. In fact, the blame game can keep you and me from ever addressing the real issues we need to face head on. We think we can deflect God's piercing gaze from our own lives and onto others, hoping to escape conviction, but until we allow His light to shine on our own hearts, lasting change is impossible.

Read: John 21: 18-23

Are you blaming anyone else for issues that you need to grapple with before God?

A Searching Moral Inventory

"Therefore consider the members of your earthly body as dead to immorality, impurity, passion, evil desire, and greed..."

COLOSSIANS 3:5

My dad ran a country store. Once each year we'd close down the store to take inventory...and inventory was no fun. Everything had to be counted: nails, potatoes, rope, everything. The work was tedious. Time-consuming. Exacting. I think of this dreaded process every time I hear the word "inventory."

But what about taking an inventory of your life? Have you ever gotten still and quiet for the purpose of examining your life, letting God shine His holy light into your very heart? It's not everyone who can be bold and adventuresome enough, faithful and honest enough, to take a searching and fearless moral inventory of his or her life. A person's willingness to do so is an indicator of that willingness to grow.

If you believe you are ready to blast out of comfortable Christianity, to hear the sound of the trumpet in the morning, to begin to walk in a new kind of life that you've never known before, let me encourage you to take inventory. Begin with the classical seven deadly sins. Evaluate your victories and failures with regard to each, making notes as you go through them thoughtfully and thoroughly. The sins I'm referring to are these: Slothfulness or laziness. Gluttony. Greed. Lust. Envy. Anger. And the deadliest sin of all: pride. How about it? Are you ready for inventory?

Read: *Colossians 3: 1-6*

Begin your inventory today.

I Confess...

MEMORIZE

*"...confess your sins to one another and pray for one another,
so that you may be healed..."*

JAMES 5:16

"Confession is good for the soul," or so the old saying goes. When we are struggling with an area of insanity in our own lives, there is great freedom and power in being able to tell another human being, "This is where I am. This is my addiction, my problem, my sin." When a person comes into a meeting of Alcoholics Anonymous, he introduces himself by saying his name, and calling himself an alcoholic. I, for example, would not say, "I'm Edwin, and I drink a little too much from time to time." That would not cut it. "I'm Edwin, and I'm not sure I need to be here," wouldn't do either. For healing to begin, I would need to say the words, "I'm Edwin, and I'm an alcoholic." At some point in the recovery process with AA, each addict selects a sponsor—someone to whom he or she will be accountable and honest about their addictive behavior.

Jessica McClure was an eighteen-month-old girl who fell down an abandoned well pipe a few years back. It took nearly 400 rescuers in her hometown of Midland, Texas, some fifteen hours to pull her from the well, with only a few bumps and bruises. Early in the rescue process, a key decision was made about how to save baby Jessica. First, they sent someone down to be with her while the rescue took place, so she would not be frightened by all the noise and machinery and manpower it would take to save her. Panic, disorientation, anxiety—all could have been life threatening for her, so they sent someone down to get next to her and comfort her.

This is what happens when we confess our sins to one another. It's like having someone else down in the pit with us, providing a face and a form to comfort and listen as we go through the process of recovery. We have the mistaken idea that if we let someone else know we are struggling, somehow our credibility as a Christian will be ruined, and that no one will trust us again, or believe in us. But confession to a Christian brother or sister who will pray and encourage is not a damaging process, but a healing one.

QUESTION

Read: James 5: 13-20

Who in your life could hear your confession, and be faithful to pray for you?

Half-Hearted Devotion

MEMORIZE

"And he did right in the sight of the Lord, yet not with a whole heart."

II CHRONICLES 25:2

Partial obedience, half-hearted devotion, diminishes the effectiveness of any Christian's life, and weakens his witness to the world.

Amaziah was a young man when he became king of Israel, and the Bible says he did right in God's eyes—but not with his whole heart. He was committed…but not totally. He was interested…but not sold out.

Amaziah successfully led the nation of Israel in battle against the Edomites. But Amaziah's divided loyalty became evident when he brought all the household gods of the Edomites home with him as spoils of war. Following his example (he was king, after all) the people began to worship these other gods, along with Jehovah.

Amaziah won the victory in the battlefield, but he lost to the Edomites in his mind and heart. He conquered their army; their little gods conquered his heart. What happened? An old Chinese proverb says, "Enemies trade vices." When we do battle with the world, it is amazing what sticks with us. A little sign over my desk says, "Beware the habits learned in controversy." When we fight a monster (and sin is a monster), we can become monster-like ourselves. Slowly, imperceptibly, we can assume the religion of our enemy. We can fight in the name of God, then bring home the same "toys" and idols that our enemy loves. Beware the habits learned in controversy!

ACTION

Read: II Chronicles 25: 14-16

Make a list of idols that you share with your enemy, the world.

Between Two Worlds

MEMORIZE

*"I have set before you life and death, the blessing and curse. So choose life
in order that you may live, you and your descendants."*

DEUTERONOMY 30:19

So much for shortcuts. God's people embarked on a trip that should have taken just a few days, but forty years later, Israel was still wandering around the wilderness of Sinai! Why? Because they were disobedient. They incorporated pagan gods into their worship. They made gods of their own invention. They intermarried. They lost their hearts to other things. Each time they sinned, Moses interceded for them and they renewed their covenant with God; but they abandoned their original sense of calling for a kind of lazy syncretism, drifting further and further into disobedience.

Instead of Canaan being their destination, Sinai became their home. They lived between two worlds: they were out of Egypt, but not yet in the Promised Land. An entire generation was lost during those wandering years, and many on the journey probably never knew why they were traveling at all. Dr. Bruce Wilkinson likens their course to our generations today. There was a generation whose relationship with God was vital—perhaps like our parents. Then the next generation was only marginally committed—and the next generation was openly rebellious. The further we get from a vital relationship with the living God, the more comfortable we become living between two worlds. We don't feel tension. We feel ease.

Beware of a borrowed or inherited faith in God. The youngest Israelites of the Exodus never knew that Canaan was their destination. God was present in the cloud, the pillar of fire and the manna—but He was not personal. They had unknowingly moved away from His purpose and His plan, until their lives looked very much like the lives of those who never knew Him at all.

ACTION

Read: *Deuteronomy* 30: 15-20

If you have become comfortable living between two worlds, perhaps it is time to choose one or the other.

I Did It My Way

"That which proceeds out of the man, that is what defiles the man."

MARK 7:20

Do you have a cabinet? I don't mean do you have a covered shelf—I mean, do you have a cadre of trusted advisors whose opinions you weigh carefully and whose advice you welcome? Trusting only self—consulting with only old number one—is a dangerous practice.

What happens when we listen only to ourselves? When I was growing up, we listened to music on phonographs, and then on "record players." We enjoyed it. There was no noise reduction then, no surround sound or complex balancing of treble and bass, but ignorance was bliss! We enjoyed what we heard. Now those in my generation have developed a more "sophisticated ear." Phonographs and record players are obsolete. The "flat" sound we listened to as teenagers has been given a whole new dimension by compact discs, digital recording, and stereos with instrument panels that resemble that of a 747.

When we listen only to our own voice, we live by a flat sound. When we pass up the symphony of other voices in favor of our own solo, we are operating at a disadvantage. My heart is wicked. Yours is, too. We need the straight stick of God's Word to live by, and the voices of other, trusted friends to tune our lives to play out the music of His grace.

ACTION

Read: *Mark* 7: 14-23

Make a list of the friends or advisors you can count on for solid, biblical advice.

When More Becomes Less

MEMORIZE

*"All that my eyes desired I did not refuse them.
I did not withhold my heart from any pleasure."*

ECCLESIASTES 2:10

A re you familiar with the law of diminishing returns? Simply stated, in a consumptive lifestyle, more and more is needed to maintain the same level of satisfaction. King Solomon discovered this when his pursuit of pleasure required more wives, more horses, more food, more wine and more land. His self-styled "pleasure safari" quickly escalated beyond control.

Maybe it's hard for you to relate to King Solomon's dilemma—but the law of diminishing returns is easily illustrated in other ways. It could apply to golf, for example. I like golf. I like being outdoors and moving around. I like competition, even if it's just competing with myself to improve last week's score. But one of the first things I learned when I began to play golf is that there are golfers, and there are golfers. I recently saw a needle-pointed pillow which stated: "Life is a game—golf is serious." Whoever owned that pillow probably started out as I did—borrowed clubs, any course I could get on, make-shift attire—but now they have gone beyond that take-it-or-leave-it stage.

"Hacking" isn't fun anymore, so now they succumb to the theory of escalation: "If you look good, you feel good; if you feel good, you play good; if you play good, you win." The time comes when only Ping irons will do. And Callaway woods. Without these "necessities," the game just isn't fun anymore. Get the picture? The law of diminishing returns says the same effort produces less satisfaction. So we put more into our passion—whatever it may be—just to enjoy it as much as we did yesterday. Pleasure is a lousy god. It's just never satisfied.

ACTION

Read: *Ecclesiastes* 2: 1-11

Make a list of your passions. Are you experiencing the law of diminishing returns in any of them?

Pleasure-Seeking Myths

"He who loves pleasure will become a poor man;
he who loves wine and oil will not become rich."

PROVERBS 21:17

Joy Davidman, wife of C. S. Lewis, had this to say about pleasure-seeking as a vocation: *"Living for his own pleasure is the least pleasurable thing a man can do. If his neighbors don't kill him in disgust, he will die slowly of boredom and powerlessness."* We live in a culture that enables pleasure-seeking. Are you a teenager who is curious about sex? Your school nurse's office has free condoms just waiting for you. Interested in a non-committal arrangement where you "try on" a potential mate like a pair of shoes? By all means, our society would say, "live together." Would you like to experience the sensation of free-falling through life? There are legal and illegal substances available to assist you in your descent.

But I believe there are two big lies or myths related to the pursuit of pleasure. Christians tend to tell one; non-Christians espouse the other. Both are untrue. In an effort to curb what they view as harmful and ungodly behavior, some Christians have tried to convince the world that sin is not pleasurable. But sin is pleasurable...at least for a while. Otherwise, what would the temptation be? But sin's pleasures are temporary, and sin's consequences are inevitable. This fact contradicts the second big myth about pleasure-seeking: that as long as you do not intentionally hurt another person, whatever you choose to do with your body and your life is fine. But God's Word clearly states that sin is a death sentence, although its consequences may not be immediate.

So if sin is pleasurable (at least temporarily), and its consequences can be delayed, why not live for pleasure's sake? Because, as Joy Davidman so eloquently stated, living for pleasure is not really living. It doesn't satisfy the deepest needs of the human heart, and it never will.

Read: Romans 6: 16-20

 How are you currently seeking pleasure in ways that will not satisfy?

Whose Birthday Is It, Anyway?

MEMORIZE

*"...She shall bear a Son; and you shall call His name Jesus,
for it is He who will save His people from their sins."*

MATTHEW 1:21

There was once a land that was backward. Everything was switched, everything seemed just a little off-kilter. In this place, the children didn't play football, they played knee-ball. Kids did not go to schools; teachers went to homes. In this unusual place, trees and flowers bloomed in the winter, and lakes froze in the summer. And in this place, a little guy named Jason had a birthday.

His grandparents came, but he never saw them. His mother baked a birthday cake, but she gave it to the mailman. All of Jason's friends gave presents to each other—not to Jason—in honor of Jason's day. Finally, he'd had all he could take. Jason got a megaphone, got on his bike, and rode through the main street of town, saying, "Whose birthday is it, anyway? Whose birthday is it, anyway?"

Some folks miss the point of Christmas. Oh, decorations are displayed. Parties are attended. Gifts are bought and exchanged. But somehow it never dawns on them that it is someone's birthday. And that someone is Jesus Christ. How about you? Have you missed Christmas because you've missed Jesus Christ? He is God's gift to you. Jesus Christ the Savior came to forgive us and cleanse us of all our sin. Have you received Him? And if you know whose birthday it is, what gift do you have for Him this Christmas? Does the One who has everything have your heart? Why not give Him that?

ACTION

Read: *Galatians* 4: 1-7

Don't miss Christmas. Make your heart a manger for the Son of God this year.

Away In A Manger

"And she gave birth to her first born Son; and she wrapped Him in swaddling clothes and laid Him in a manger..."

LUKE 2:7

"Away in a manger, no crib for a bed, the little Lord Jesus lay down His sweet head..." We sing such warm words about the manger, and have such loving thoughts toward the little baby it held. But we shouldn't try to keep Him there. He is no longer a baby, but a king. He is not in the manger anymore. He lives in us.

Class 202 was full of wealthy children from old-money families. Their teacher loved them, and knew each one well. One day, a new child came to class. He was not like the rest of the children. His clothes were old and mended. He needed a haircut, and he didn't smell very good. He arrived with a note from the principal, explaining that he was the son of a migrant family of fruit-pickers, admitted as a goodwill gesture in hopes of generating favorable publicity for the school. His name was Daniel; he would only be in school for a short while.

In class, the other children snickered at him, but at recess, Daniel's stock went up. He led off the kickball game with a homerun, and followed with a double. When the worst player on the team came to bat, the other children groaned, but Daniel encouraged him. "Don't let them bother you, kid. Step up there and kick it—you can do it!" At that moment, Daniel became more than "the new kid." He became a leader. It wasn't long before the whole class gravitated toward Daniel. At Christmas the teacher received the usual expensive gifts from her students. On the last day before holiday break, Daniel stayed until everyone else had gone. He came to the teacher's desk with a polished rock and said, "This is for you. I found it and cleaned it up real nice. And teacher, tomorrow we're moving on...but I'll miss you." She never saw Daniel again, but this teacher told her students his story each year at Christmas. Inevitably, one of them will say, "I wonder where Daniel is today? I bet he's somewhere real good!" She always says she thinks so, too...and then whispers to herself, "He's in my heart."

Read: I John 5: 10-13

Where is Jesus today? Is He "away in a manger," or alive in your heart?

Born To Be King

MEMORIZE

"For in Him all the fullness of deity dwells in bodily form."

COLOSSIANS 2:9

I n 1940 and 1941, British author Dorothy Sayers was commissioned to write a series of plays entitled "The Man Born to be King." These plays about the life of Jesus Christ were later produced and broadcast by the BBC. But before they were ever heard, they caused quite a national stir. The language was modern. The dialogue was fictionalized. And many accused Miss Sayers of blasphemy by "personifying the Godhead" by portraying the voice of Christ over the airwaves. But when the first play, "Kings in Judea," aired in December of 1941, public response was overwhelmingly positive.

I am not surprised. You see, when it comes to sheer, powerful story-telling—nothing beats the Gospel. There is just no better story, because there is no better Storyteller. "Kings in Judea" took the Christmas story out of the church pews and into the homes of hundreds of thousands of men, women and children who somehow heard it with brand new ears.

At Christmastime and all year long, I challenge you to weave the wonder of the incarnation into every moment of every day. Tell the story. Tell it in your language. Tell it truthfully, but tell it in a way that only you can. Tell it in a gesture, a smile, a hug or a bedtime story. Tell it in a song, a gift, or a selfless act of patience. Tell it with all the wonder of an eyewitness, like Sayers' King Balthazar, who gazed into the eyes of the baby he came to honor and exclaimed, *"I looked at the Child. And all about Him lay the shadow of death, and all within Him was the light of life; and I knew that I stood in the presence of the Mortal-Immortal, which is the last secret of the universe."* Always keep looking at Jesus, and tell others what you see.

ACTION

Read: *Galatians 4: 4-7*

Memorize the Christmas story as a family, and have one member recite it on Christmas Eve.

Wanted: Child To Adopt

MEMORIZE

"God sent forth His Son...in order that He might redeem those who were under the law, that we might receive the adoption as sons."

GALATIANS 4:4-5

You may have never noticed it, but the classified sections of most big city newspapers have a section called "Adoptions." It does not announce who has been adopted, but who wants to adopt. Couples who do not have children advertise to pregnant women who may be considering giving their child away. Listen to these entries: *"California doctor-dad, at-home mom wish to adopt newborn. Will provide love, security, and opportunity. Call Steve and Elaine."* And another one: *"Desire baby to adopt. Outdoorsman dad, stay-at-home mom, one crazy dog, wish to provide love and financial security and a great home to your newborn."* Then this one: *"Adoption. Joan, a Texas elementary art teacher. David, a successful professional, wish to adopt your baby and provide a wonderful life filled with love and stability. Will share photos through the years. Please call."* Do these pleas touch your heart the way they do mine?

God is in the adoption business. He has an ad in His paper for people like you and me, and for all who are away from Him, pleasure-seekers included. It goes something like this: "Behold, I stand at the door and knock; if anyone hears My voice and opens the door, I will come in to him and will dine with him, and he with Me. He who overcomes, I will grant to him to sit down with Me on My throne, as I also overcame and sat down with My Father on His throne." (Revelation 3: 20-21) It promises not temporary gratification, but lasting joy. It promises a place with Jesus, in whose presence is fullness of joy, and in whose right hand are pleasures forever.

REFLECTION

Read: *Galatians* 4: 5-9

How does it feel to realize you are adopted into God's family? Think about what lengths He went to, to bring you home.

Planting And Pulling Up

MEMORIZE

"There is an appointed time for everything...a time to plant,
and a time to uproot what is planted."

ECCLESIASTES 3:1-2

Have you ever planted caladium bulbs? Caladiums are a horticul-
tural staple in Houston, Texas, during the spring and summer
months. Yard after yard in our city is accented by caladiums—
white, pink, and green—and each time I see them I think, *someone waited.*
Caladium bulbs are gnarled and ugly, and after you plant them, you wait.
First, small, blade-like shoots appear, and then the shoots unfold into
leaves. They flatten out and "show their colors," and you're on your way to
Yard-of-the-Month. (Maybe.)

When caladium season is over, you can dig up your bulbs, store them in
a cool, dark place, and replant them again next year. But if you miss a few
bulbs, come spring you'll see caladiums inching through your ground cover
in your flower beds, and the asymmetrical effect may not be what you had
hoped for.

Solomon observed that there is "a time to plant, and a time to uproot
what is planted." There is a time to plant, and a time to harvest. They cannot be switched. A pattern exists, and it must be followed to achieve the
desired results. What is planted must remain planted, too. The process cannot be hurried along. "Leave the bulbs alone," wrote C. S. Lewis, "and the
new flowers will come up. Grub them up and hope, by fondling and sniffing,
to get last year's blooms, and you will get nothing." There is a time to plant,
and a time to uproot.

QUESTION

Read: *Ecclesiastes* 3: 1-5

Are you planting more or harvesting more in your life right now?

A Time For War,
A Time For Peace

MEMORIZE

"There is an appointed time for everything...a time for war and a time for peace."

ECCLESIASTES 3:1,8

I thought I was a pacifist at one point in my life, but I know now that I am not. There is a time to stand for what is right and what is of God, even if others oppose it. The nation of Israel faced war early in her history when God commanded the Israelites to enter the promised land of Canaan and drive out its inhabitants. (I think some of God's chosen people may have been surprised to find out that the land had inhabitants!)

They were commanded to fight in order to receive what God had already stated would be theirs, and they were instructed that the "clearing" of their land would not be accomplished in a single battle. "I will not drive them out before you in a single year...I will drive them out before you little by little, until you become fruitful and take possession of the land." (Exodus 23:29-30)

Peace, too, is a great enterprise, and Solomon noted there was a time for it, as well. Peacemakers are not always heralded in the way victorious warriors are, but they are just as significant. They are quietly behind the scenes, working and praying for God's truth and His justice to prevail. There is a time for war and a time for peace...a time for warriors and a time for peacemakers.

ACTION

Read: *Ecclesiastes 3:6-8*

If you are in a time of peace, thank God for it. If you are fighting to "clear the land" in your life, trust God for the victory.

Chance, Choice, Or Chosen-ness?

MEMORIZE

*"I know that everything God does will remain forever;
there is nothing to add to it and there is nothing to take from it..."*

ECCLESIASTES 3:14

How do you explain the "random-ness" of this life under the sun? Solomon had the same options any one of us has in explaining why things are the way they are. These choices could be called "philosophies of life," and they go by many names, although I will suggest three generic terms for them: chance, choice and chosen-ness.

Which of them is the answer? I believe it is a combination of the last two. Life is chosen—not by fate or a nebulous "higher power," but by God Himself. Yet in His chosen-ness, there is personal choice. Suppose, for example, that winter is coming. I could choose, in the middle of winter, to put on a bathing suit and jump into an outdoor pool. That would certainly be a choice. Winter is "predetermined," but I can choose how I respond to winter. Much about our lives has already been determined. Our gifts and abilities, our talents, the families into which we were born—these things were chosen for us by God. But within that chosen-ness, we have choices. We are free moral agents, or, as R. C. Sproul has said, "We are free subjects who serve a sovereign king."

We live on the backside of life's tapestry, trying to make sense of the weaving with one colored strand or another of philosophy. We see the threads of life, but not its grand design. When do we understand? Only when we view the tapestry from the upper side—above the sun. From that perspective, the pattern is nothing less than perfect: *He has made everything beautiful in its time. He has also set eternity in the hearts of men; yet they cannot fathom what God has done from the beginning to end.*

ACTION

Read: *Ecclesiastes* 3: 1-11

Trust God for the beautiful work He is making of your life.

Re-Runs

MEMORIZE

"Is there anything of which one might say, 'see, this is new?'
Already it has existed for ages which were before us."

ECCLESIASTES 1:10

"**R**ow, row, row your boat, gently down the stream. Merrily, merrily, merrily, merrily, life is but a dream." I never stopped to think how depressing that sounded as a child, did you? The idea that life is but a dream—a series of re-runs played over and over again—is a recurring theme in ancient and modern literature. "Is there anything new under the sun?" King Solomon asked. "Or is all of life just 'more of the same'?"

The secular humanists tell us that mankind is moving toward our ultimate potential; that it is just a matter of time before we make right all that has been wrong. But Solomon would disagree. "That which has been is that which will be. And that which has been done is that which will be done." Man's fallen nature is still the same. And even the events of history have a remarkable sameness about them. Leon Uris, author of *Exodus* and *The Haj* has written a book on the history of Ireland called *Trinity*. At the conclusion of this book that chronicles over three hundred years of Gaelic history, he states, "There is no future for Ireland, only the past happening over and over again." So is there any way out of re-run city? Can we hope for any new scenery in the journey of life?

We can. God never meant for us to have a circular existence. From our beginning recorded in Genesis, man was built for linear living. We were created to go somewhere—with purpose. Solomon said life is pointless. God says life is full of purpose. We were meant for linear living, but sin has forced us into a circular pattern. We are meant to live in relationship, but our sin has forced us into hiding, and isolation. Thank heaven (literally!) for Jesus Christ, whose life, death and resurrection broke the cycle of sin we were doomed to repeat. He is our way out of the endless re-runs of meaningless living.

ACTION

Read: *Ecclesiastes* 1: 1-10

Ask God to get you off the treadmill of re-runs, and to help you walk in newness of life.

Conventional Wisdom

*"For My thoughts are not your thoughts,
neither are your ways My ways, declares the Lord."*

ISAIAH 55:8

Most of us want enough wisdom to satisfy the mind, enough ethics or philosophy to satisfy the conscience, enough hedonism or pleasure to satisfy the body, enough materialism to satisfy the pocketbook, and enough religion to satisfy the spirit. Wisdom, ethics, hedonism, materialism, religion—they are contemporary, are they not? There are those today who give themselves to wisdom, those who give themselves to pleasure, and those who give themselves to wealth and power. There are those who give themselves to sex, those who give themselves to political reform, and those who give themselves to spiritual enlightenment.

Many in our day attempt to give meaning to life through a general, nebulous, non-threatening belief in God—a God that makes no requirements on the way we live. Consider the appeal of this ad that appeared in a Houston newspaper: *"Most people in my generation see religion as too much of a hassle. We're finally starting lives of our own—beginning our careers, entering relationships, building our families—and we're not looking for any more burdens or responsibilities. That's how I saw religion, until I learned more about [name of the congregation]. Here was a religion that gave me room to breathe. They offer services that are relevant to my life. Their philosophy encourages me to explore my inner spirituality. And their belief in activism and social justice inspires me to look outward."*

Have you ever heard such an empty, self-centered commentary? The God-as-an-accessory mentality of our modern world must offend Holy God and break His heart. The conventional wisdom of the day can never approach the mind of God. And nothing but the true and living God can satisfy the deep longing in man's heart.

Read: *Isaiah 55: 8-11*

What are you seeking that you hope will give your life a sense of meaning? How important is it in comparison to your relationship with Almighty God?

Why Are We Here?

MEMORIZE

"His bondservants shall serve Him; and they shall see His face,
and His name shall be on their foreheads."

REVELATION 22:3-4

Ask a hundred people the meaning of life, and be prepared for a hundred different answers—each of them from a particular point of view. Several years ago, *Life* magazine queried readers for its holiday issue, asking, "Why are we here?" Listen to some of the replies. Jose Martinez, a taxi driver, said "We're here to die, just live and die. I do some fishing, take my girl out, pay taxes, do a little reading, then get ready to drop dead. After you're gone, other people will come. The only cure for the world's illness is nuclear war—wipe everything out and start over." Jason Gaes, a young cancer victim, saw it this way: "I think God made each of us for a different reason. If God gives you a great voice, maybe he wants you to sing. Or else, if God makes you seven feet tall, maybe he wants you to play for the Lakers or Celtics. I used to wonder why did God pick on me and give me cansur (sic). Maybe it was because he wanted me to be a dr (sic) who takes care of other kids with cansur (sic)."

Ordinary people answered. Famous people gave it a shot. Author and humorist Garrison Keillor offered this response: "To know and serve God, of course, is why we're here, a clear truth that, like the nose on your face, is near at hand and easily discernible but can make you dizzy if you try and focus on it too hard. But a little faith will see you through."

Jose observed life from the inside of a taxi cab. Jason saw it from the eyes of a child in a hospital cancer ward. Garrison Keillor's perspective combines an evangelical, mid-western upbringing with a keen sense of humor. Saint Augustine said that the chief end of man—the main reason we are here—is to love God, and to glorify Him forever. John's vision of Heaven in Revelation bears that out. We who are His will love, glorify and serve Him forever…reigning with Him in the glory that was His before the world began. With that end in mind, how should we then live?

ACTION

Read: *Revelation 22: 1-7*

 Live with the end in mind. If you were made to love and glorify God, why not begin now?

Saved By Love

"For God so loved the world, that He gave His only begotten Son..."

JOHN 3:16

Every teacher has students that are harder to love than most, and Teddy Stoddard was one of those students for Jean Thompson. Teddy came to class dirty, was unresponsive, and turned in abominable work. Mrs. Thompson returned many of Teddy's papers with a large, red "F" on the top. If she had read Teddy's permanent record, she would have seen a history of trouble from first grade on. His home life was in turmoil. His mother became terminally ill, then died the next year. The school counselor noted his depression, and recommended psychiatric help. It was all in the record...but Mrs. Thompson never read it.

On the last day before the Christmas holidays, Mrs. Thompson received gifts from all of her students, including Teddy. His was crudely wrapped in brown paper, and contained a rhinestone bracelet with a few stones missing, and a half-used bottle of perfume. The other children laughed as Mrs. Thompson put on the bracelet, and dabbed the perfume on her wrist. "Isn't this lovely," she said, nodding to Teddy with a smile. After class, Teddy approached her desk. He had never come forward before. "Mrs. Thompson," he said, "thank you for liking my presents. You smell like my mother used to smell, and her bracelet looks good on you, too." When he walked out, Jean Thompson sank to her knees and prayed, "God, I sought to be a teacher of facts and not a lover of children. Forgive me for misunderstanding Teddy. Help me to love him more."

The next morning Jean Thompson arrived in class a changed teacher, and Teddy Stoddard was a changed boy. She tutored him so he could catch up with the other students. She looked for things she might praise him for, no matter how small. He had never encountered that kind of love before, and he blossomed under her care. At the end of the year, Teddy graduated into the next grade, but Mrs. Thompson received notes from her student for many years after that. The last one read, "Dear Mrs. Thompson: You can now call me Theodore J. Stoddard, M.D. Would you ever have believed it? By the way, I'm getting married July 26th, and I would love for you to come. You can sit where my mother would have sat. You're all the family I have. My dad died this year. Hope to see you soon. Love, Teddy." Teddy was saved by love. And so are we.

Read: John 3: 16-18

 Are you saved by love? Then love.